REAL WORLD
GOOGLE
SKETCHUP 7

MIKE TADROS

PEACHPIT PRESS
BERKELEY, CALIFORNIA

REAL WORLD GOOGLE SKETCHUP 7
Mike Tadros

Peachpit Press
1249 Eighth Street
Berkeley, CA 94710
510/524-2178
510/524-2221 (fax)

Find us on the Web at: www.peachpit.com
To report errors, please send a note to errata@peachpit.com

Peachpit Press is a division of Pearson Education.

Editor: Becca Freed
Production Editors: Lisa Brazieal and Tracey Croom
Development Editor: Dan J. Foster
Copyeditor: Dan J. Foster
Proofreader: Patricia J. Pane
Compositors: David Van Ness and Owen Wolfson
Indexer: Valerie Perry
Cover design: Charlene Will
Cover Illustration: Ryan Alden; www.ryanalden.com
Cover model of Dry Van Trailer courtesy of Sam J. Wipf

ISBN-13 978-0-321-66031-2
ISBN-10   0-321-66031-5

9 8 7 6 5 4 3 2 1

Printed and bound in the United States of America

TABLE OF CONTENTS

INTRODUCTION

I started using SketchUp about six years ago after a friend convinced me to give it a shot for some of the architectural design work I was doing while working for a firm in Los Angeles. At the time, I was spending about half of my time on the verge of falling asleep drafting in AutoCAD or stressed out about how much time I would have to spend in 3DS Max, Photoshop, and Illustrator to put together my next presentation. By all comparisons, SketchUp was simply *fun*! And that was the initial reason why I was compelled to figure out a way to use it to do just about *everything*.

Soon after plowing through my first few SketchUp projects, I was presented with an opportunity to join the SketchUp team as a software trainer. Over the past six years I've spent countless hours traveling the world, teaching people to use SketchUp, and I have continued to use SketchUp for the design and 3D modeling projects that we work on at my company, Igloo Studios.

I wish I could take full credit for having conceived of everything you'll read in this book, but, in fact, the following pages are an amalgamation of having met and shared ideas with thousands of professionals across all sorts of professions, from elementary school teachers who work with kids on the autism spectrum, to CAD managers at Skidmore Owings and Merrill—as well as landscape, graphic, interior, and kitchen & bath designers, contractors and construction managers, building product manufacturers, city and regional planners, packaging designers, and tech savvy do-it-yourselfers.

Having reached the point some years ago when SketchUp became not only fully integrated into our professional workflow but the central tenet around which all other software and processes revolved, a paradigm shift occurred in the efficiency and ease with which we were able to communicate with our clients and deliver solutions that exceeded expectations.

What follows is a summary of some of the workflow methods and practices that have proven successful for the work that my colleagues and I have done, as well as methods that have proven successful for others whom I've taught and who have reported their success stories back to me.

This isn't a basic intro to SketchUp that talks about how to use the Pencil tool or the Push/Pull tool; there are already a few other books out there that you can buy for that stuff. This is a book that covers the issues you probably don't even know you have, especially with regard to all the time you're probably wasting by not having had a chance to fully think through the workflow and interoperability of using SketchUp in conjunction with other design practices and software programs.

This book is broken up into four main sections that are intended to focus on the issues most relevant to taking it up a big notch when it comes to spending less time banging your head against the wall and spending more time wowing the pants off our clients: 1) Setting up your SketchUp preferences; 2) Importing stuff into SketchUp; 3) Working on and managing your SketchUp models efficiently and; 4) Exporting stuff from your SketchUp models.

If you're new to SketchUp, you'll probably be able to get through the next couple hundred pages without too much trouble, but you'll certainly have a much easier go of it if you've already got a basic understanding of how SketchUp works. That is why this book comes with a DVD loaded with supplemental video tutorials intended to help ensure a successful journey through the examples contained herein. I've also included URLs throughout the book that link to online resources that will help you build up solid fundamental SketchUp skills while chugging through the more advanced stuff outlined in this book.

Some of the videos you'll find on the DVD are episodes of *The SketchUp Show* video tutorial series (which is also available on YouTube, iTunes, and our Web site, www.go-2-school.com). The DVD also includes snippets from other SketchUp Training DVDs that we've produced at *School*.

On our *School* Web site, you'll find dozens more episodes of *The SketchUp Show* as well as a variety of other training products and services for Google SketchUp, Google Layout, and Google Earth, such as Training DVDs, Webinars, and options for live, in-person SketchUp training.

I tried hard over the past six months of writing this book to ensure that it included information that even a seasoned SketchUp veteran could benefit from. This is my first time writing a book and I'm more than happy to receive your feedback about it. If you buy this thing and think there's room for improvement, I'd like to know. (Seriously, please email me at mike@go-2-school.com if you think this book sucks and tell me how I could have made it better. If this thing sells enough copies, there's a chance I might get to do this again someday.)

I've long subscribed to the notion that for any of us to stand a chance of evolving personally or professionally, we have to try to fulfill our responsibility to help each other get better at what we do. This book, as well as the rest of the work that my colleagues and I do at *School*, is focused on trying to catalog as much information as possible for helping people integrate SketchUp into their own professional workflows—with the hope that ultimately we may all benefit from any further evolution that's inspired by the work we've done, the discoveries we've made, and the things we've learned.

I accepted the offer to write this book because I knew there were things in my head that weren't in any other SketchUp books out there and I thought I stood a good chance of putting something together that could benefit the folks who got their hands on this book you're holding right now.

My sincere hope is that you find the information contained herein to be helpful, inspirational, and fun! I also hope that you'll be able to use this book to guide further discovery and that you'll perhaps then have an opportunity to experience the thrill of sharing those discoveries with others.

Happy Sketching!

Acknowledgments

I would like to extend a special thanks to the following people who have all in some way or another contributed to my opportunity to write this book:

Thanks to my family for their encouragement—especially my parents, Elaine and Tad, who have always been there to support me in anything and everything I've ever set out to do.

To my wife Suzanne for all of her love and support. I truly would not be where I am today without her.

To all of my colleagues at Igloo Studios (past and present) for helping to create a company that has afforded me the opportunity to help others.

To all of the great teachers in my life who have instilled in me a desire to teach others.

To all of my employers and co-workers throughout the years who so willingly shared their knowledge with me.

To the *entire* Google SketchUp team (past and present) for their support—especially Mark Carvalho for seeing in me what I may never have seen in myself, and to Brad Schell and Joe Esch for creating the kick-ass program that has inspired us all.

To Peachpit for giving me the opportunity to write this book—especially Becca, Dan, Nancy, Pat, and Bil for helping turn my ideas into something legible.

CHAPTER ONE

Setting Your SketchUp 7 Preferences

Setting up preferences is one of the first things that anyone who uses SketchUp at a high level should get squared away. The Preferences dialog is filled with options that can save bits of time here and there, increase the functionality of SketchUp, allow you to work more intuitively, protect your work and your files, and optimize the performance of your hardware.

Almost all the preferences discussed in this chapter are modified in the Preferences window. On a PC, choose Window > Preferences (**Figure 1.1**); on a Mac, choose SketchUp > Preferences (**Figure 1.2**). In this chapter we'll go through all the panes in the Preferences window and pick the best options in each.

Figure 1.1 On a PC, the Preferences window is opened from the Window menu.

Figure 1.2 On a Mac, the Preferences window is opened from the SketchUp menu.

APPLICATIONS

If you've applied image-based texture maps (such as JPEG or TIFF files) to your models (a process that will be explored in detail in Chapter 6), you may find you need to edit those images in their native form. The Applications preference is a new feature in SketchUp 7 that makes it easy to jump out to your favorite image editing application for this purpose (**Figure 1.3**).

Click Choose and navigate to the image editing application you want to use. For example, you might navigate to C:\Program Files\Adobe Photoshop CS4\Photoshop CS4 on a PC, or Main HD/Applications/Adobe Photoshop CS4/Photoshop CS4 on a Mac.

DRAWING

The Drawing preferences (**Figure 1.4**) are a straightforward set of options that allow you to customize the way you work in SketchUp. Tinkering with these settings can help make your work in SketchUp more intuitive, depending on whether you've got some kind of latent muscle memory built up from using your mouse or trackpad in a particular way in other design, illustration, modeling, or rendering programs. The preferences in Figure 1.4 are what work for me: Enable "Auto detect" and "Continue line drawing" under Click Style, and select "Auto-activate paint tool" under Miscellaneous.

Figure 1.3
The Applications preferences dialog.

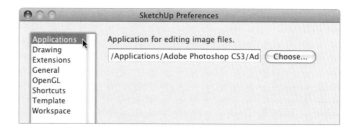

Figure 1.4
Suggested settings for the Drawing preferences.

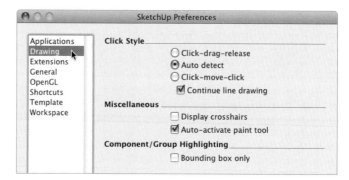

EXTENSIONS

This part is easy—just check *all* the boxes in the Extensions preferences dialog (**Figure 1.5**)! In SketchUp, extensions include both Ruby scripts and plug-ins, and we'll install and explore various ones throughout the book. When an extension is enabled, any toolbars associated with it will be accessible under the View > Toolbars menu. To disable an extension, first uncheck the extension in this pane, and then restart SketchUp.

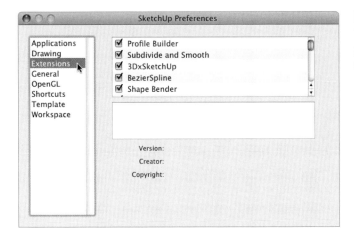

Figure 1.5
The Extensions preferences dialog.

FILES

The Files pane (**Figure 1.6** on the next page), which lets you specify where you want various files to be saved, and where your various libraries will be organized, is available only on the Windows version of SketchUp. This is one of the most important preferences to customize if you are sharing SketchUp files with colleagues via a file server.

- **Models** This field is where you tell SketchUp where to autosave your files. I have this set to save files to the desktop. Most IT guys would shudder at the thought, but I keep a tidy desktop, so when SketchUp crashes, the autosaved file is one of the only things there, and I can find it quickly and get back to work.

  By default, the Files preferences will point to your My Documents folder.

Figure 1.6 The Files preferences dialog (PC only).

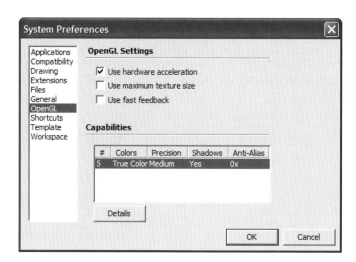

- **Components** Component libraries can be maintained locally, or they can be shared across a network. To set up your File preferences to reference libraries that are managed centrally on a company file server, copy your components library to a folder on the server and then set the components directory to that location. You can add new subfolders within the component folder to organize components by type, or on a per-project basis, or both.

    By default, the component library directory is C:\Program Files\Google\Google SketchUp 7\Components.

- **Materials** Material libraries can also be maintained locally or across a network. For network setup, copy your Material library to the server and then set the Materials directory to that location. You can add new subfolders within the Materials folder to organize components by type, or on a per-project basis, or both.

    By default, the material library directory is C:\Program Files\Google\Google SketchUp 7\Materials.

- **Styles** Style libraries can also be maintained locally or across a network. For network setup, copy your Styles library to the server and then set the Styles directory to that location. You can add new subfolders within the Styles folder to organize components by type, or on a per-project basis, or both.

    By default, the styles library directory is C:\Program Files\Google\Google SketchUp 7\Styles.

NOTE If the computer you're setting up is a laptop that is sometimes plugged into a file server but is also used in the field or offline, be sure to have the files you need available on the local hard drive so that you can direct SketchUp to the local folders when needed.

General Preferences

There are lots of options to modify in the General pane of the Preferences dialog—some more helpful than others (**Figure 1.7**). We'll touch on each of them in this section.

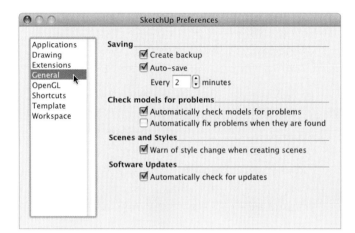

Figure 1.7
Suggested settings for the General preferences.

Saving

Create backup Those of you who work on a PC may have wondered about the difference between the .skp and .skb file extensions. And those of you who work on Macs may have noticed that some of your SketchUp files include a tilde symbol (~) at the end of the filename. Both the .skb files on the PC and the tilde (~) files on the Mac are backups.

The Backup function in SketchUp is just an insurance policy. If something ever goes sideways with your SketchUp model, you're all set with a shiny new backup file. In over six years of using SketchUp, I've been fortunate to have only ever needed to use my backup file twice, but, man, was I psyched each time when that backup file opened. In both instances, something had gone awry while SketchUp was trying to save a rather large file, and the saved file became corrupted. After being corrupted, the SketchUp model appeared to save and close like normal, but then the model wouldn't open back up. Despite the issues with the original model, the most current backup file opened just fine. I would have lost about 10 hours of work in both cases.

A backup is created as soon as you save a file for the first time. Every subsequent save automatically updates the backup file. If you delete the backup, a new one will be created the next time you save. You'll probably trash about 99.9 percent of your ~.skp/.skb

NOTE If SketchUp crashes while you're working on a new, untitled file that has yet to be officially saved, the autosave file will be saved to the default Files directory. On a PC that directory is My Documents (unless you changed it per the Files preferences discussed earlier in this chapter). On the Mac the folder is User/ Library/Application Support/Google SketchUp 7/SketchUp/ Autosave.

files, but that 0.1 percent of the time you end up using a backup file makes it totally worth it.

Auto-save Another little good-luck charm you can have in your back pocket is the Auto-save feature, which kicks in when SketchUp crashes. By default, the Auto-save feature is set to automatically save your model every 5 minutes. SketchUp keeps a little timer running, and if you've neglected to save after working for 5 minutes, Auto-save will record the current state of the model, just in case. If SketchUp actually crashes, it will create a new file, which will be located in the same folder or directory as the original .skp file. The Auto-save filename will have the syntax Autosave_OriginalFilename.skp.

If or when this scenario occurs, you'll find that the autosaved file is typically the most current version of your SketchUp project. When you open the autosaved file, you should do a Save As and rename the file without the Autosave prefix.

As for setting the Auto-save frequency, I have my Auto-save preferences set to 2 minutes (instead of 5). Why? I'm not a huge fan of having to doing stuff twice.

Workflow Tip: Save a Copy (at Least Once a Day)

When I'm working on a project over the course of a few days, weeks, or months, I try to get in the habit of using Save As to create a version of the file for each day that I work on the project (in some cases I might save a couple versions each day).

I've found that the following file-naming convention helps keep track of projects (especially when there's more than one person getting their grubby hands on them).

Pattern: Date_Description_Version_Initials.skp

Example: 050609_SITE MODEL_01_MT.skp

The six-digit date code makes it easy to tell which files are the most current. The two-digit version code lets you track multiple versions that may evolve over the course of the same day.

And the initials stamp lets you know who to point fingers at when something goes wrong.

NOTE Mac users: When you save a model in SketchUp, make sure you check the Custom Icon check box (**Figure 1.8**). A custom icon can save you the trouble of having to open and close files to figure out what's in each model.

Figure 1.8
Make sure to check the Custom Icon box in the Save dialog.

 TIP In some cases, you may even want to open old files and save and close them just so you can create custom icons for them (**Figure 1.9**).

Figure 1.9 SketchUp's default icon (left) always looks the same, but a custom icon (right) is like a mini-preview of your file's contents.

Check Models for Problems

Automatically checking models for problems is generally a good idea. When SketchUp finds a problem, I prefer to approve the fixing of said problems. It makes me feel like I contributed to the solution. If you'd rather just have SketchUp do its thing, you can check both boxes. To check the model for problems manually, you can choose Window > Model Info > Fix problems.

Scenes and Styles

This is a good option to have turned on. In Chapter 8 we'll dig into the options for style changes when creating and updating scenes.

OPENGL

When it comes to SketchUp, it's possible that OpenGL settings have been the source of more performance questions about hardware specs than any other preference.

What Is OpenGL?

The term OpenGL stands for *Open* Graphics *Library*.

OpenGL plays a critical role in deciphering and displaying the graphical information required for you to see a 3D computer model on your screen (instead of just a bunch of illegible code). Wanna see your 3D model in perspective? Use Orbit, Pan, and Zoom? Turn on the shadows? Toggle into and out of X-Ray mode? Apply sketchy edge styles? Or apply an image texture to a surface? Well, you're gonna need OpenGL for all of that, as well as for anything else you do in SketchUp that you would expect to be able to *see* on your screen.

What's It Got to Do with You?

Well, for starters, it certainly helps if your computer is capable of using OpenGL to translate the information it's getting from SketchUp so that it can properly display your model on your computer screen. If there's a breakdown in the communication pipeline between SketchUp and OpenGL, any of a number of screwy things might happen in SketchUp:

- You may notice shadow relics that follow the cursor or SketchUp model when you draw, orbit, etc.

- The drawing cursor might be replaced with white boxes, instead of mimicking the Tool icons.

- Surfaces might not render at all.

- SketchUp will be slow to respond to commands and will feel clunky.

How Do You Avoid an OpenGL Breakdown?

First off, your best protection is to have a computer with a graphics card or graphics processor that is OpenGL compliant. If you bought your computer in this millennium, it probably supports some form of OpenGL, but that alone may not be good enough. You need to meet SketchUp's minimum hardware requirements (see the URL below for details), and you need to make sure you have the most current driver for your graphics processor. Second, you'll want to make sure you've got the most up-to-date OpenGL graphics card drivers installed. (As of this book's publication date, OpenGL is in version 3.1.)

Hardware Requirements

Check out this page on the SketchUp Web site for the minimum hardware requirements for SketchUp and a list of recommended hardware upgrades:

http://sketchup.google.com/support/bin/answer.py?answer=36208&cbid=1rzs4r4c9csiw&src=cb&lev=answer.

On Mac systems, the OpenGL updates are typically included with operating system updates.

PC users should check their system profiles to get the make and model info about their graphics card (**Figure 1.10**). Equipped with that info, it's possible to download and install the latest OpenGL drivers from your graphics card manufacturer's Web site.

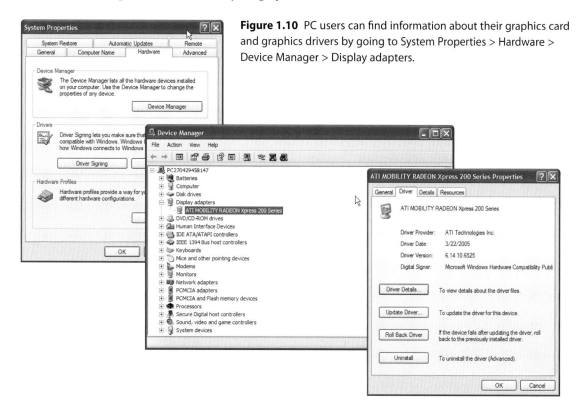

Figure 1.10 PC users can find information about their graphics card and graphics drivers by going to System Properties > Hardware > Device Manager > Display adapters.

If for some reason your computer has a graphics card or graphics chip set that cannot support OpenGL, you have a few options:

- Use it as an excuse to get a new computer.

- Get a new graphics card (typically not an option for Macs).

- Uncheck these options in the OpenGL preferences pane (**Figure 1.11** on the next page): "Use Hardware acceleration," "Use maximum texture size," and "Use fast feedback."

Figure 1.11
Suggested settings for default OpenGL preferences.

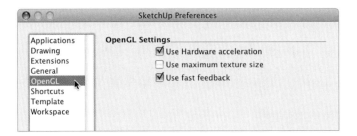

Use Hardware acceleration   This option is useful for speeding things up only if your computer's graphics card or chip set is OpenGL compliant.

Use maximum texture size   This option directs SketchUp to display the maximum allowable image resolution for the image-based textures that have been imported into the model, which may cause SketchUp to run a bit slower than it would otherwise. You'll probably have this turned off most of the time when you're working, but you might turn this option on for presentations and renderings.

Use fast feedback   This option is also useful for speeding things up if your computer's graphics card or chip set is OpenGL compliant.

Reverse Driver Picking Bug (PC only)   The driver-picking bug presents itself when the computer's graphics card is not OpenGL compliant. The most common symptom of the bug is when the Select tool picks an object behind one that you click rather than selecting what you clicked. In most cases, turning this option on will help fix that bug.

Taking the preceding into account, even the best graphics cards—with totally up-to-date drivers—have their limitations. Because SketchUp requires OpenGL to translate information, and since your computer's graphics card is often the hardware that SketchUp uses to facilitate that process, it's not very hard to reach the threshold at which your graphics card's little brain starts freaking out. The following graphics display factors contribute to the speed with which OpenGL can keep up with you as you're working in SketchUp:

- The number of polygons being displayed on the screen

- Whether there are any colors or image textures applied to the surfaces in the model

- Whether any artistic display styles are applied to the model

- Whether the shadows are turned on in the model

In short, the more information you require OpenGL to process, and the bigger the burden you place on your system's graphics card, the slower SketchUp will be to respond. Throughout this book, we'll look at ways to better manage and mitigate the graphical stuff so you can work faster without having to sacrifice all the fun of SketchUp's great rendering options.

To check out all the geeky details about OpenGL, a thorough history, and more, visit the OpenGL Wikipedia page: http://en.wikipedia.org/wiki/OpenGL#Post_OpenGL_3.1.

SHORTCUTS

Setting, learning, and using keyboard shortcuts can greatly increase the speed with which you're able to work in any program, including SketchUp.

To find the default keyboard shortcut for a tool, just hover your cursor over the icon in the toolbar, and if the tool has a shortcut assigned to it, the shortcut will appear in brackets next to the tool name when the tool name pops up.

The default shortcuts are also listed on the SketchUp Quick Reference Card. You can view or download the quick-reference cards for both the PC and Mac versions of SketchUp here:

http://sketchup.google.com/support/bin/answer.py?hl=en&answer=116693

Setting Custom Shortcuts

Keyboard shortcuts in SketchUp can be assigned as a single letter (M for Move, for example) or as a letter plus modifier key(s) (such as Shift+M or Ctrl+Shift+M for Move). Shortcut combinations can't contain more than one letter, so MOV wouldn't be an option for Move, for example.

Shortcuts are more effective when they're intuitive and easy to remember, so if the default shortcuts don't make sense, or if you're a Photoshop user and you find yourself consistently pressing the V key expecting to activate the Select tool, don't hesitate to change your SketchUp shortcuts so that they work the way you work.

To set a new keyboard shortcut on a Mac or PC:

1. All the tools and commands that can have a keyboard shortcut are listed in the window and arranged alphabetically by main menu heading. You can use the search field to narrow the list. For example, type **Select** to locate the Select tool (**Figure 1.12** on the next page).

2. Select the tool in the list that you want to (re)assign (such as Tools/Select).

Figure 1.12 You can search or browse for commands for which to set keyboard shortcuts, and then type keyboard combinations you want to use (Mac).

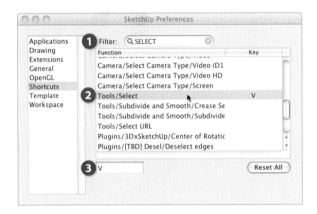

3. Type the keyboard letter you would like to use into the Shortcut field (the letter V, for example).

4. (*PC only*) Make sure that you click the + button to assign the keyboard shortcut (**Figure 1.13**).

Figure 1.13 It takes a few additional steps to save a keyboard shortcut in the Windows version of SketchUp.

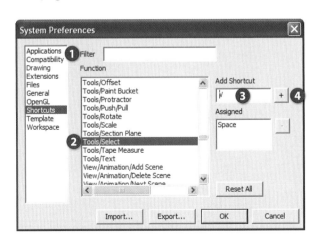

5. (*PC only*) Click OK to save your new preferences.

Congrats! At this point you could use the V key to call up the Select tool.

Keyboard Shortcut Suggestions

Table 1.1 shows my own list of preferred keyboard shortcuts. This is a mixed bag that includes some shortcuts that I learned by using other programs. For example, in Photoshop V is the Select tool and N is the Rectangle Marquee. Some others make more sense to me than the defaults (such as R for Rotate), and some are based on keys

Table 1.1 Recommended SketchUp Keyboard Shortcuts

Key combination*	Command	Key combination*	Command
Q	Push/Pull	Cmd+G	Make Group
W	Walk	H	Pan
E	Erase	Shift+H	Hide Rest of Model
Shift+E	Hide	Cmd+Shift+H	Unhide All
Opt+E	Soften Smooth	L	Line
R	Rotate	Z	Zoom
Shift+R	Protractor	Shift+Z	Zoom Window
T	Text	X	X-Ray View
Shift+T	3D Text	Cmd+X	Cut
Y	Look Around	C	Circle
I	Intersect with Model	Cmd +C	Copy
Shift+I	Interact with Model	V	Select
Cmd+I	Entity Info	Cmd+V	Paste
O	Offset	Opt+Shift+V	Paste In Place
Cmd+O	Open	N	Rectangle
P	Paint Bucket	M	Move
A	Arc	Cmd+1	Top View
Shift+A	Axes	Cmd+2	Bottom View
Cmd+A	Select All	Cmd+3	Front View
Cmd+Shift+A	Select None	Cmd+4	Back View
S	Scale	Cmd+5	Left View
Cmd+S	Save	Cmd+6	Right View
D	Tape Measure	Right Arrow	Lock Red Axis
Shift+D	Dimension	Up Arrow	Lock Blue Axis
F	Follow-Me	Left Arrow	Lock Green Axis
G	Orbit	Down Arrow	Lock Blue Axis
Shift+G	Make Component		

* Opt (Option) and Cmd (Command) are Mac keys. The Windows equivalents are Alt and Ctrl.

that are more conveniently located on the keyboard (such as Q for Push/Pull). Note that my list is ordered to follow the arrangement of keys on a QWERTY keyboard.

Review the list to find the tools you use most often, and set keyboard shortcuts for them. A great way to learn the shortcuts is to pick one or two tools per day and challenge yourself to use only the keyboard shortcut to invoke that tool.

Importing and Exporting Shortcuts

Setting up office-wide standards for keyboard shortcuts can help bring new SketchUp users up to speed more quickly and make it possible for anyone to work efficiently on any computer in the office.

Once you've agreed upon an office-wide list of keyboard shortcuts, you can program them on one machine and then simply transfer them to all the other computers in the office.

Shortcuts can be transferred from one PC to another or one Mac to another, but they can't be transferred from a Mac to a PC, or vice versa.

To copy shortcuts from one PC to another:

1. Click the Export button in the Preferences > Shortcuts window to save the preferences as a .dat file (**Figure 1.14**). You might consider giving the file a name such as *YourOfficeName*.dat.

Figure 1.14
Exporting short-cuts is a two-step process in the Windows version of SketchUp.

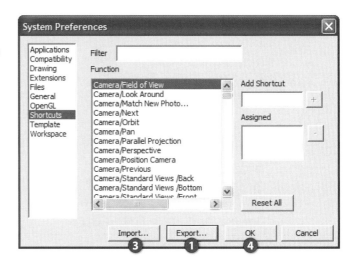

2. Transfer the .dat file to any other PC (copy it over a network or via a flash drive, or e-mail it—it doesn't matter).

3. On the other PC, click the Import button in the Preferences > Shortcuts window to import the *YourOfficeName*.dat file.

4. Click OK to close the Preferences > Shortcuts window. The new shortcuts should be ready to go.

To copy shortcuts from one Mac to another:

1. Locate the Shortcuts.plist file on the Mac you've set up with custom shortcuts. The file is located in Users/*User*/Library/Application Support/Google SketchUp 7/SketchUp/Shortcuts.plist.

2. Copy the .plist file to the same location on any other Mac.

3. Restart SketchUp on the Mac to which you copied the .plist file, and then SketchUp will load the new shortcuts.

For more information about setting up keyboard shortcuts, check out Episode 10 of *The SketchUp Show*: "Setting Keyboard Shortcuts and Working with Large Files" online at www.go-2-school.com/Real-World-Google-SketchUp-7.

TEMPLATE

The template is the file that opens up each time you start a SketchUp project. A number of preconfigured templates are included, and you can choose the one that best fits the types of projects you typically work on (**Figure 1.15**). To change your template, simply click the one you'd like to work with, close the Preferences window, and then open a new SketchUp file.

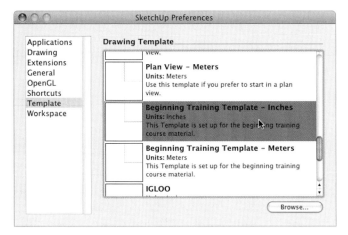

Figure 1.15
The Template
preferences pane.

In addition to the default template library, you can save any SketchUp file as a custom template.

There are so many things you can customize for each template that the topic deserves its own chapter—so we gave it one, and it's coming up next.

WORKSPACE

SketchUp v7.1 has a new pane in the Preferences window, the Workspace pane (**Figure 1.16**). This pane has most of the settings that let you manage your workspaces efficiently. But before we review the options available in the Workspace pane, I'll show you my preferred screen arrangement and give Mac users a tip on saving custom workspaces.

Figure 1.16
The Workspace
preferences pane.

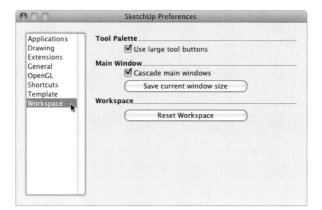

Tool Palette

The "Use large tool buttons" option is useful if you actually use the Tool palette. If you've got a small screen, typically use keyboard shortcuts, or have eyes like a hawk, then you may prefer to uncheck this setting.

Main Window

This option applies only to Mac users. But it's a good one, so hopefully you Mac folks are paying attention. By default, the Mac version of SketchUp is set up so that when you open a new SketchUp file, the default size of the Drawing window is 800 pixels by 600 pixels. The bigger your drawing window, the better. To set SketchUp so that each drawing window will open full screen, follow these steps (**Figure 1.16** and **1.17**):

1. Pull the main toolbar in from the side of the screen.

2. Pull any dialog windows in from the side of the screen.

3. Maximize the drawing window by clicking the little green circle in the top-left corner.

4. Click the "Save current window size" button in Preferences > Workspace (Figure 1.16).

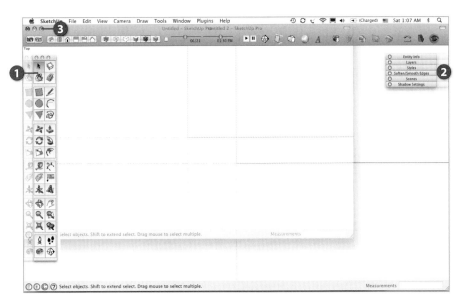

Figure 1.17 Pull in toolbars and dialogs, and then click the green Zoom button to maximize the drawing window.

Workspace

It's commonplace nowadays to find yourself in a situation where you need to switch up your workspace and/or display settings on the fly. It's possible, when modifying your display settings, that some of your windows and/or toolbars may disappear during the switch, such as in the following two situations:

*   If you're working on a high-resolution display with windows and/or toolbars out at the far edge of the screen and you switch to a lower-resolution setting

*   If you switch from a dual-monitor setup—with windows and/or toolbars located on the secondary display—to a single display setup

*   If, for whatever reason, you think you have have lost one or more of your windows, you can use the Reset Workspace button to bring everything back into view.

CHAPTER TWO

Creating Custom Templates

Whenever you start a new project, SketchUp creates a new, untitled file by creating a duplicate of whichever template you've selected as the default.

As mentioned at the end of the previous chapter, you can set or change the default template by selecting from the list located in SketchUp Preferences > Templates. (In case you're wondering, the examples in this book were created using the "Beginning Training Template - Inches" template.)

You'll probably find that a number of templates seem to work pretty well for the kind of work you do, or plan to do, in SketchUp. Over time, however, it is likely that you will refine the types of projects that you work on, and the ways in which you work on them.

If you've ever been working on a project and thought to yourself, "What were the animation settings I used on that project a couple weeks back?" or "What were those dimension settings I had figured out for that last project?" you'll be happy to know that you can largely avoid those types of investigations. You just have to take the time to set up your own custom template.

Creating a custom template doesn't have to be a lengthy process. In fact, if you currently use either of the Architectural Design templates and you're tired of seeing Sang standing in the middle of the screen every time you open a new model, grab the Eraser tool and erase him (just as usual). Then choose File > Save as Template. Check the Save as Default Template box to start a new life sans Sang.

Perhaps the most important concept that you should take away from this chapter is that a template can be anything from a blank screen to an entire scene with buildings and cars and people. The template files are just like any other SketchUp model; the only difference is that template files are stored in the Templates folder on your computer's hard drive. On a Mac, the Templates folder is located at *Main HD*/Users/*User*/Library/Application Support/Google SketchUp 7/SketchUp/Templates. On a PC, the Templates folder is located at C:\Program Files\Google\Google SketchUp 7\Resources\en-US\Templates.

While bidding adieu to Sang might have given you a bit of instant gratification, you should pause to think a bit before you go nuts creating new templates. If you work in a collaborative professional environment, templates can be a great quality control measure that you'll want to employ with forethought and care. The purpose of this chapter is to help you determine how to use templates intelligently in your own work environment. You may decide that your workflow could benefit from a handful of custom templates for different types of projects, or for different departments in your office that may use SketchUp at different stages of typical projects. We'll take a tour through some of the most popular options that you should think about when setting up a template for yourself or for your office.

Model Info

The Model Info dialog contains some basic settings that are likely to be common to many of your models, so it's a good place to start tweaking your templates. You can open the Model Info window by choosing the sensibly located menu option Window > Model Info.

Just about everything you tinker with in the Model Info window can be saved as a part of your SketchUp template.

Animation

The Animation settings determine the scene transitions and scene delays during an animated playback of whichever scenes you've configured in your SketchUp model. The default settings are all right, but for most fly-through type animations you may be more likely to use a scene transition of around 4 seconds and a scene delay of 0 seconds (**Figure 2.1**).

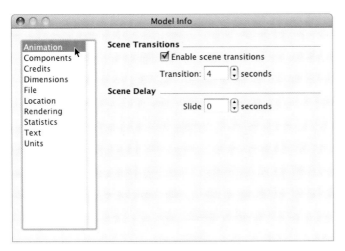

Figure 2.1
Animation
settings can
affect the timing
for transitions
and delays
between scenes.

Components

In the previous chapter we explored the setup and use of keyboard shortcuts (see
"Shortcuts" in Chapter 1). One of the recommended shortcuts was for the command
View > Component Edit > Hide Rest of Model. Notice the check box highlighted in
Figure 2.2: That check box controls the same option. When editing a group or component instance in the model, you can use the slider to control how faded you want the
rest of the model to look. If you check Hide, everything in the model, aside from the
group or component that you are editing, will disappear. As soon as you close the
component or uncheck the box, the rest of the model will reappear.

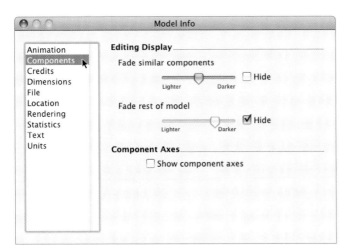

Figure 2.2
Component
settings can alter
the way a model
is displayed
while in Edit
Component or
Edit Group mode.

Credits

Disclaimer: Information entered into the Credits pane won't be saved as part of your template, but since we're here, it's worth a few words.

The Credits feature (**Figure 2.3**) allows you to claim authorship of a SketchUp model and also lets you see who else might have contributed to a project. You must be connected to the Internet to utilize this feature. If you're online, you can claim credit for a model by inputting your Google ID (Gmail address and password). The authorship information will stay with the model as it changes hands throughout a project, and the authorship information is automatically transported when models are uploaded to and from the Google 3D Warehouse. Any other modelers who manage to get their grubby little hands on your file will have a chance to add their names to the author list if they make a revision to the file. You'll notice that the author names of SketchUp modelers will appear when you download components from the Warehouse and add them to your projects. It's actually a cool feature for being able to figure out who to call when the model goes sideways (but it's also a good thing to keep in mind before telling someone about your "original" masterpiece).

Figure 2.3
SketchUp 7 allows users to assign authorship credits to their models.

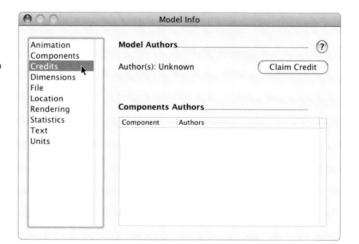

Dimensions

Dimensions settings (**Figure 2.4**) can be a real pain to switch around halfway through a project, especially if you've already added a bunch of dimension strings to your project. For example, if you've laid out a series of dimensions in such a way that the spacing between the strings works great with a 12-point font and dimensions aligned to the screen, you may have to go back and adjust the position of all the strings if you later decide to use a 14-point font with dimensions aligned to the dimension lines. Changing from dots to slashes may cause a ripple effect of having to change the font size and so on down the line.

Before you set your template preferences, think for a minute about whether you'll be more likely to use dimensions in elevation and plan views of your models, or whether you prefer to add dimensions while in perspective views. These two alternatives are likely the basis for a few options that you have for customizing your dimensions settings.

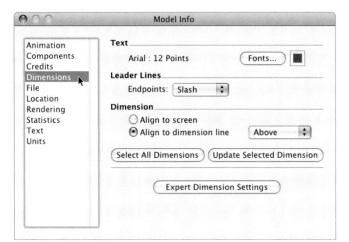

Figure 2.4
The Dimensions settings pane.

The Expert Dimension Settings tab is great for models with dimension strings that have been drawn for multiple views of the model.

I suggest enabling both the "Show radius/diam prefix" and "Hide when foreshortened" options, as shown in **Figure 2.5**.

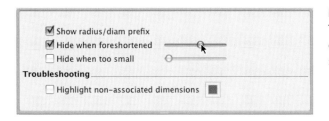

Figure 2.5
The expert dimension settings.

TIP To learn the basics of using SketchUp's Dimensions feature, watch this online video tutorial: www.youtube.com/watch?v=xKLc3hb9Crk.

File

The information and options in the File pane (**Figure 2.6**) are a bit more relevant when you're working with component files than when setting up templates. For that reason, we'll look more closely at these options in Chapter 8, "Mastering Components."

Figure 2.6
File settings.

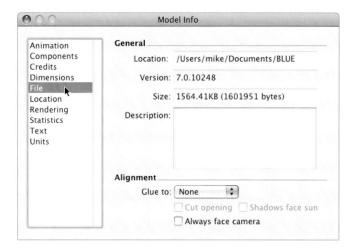

Location

Boulder, Colorado is set as the default location for all the templates that come bundled with SketchUp. The reason (in case you didn't already know) is that Boulder is the gravitational center of the (SketchUp) universe. It's also the city where a couple of dudes named Brad Schell and Joe Esch co-founded @Last software, the company that originally developed SketchUp, prior to Google's subsequent acquisition. Despite Google's acquisition, the SketchUp (and Layout and 3D Warehouse) development teams have remained in Boulder, as has the default location for SketchUp model templates.

You could leave the default location alone (**Figure 2.7**), but setting the location of your SketchUp model influences a number of aspects of your model, including the path that the sun travels while casting shadows. It also determines where a model shows up when it's exported to Google Earth. For those reasons you may be inclined to set the default location to a city where your projects are likely to be located. For example, since I live and work in Southern California, I have my default template location set to Los Angeles.

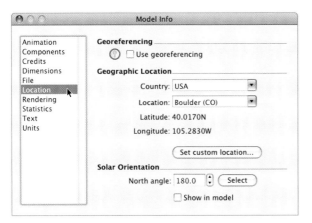

Figure 2.7
You can set a
default location
for your template
by changing the
Location settings.

There are a number of ways to set a new default location for your template.

1. Select the Country and Location (city) from the drop-down menu lists. SketchUp will determine the Latitude and Longitude coordinates based on the geographical center of whichever city you pick from the list (**Figure 2.8**).

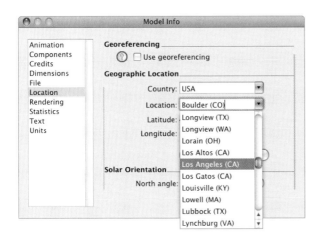

Figure 2.8 SketchUp has a fairly comprehensive list of countries and cities to set as your model's location.

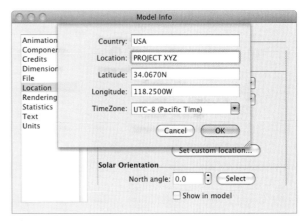

Figure 2.9 You can enter specific site location information for a project.

2. Click the Custom Location button, and enter specific latitude and longitude coordinates for your location (**Figure 2.9**).

3. If you have Google Earth open, search for a specific location and then import it into SketchUp using the Get Current View tool 🌐. SketchUp will register the latitude and longitude coordinates from the center of your view in Google Earth (**Figure 2.10** on the next page).

NOTE For quick access to the location settings, click the Georeferencing icon ⊙ in the bottom-left corner of your drawing window.

Figure 2.10
When you geo-reference your model to a specific location in Google Earth, the location fields will read "N/A," but the Latitude and Longitude coordinates will be on point.

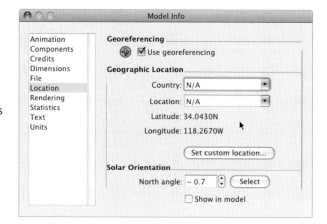

Rendering

SketchUp 7 introduced a new rendering option (**Figure 2.11**) for displaying anti-aliased textures that, depending on your graphics card, may not only improve the way textures look, but might also improve performance. Unless you notice a significant degradation in performance, I'd recommend leaving this option turned on.

Figure 2.11
Rendering settings.

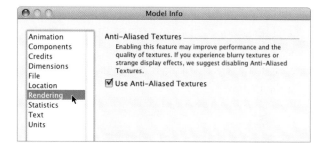

Statistics

As its name suggests, the Statistics pane (**Figure 2.12**) displays a list of stats about your model. One of the most common stats you'll hear people refer to is the polygon (face) count of a model. The "Purge unused" button in the Statistics pane will purge the entire model of any unused components, materials, styles, and layers. It's a great option for reducing the file size of a model before sharing it, but you may find that any unused components, materials, or styles (as well as any unused layers) in your In Model Components library might also end up being purged—so make sure you're not throwing away things you or your colleagues will need later.

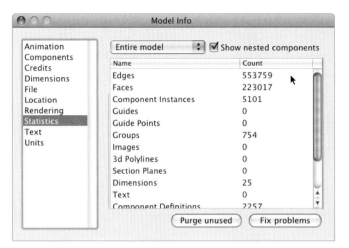

Figure 2.12
Here are the stats for one of the larger projects I've worked on.

Text

The Text pane (**Figure 2.13**) lets you control the default appearance of floating text, leader text, and leader lines by establishing preferences for the font, size, and color of your text objects. Click the Fonts button to choose a default font and size, and click the color box to select a font color.

Once you've added text objects to your model, you can then use the Text preferences pane to globally select and modify your text display preferences. To alter the appearance of individual text objects, it's probably more convenient to right-click them and make changes via the Entity Info window.

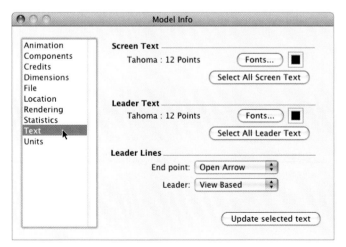

Figure 2.13
Text settings.

NOTE To learn the basics of using SketchUp's Text tool, watch this online video tutorial: www.youtube.com/watch?v=ClHdYWFczgU.

I've found that text preferences vary widely across a spectrum of professional standards and personal tastes. For my projects, I'm a fan of 12-point Arial for onscreen text and 14-point Arial for leader text. I also like using the Open Arrow style for end points, and view-based leader lines. Those aren't prescriptions—just my personal preferences.

Units

The topic of units has come up in just about every SketchUp class I've taught over the past five years. The most frequent question that leads to a conversation about units: "How do you set the scale for your model?" The answer to that question is "You don't set a scale, you set the units."

SketchUp understands a wide range of unit inputs, including both English and metric units, as well as both fractional and decimal units. The Units pane (**Figure 2.14**) simply allows you to select the default units of measurement for your project.

Figure 2.14
Specify which units of measurement you want to use for your model in the Units pane.

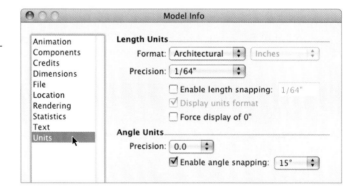

The units you choose for your SketchUp model will affect the following:

- The default unit of measurement for dimensions entered in the Measurements box. For example, if the default units are set to Architectural (Inches) and you specify the length of a line as simply "36," the input will register as 36 inches. On the other hand, if the default units are set to Decimal (Meters) and a length of 36 is entered, the input will register as 36 meters.

- The default unit of measurement for dimensions displayed in and entered into the Entity Info window.

- The default unit of measurement displayed in any dimension strings throughout the model.

- The unit of measurement displayed in the default text that appears when leader text is drawn from On Face or On Edge inferences.

The units will not affect the scale of your model, whether you draw a line and specify a length of 3.28 feet, or whether you specify a length of 1 meter. The line will still be the same length.

Since you have the ability to simply draw objects at their real-world size while working in SketchUp, you don't have to worry about a drawing scale (such as 1/4" = 1'0"). In other words, if a table is 6 feet long, draw it in SketchUp as being 6 feet long. If a door is 7 feet tall, make it 7 feet tall.

Should you ever need to print or export your SketchUp model to scale, you most certainly have that option. We'll discuss exporting your SketchUp model to scale in Chapter 10.

DEFAULT FIELD OF VIEW

The field of view for most of the default templates is set at either 30 or 35 degrees (such as in **Figure 2.15**). The field of view determines the visible limits of the model, based on the position of the camera in the model. The larger the degree angle, the more you can see.

Figure 2.15
View of model with 30-degree field of view.

The Walk tool is the only navigation tool in SketchUp with built-in collision detection, so setting a larger field of view angle may help avoid those times when you inadvertently find yourself having orbited into another room, or through a wall.

To change the field of view, you can either:

- Select the Zoom tool 🔍. Hold down the Shift key and then click and hold down on the left (primary) mouse button while dragging the mouse to change the field of view. Drag the mouse down to increase the field of view, or drag the mouse up to decrease it.

- Select the Zoom tool 🔍. Type in the desired field of view angle followed by the letters *deg* (like this: **45deg**) and press Enter.

The bigger the field of view, the easier it'll be to work on interiors and other small spaces. You'll probably find a field of view around 45 degrees (as in **Figure 2.16**) to be much more accommodating.

For all you old-school CAD monkeys out there, if perspective isn't your thing, you could set the default model view to Parallel Projection mode, with the perspective turned off. To turn off the perspective, go to Camera > Parallel Projection mode. (Note: If you ever want to turn the Perspective view mode back on, go to Camera > Perspective.)

Figure 2.16 View of model with 45-degree field of view. The camera is located in the same place here as it is in Figure 2.15. The larger Field of View degree angle lets you see more of the model.

MORE TEMPLATE SETTINGS

Here are more elements you should consider adding to your template. They are located under a variety of SketchUp's menus, not neatly gathered in one dialog like the Model Info settings. Several of these options will be discussed in more depth in later chapters.

In Model Components

If you find yourself diving into the Components browser every time you feel like dropping in your favorite model from the People folder (Walking_Woman_01, for example), or if you have yet to create a model that doesn't include your favorite 40-foot palm tree, or if your national sales reps consistently need access to the same product catalog in every SketchUp model, then you may consider dragging your "must-have" components into the In Model Component library before saving your SketchUp template.

To add components to the In Model library:

1. Go to Window > Components to launch the component browser.

2. Click the Secondary Selection Pane icon ⯐ in the top-right corner of the component browser to open a secondary browser window.

3. Click the House icon above the primary browser window to open the In Model library.

4. Use the secondary browser window to browse through libraries or search the 3D Warehouse for components you want to add to your template.

5. When you find a component you want to keep, drag it from the secondary window and drop it in the primary window.

The upside to adding components to the In Model library is that your In Model library will always contain your favorite components—even if your component libraries suddenly evaporate or you have to go offline and do not have access to your file server or the 3D Warehouse.

The potential downside is that all of your In Model components are automatically embedded in every new SketchUp project file. Having too many In Model components may unnecessarily increase the file size of some of your projects. If you later decide to pare down the selection of components from the In Model library, you can right-click any of the components listed in the component browser and choose Delete. Then just resave your template and you'll be good to go.

We'll explore more advanced organization and use options for the component browser later in Chapter 4.

Styles

The Styles palette is where you get to pick all sorts of settings pertaining to the way your SketchUp models are rendered onscreen. Line widths, sky and ground colors, watermarks, and numerous other color and display preferences are all housed in the Styles palette. For now, just keep in mind that you can alter the appearance of the default style by going through and determining your preferences under each tab and then clicking the Update Style icon in the Styles palette. Any changes will then be saved as part of your custom template.

As is the case with components, you've also got the option to gather your favorite rendering styles into the In Model folder of your Styles library. Once you save your template, any styles in the In Model library will be readily available for each new model that you start working on.

NOTE Some styles may include background images, artistic line types, or other graphical elements that will increase the file size. As mentioned in the previous section, you may want to consider purging your files before transmitting them. The option found in Model Info > Statistics > Purge Unused will get rid of any unused Styles.

Layers

In just about any office for which I've worked or consulted, layers and layer management are a big deal in almost any program that has a layer function.

In Chapter 5 we'll explore the utilization of layering conventions and gain a better understanding of how to get the most out of what layers have to offer. For now, just keep in mind that you can set up a standard list of layers for your models and save them as a part of your template. Establishing a preset list of layers with which to work will establish a framework and potentially avoid the kind of confusion and widespread panic that ensue when people working together in an office or on a project make up a new set of layers for each new project.

Generally speaking, when it comes to using layers in SketchUp, you'll find they work a bit differently than in other programs. You might intuitively want to be able to mimic the same layers in SketchUp that you use in other CAD applications, but in most cases it's just not worth it. Chances are, you'll be able to work more efficiently in SketchUp if you create a list of layer names that describe the parts of the model being placed on the corresponding layer. For example, if you typically add People to your SketchUp models, create a layer called *People*.

Figure 2.17 shows an example list of commonly used layers that you may want to consider making a part of your SketchUp template.

Figure 2.17 A sample list of layers for a typical two-story building.

Shadow Settings

By now I'm guessing you get the idea: Change a setting, and then save it as part of your template. Of course this goes for the Shadow settings. You can pick a date, time of day, brightness of highlights (the Light slider, with 1 being darkest and 100 brightest), and darkness of shadows (the Dark slider, with 1 being darkest and 100 brightest). The following are my preferred settings (as shown in **Figure 2.18**):

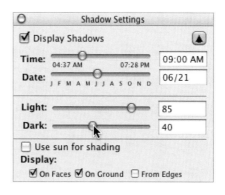

Figure 2.18 Suggested Shadow settings.

- Time: 9 a.m.

- Date: June 21

- Light: 85

- Darkness: 40

Scenes

Scenes are a whole big ball of fun and games, so much so that we've got the entirety of Chapter 9 set aside to get into all sorts of trouble. For now, I just wanted to mention that scenes are another thing you can put on your list of things to consider saving as part of your templates.

You can use scenes to save views with different camera locations, visible layers, active section planes, styles, shadows, and more (**Figure 2.19**). Saving scenes as part of your template is probably more beneficial if you find yourself needing to re-create the same standard views for your presentations. For example, I've helped a number of interior designers and kitchen and bath professionals create templates that include preconfigured views for creating a series of interior elevations.

Figure 2.19 The Scenes dialog.

CHAPTER THREE

SketchUp Extensions

As with Photoshop, AutoCAD, and many other programs, third parties (and Google) have extended SketchUp's capabilities with add-ons. These extensions do a multitude of things, but this chapter focuses on a selection of additional tools for integrating SketchUp more fully within a professional workflow and expediting your work. In addition to profiling my top picks among extensions, I'll discuss how to install and enable them.

Extensions are typically lumped into one of two main categories: Ruby scripts and plug-ins.

RUBY SCRIPTS

Ruby scripts are custom tools or functions that, in SketchUp, are programmed to execute commands. The Ruby programming language originated in 1995 and in addition to being used to create scripts for SketchUp, is popular for Web application development. A Ruby application programming interface (API) was introduced as part of SketchUp version 4. Ruby scripts can be created using a basic text editor, and they can be tested and debugged within SketchUp using the Ruby Console (choose Window > Ruby Console).

Having some programming knowledge certainly helps when it comes to creating your own Ruby scripts for SketchUp. For the avid and aspiring programmers among you, I've listed some great online resources for learning Ruby scripting later in this chapter. Figure 3.2 (on the next page) shows the Ruby Console, along with some code that provides a taste of the fun and excitement of Ruby scripting. If you're like me, and learning Ruby just never seems to make it to the top of the to-do list, you'll be glad to know that there's an incredible community of Ruby programmers who have already written hundreds of scripts for you to use.

If you want to tinker with some rudimentary Ruby scripting, try typing the following line into the Ruby Console: `UI.messagebox("PeachPit told me to!")` <Enter> (**Figure 3.1**).

Here's another super-easy script to try. Type the following lines into the Ruby Console (**Figure 3.2**):

Figure 3.1 The results of a simple Ruby script.

```
pt1 = [0, 0, 0] <Enter>
pt2 = [15, 15, 15] <Enter>
model = Sketchup.active_model <Enter>
model.entities.add_line(pt1, pt2) <Enter>
```

Figure 3.2
The SketchUp Ruby Console.

```
> UI.messagebox("PeachPit Told Me To!")
1
> pt1 = [0, 0, 0]
[0, 0, 0]
> pt2 = [10, 10, 10]
[10, 10, 10]
> model = Sketchup.active_model
#<Sketchup::Model:0x1ef85bb0>

model.entities.add_line(pt1, pt2)
```

Where to Find Ruby Scripts

If you think SketchUp is perfect just the way it is, you're welcome to skip through to Chapter 4. But if you're like the rest of us, you've probably encountered a time when you were working on a project and thought to yourself, "SketchUp would be way cooler if only there was an easy way to draw *x* (a two-point circle, for example)." Well, as it turns out, you can—but only after you download and install the Two-Point Circle Ruby script.

I think it was Captain Obvious who once declared "Google it!" A Google search for "2ptCircle Ruby" will lead you right to the Web site from which you can download the script. The search approach works particularly well if you already know the exact name of the tool you're looking for, but perhaps less well if you're searching with only a vague idea of what a script might be called or what kind of function it might perform.

If you have nothing in mind more specific than a sense that there should be a better way to draw circles in SketchUp, you may have better luck browsing through a catalog of scripts in hopes of finding one that does the trick. Below is a list of my favorite sites for finding Ruby scripts; visiting any of them will repay the time you spend browsing by a factor of ten, thanks to the time-saving tools you'll find. I've bookmarked them and/or subscribed to their RSS feeds, so I'm alerted anytime a new script is posted.

Among these sites you'll find both free and pay-per-download scripts. Some of the sites have such large inventories of scripts that it can make your head spin. If you want to just dip a toe into Ruby scripts, start at the top of this list—the selection gets broader and deeper as you go down.

- **Google SketchUp Web Site**

  http://sketchup.google.com/download/rubyscripts.html

  The Ruby Scripts page in the Downloads section of the SketchUp Web site includes a small selection of free Ruby scripts.

- **Smustard** www.smustard.com

  This site contains a long list of professional-grade scripts; site creator Todd Burch and his colleagues are among the most talented and prolific Ruby script programmers in the world. Some of the scripts are free; some cost money. Any dollars spent here will be well worth the investment.

- **Ruby Library Depot** www.crai.archi.fr/RubyLibraryDepot

  Didier Bur's marvelous contributions to the SketchUp/Ruby community not only include a number of fantastic scripts, but also this great site, which contains hundreds of free scripts. What the 3D Warehouse is to components, the Ruby Library Depot is to Rubies.

- **SketchUcation Extensions Index** www.sketchucation.com/extensions-index

  The SketchUcation Web site has a page with an indexed list of extensions that span a number of smaller Ruby script download sites.

How to Install Rubies

Ruby scripts can be installed simply by placing the downloaded file *ScriptName*.rb into SketchUp's Plugins folder. Some scripts may also require you to place additional files or folders associated with the script (such as toolbar icons) into the Plugins folder. On a PC, the Plugins folder is located at C:\Program Files\Google\Google SketchUp 7\Plugins. On a Mac, the Plugins folder is located at Mac HD/Library/Application Support/Google SketchUp 7/SketchUp/Plugins.

> ### Special Instructions
>
> **Un-Zip It:** Some scripts are downloadable as .zip archives. I'll typically download zipped files to my desktop or downloads folder, unzip them, and then move the files to the Plugins folder (see path descriptions above).
>
> **Tools vs Plugins:** When downloading a script, check the script's Web page for any special installation instructions. On rare occasions you may be required to place the scripts into the Tools folder—rather than the Plugins folder.
>
> **Dependency Issues:** In some cases you may find a script that requires other scripts in order to work properly. Information about special dependencies is typically mentioned on the Web page from which you download the script.

NOTE In some cases, you may need to activate the scripts or plug-ins in the Extensions preferences pane in order for the tools to show up in the menus. For example, the Sandbox tools are a collection of Ruby scripts that are installed automatically as part of Google SketchUp 7, but they won't show up in the View > Toolbars menu until they're enabled in the Extensions pane.

The most efficient way to install Ruby scripts is to right-click (for Macs, Control-click) the download link and choose Save Target As (PC) or Download Linked File As (Mac). Then save the .rb file directly to the Plugins folder (per the preceding directions).

Once the scripts have been saved to the Plugins folder, you'll need to relaunch SketchUp. Any tools located in the Plugins folder will automatically load when the program launches.

The new tools and commands for a script might show up in any one of the following SketchUp menus: Edit, View, Camera, Draw, Tools, Plugins, or contextual menu (right-click). Some scripts might even include their own toolbars that can be turned on by going to View > Toolbars.

Most Rubies will also appear in the Shortcuts list, so if you've downloaded a script that you think you'll use fairly often, you might consider assigning a keyboard shortcut for it (see "Shortcuts" in Chapter 1 for instructions).

Developer Resources

There is no shortage of Ruby programming resources available for learning to create your own scripts. Here are some good places to start that adventure:

- Google SketchUp Ruby API: http://code.google.com/apis/sketchup

- Google SketchUp Developers Discussion Group: http://groups.google.com/group/google-sketchup-developers

- *Ruby: Visual QuickStart Guide* (Larry Ullman, Peachpit Press, 2008)

PLUG-INS

Plug-ins help to both improve SketchUp's interoperability with other applications and expand the kinds of output you can generate from SketchUp. Many plug-ins are created by software developers who want their applications to work well with SketchUp. On the other hand, some plug-ins exist just to extend the capabilities of SketchUp, such as IDX Renditioner (**Figure 3.3**). It lets users generate photorealistic renderings directly within SketchUp, increasing the number of available output formats and potentially saving the time required to export models for rendering in another application.

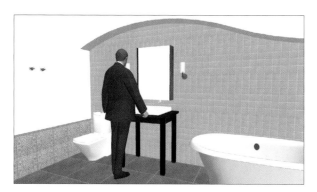 

Figure 3.3 Rendering comparison between standard SketchUp output (left) and a rendering that was created using the IDX Renditioner plug-in (right).

Where to Find Plug-Ins

Google SketchUp Web site http://sketchup.google.com/download/plugins.html

The SketchUp Web site includes a pretty thorough rundown of available SketchUp plug-ins. Almost all the links on the SketchUp site will send you to the software company that developed the plug-in.

Other software developer Web sites

As I write this, there are currently 22 different plug-ins for SketchUp that enable the program to integrate with other applications. A few noteworthy plug-ins include:

- IES VE Energy Analysis Plug-In: www.iesve.com/sketchup

- Photoshop CS3 Extended: http://labs.adobe.com/downloads

- Maxwell Render: www.maxwellrender.com/plugins/sketchup

NOTE Don't overlook the "Plugins for older versions of SketchUp" link on the SketchUp site, which takes you to this site: http://sketchup.google.com/download/previousplugins.html. There you'll find older but still useful tools such as the Film & Stage plug-in.

Many of these sites provide a bunch of great resources, such as additional plug-ins as well as reference manuals and video tutorials.

How to Install Plug-Ins

Installing plug-ins is usually easier than installing Ruby scripts, since most SketchUp plug-ins are downloaded as .exe (PC) or .dmg (Mac) installer files. Once you've run through the installers and followed the onscreen instructions, you may find that new features may have been added to SketchUp (or to whichever other application the plug-in was designed for).

After installing the plug-in, you'll need to restart SketchUp and then check the Extensions preferences pane to make sure that the installed plug-in is enabled (**Figure 3.4**).

Figure 3.4
The Extensions pane of SketchUp Preferences. Check to make sure that installed plug-ins and Ruby scripts are enabled.

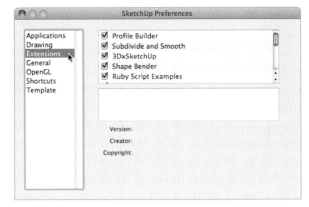

Developer Resources

If you're so inclined, you can develop Google SketchUp plug-ins using the Ruby API and/or the Google SketchUp C++ Software Development Kit (SDK), which can be downloaded from the following site: http://code.google.com/apis/sketchup/docs/downloadsdksubmit.html.

The Google SketchUp Developers Discussion Group is another valuable resource for learning and getting support for your plug-in development endeavors: http://groups.google.com/group/google-sketchup-developers.

TOP 10 EXTENSIONS

Narrowing down the 60 or so scripts in my Plugins folder wasn't easy (this could have easily been a top 30 list), but the following are the plug-ins and Ruby scripts that I think deliver the most bang for the buck (especially considering that most of them are free!).

1. **Deselect** Look in the Selection section of www.crai.archi.fr/RubyLibraryDepot.

   This tool lets you modify a selection set by selecting or deselecting edges or faces. For example, if you want to select all the edges within a component so that you could hide them, you could choose Select All, and then right-click and choose the Deselect Faces option. You'll be left with all the edges selected and then you can choose Edit > Hide.

2. **Profile Builder** www.smustard.com

   The script includes a massive library of professional profiles for finish carpenters, structural engineers, interior designers, and builders. It improves on the basic functions of the Follow-Me tool for creating profile-based extrusions. For example, it allows you to go back and edit the original path or profile of an extrusion, even after you've extruded the profile.

3. **IDX Renditioner** www.idx-design.com

   This easy-to-learn toolset allows SketchUp users to create photorealistic renderings of their models directly within SketchUp. IDX Renditioner includes functionality for adding different types of lights, and includes material-rendering options for reflectivity, and bump maps.

4. **Tools on Surface v1.3** Search http://forums.sketchucation.com.

   Tools on Surface is a set of tools that, among other things, allows you to draw primitive shapes directly onto curved surfaces. For example, with the Tools on Surface Rectangle tool you can draw a rectangle directly onto a contoured landscape surface. Great for landscape design, product design, and character modeling.

5. **Simplify Contours** http://sketchup.google.com/download/rubyscripts.html

   When you import contour line drawings that were executed in other CAD applications, SketchUp will probably convert the polyspline contours into polylines that contain hundreds or even thousands of straight-line segments. This script reduces the number of edge segments that make up the contour lines, which in turn reduces the overall file size and also makes it easier to work with the contours in SketchUp.

6. **Subdivide and Smooth** www.smustard.com

   This is a jaw-dropping series of tools for creating organic shapes and structures.

7. **Rotated Rectangle** http://sketchup.google.com/download/rubyscripts.html

   This drawing command enables you to draw a rectangle by first drawing the length (at any angle) and then the width. It's a great option for tracing sections of CAD plans and satellite imagery where buildings or parts of buildings don't align to the axes.

8. **Stray Lines** www.smustard.com

   Label, Select, Delete, or Show all the open-ended line segments in a drawing. This is an *excellent* script for assessing how much cleaning up an imported CAD drawing will need.

9. **Shape Bender** Search http://forums.sketchucation.com.

   Have you ever needed to create a curved sign (including 3D text)? I guarantee it will be easier with this tool than with any other method you've tried.

10. **Open Studio** http://apps1.eere.energy.gov/buildings/energyplus/openstudio.cfm

    Open Studio is a set of tools for assigning information to objects and entities in your SketchUp models, so you can run building performance simulations and energy analyses.

11. **FreeScale** (OK, so I couldn't resist just one more.)
    Search http://forums.sketchucation.com.

    Ever tried to scale an object that isn't aligned to the axes? Among other things, the FreeScale toolbar includes a scale function that does not discriminate based on an object's orientation.

CHAPTER FOUR

Importing SketchUp Files

You can spend less time drawing and more time designing by downloading models that are already available. This is especially helpful for adding the kinds of set dressing and detail to your model that would otherwise be incredibly time consuming to create from scratch. The best single source is the Google 3D Warehouse, which, in addition to being the world's largest online repository of 3D content, is extremely well integrated into SketchUp. Use the Google 3D Warehouse to quickly search for models of just about anything you can think of—such as people, trees, cars, furniture, and so much more—and download models from the Web directly into SketchUp. In this chapter I'll help you find what you need quickly with targeted searches and explain your options for pulling models into an existing project.

BASIC SKETCHUP FILE IMPORTING

The basic method of importing SketchUp models is the foundation for everything else I'll discuss in this chapter. As you'll see, there are other methods you can use to import SketchUp files into a project, but this basic option is still the best for projects such as assembling larger site models.

To import one SketchUp model into another, choose File > Import.

Then select the file Format option for SketchUp. Locate the SketchUp model you'd like to import in the file browser and then click the Import button (**Figure 4.1** on the next page).

Figure 4.1
The File Import
dialog.

Once you click the Import button, SketchUp will automatically activate the Move tool
. The imported model will appear in the drawing window and it will be attached to
the cursor. There's a name for the point at which the cursor has a hold of the model
being imported: It's called the *insertion point*.

The position of the insertion point of a model corresponds to the position of the axis
origin within the model being imported (**Figure 4.2**).

Figure 4.2
Relationship between
the axis origin and
insertion point for an
imported SketchUp
model.

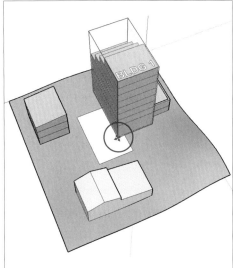

NOTE You can import SketchUp models into your drawing window by dragging them from an open file folder and dropping them into whatever project you're working on (**Figure 4.3**).

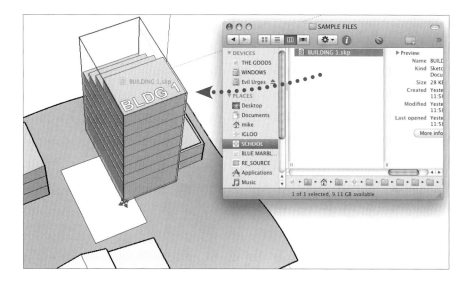

Figure 4.3 You can import files from a file folder simply by dragging them into the drawing window.

Once a file has been imported into SketchUp via the File > Import option, SketchUp will recognize the imported file as a component…which brings us to our next option.

USING THE COMPONENT BROWSER

Importing a component into your project from the component browser has the same effect as importing a SketchUp model using the File > Import command. To open the component browser (**Figure 4.4**), choose Components from the Window menu.

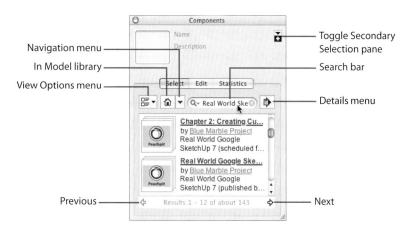

Figure 4.4 The component browser.

You can use the component browser to import models stored locally on your computer's hard drive or network file server. By default, the component browser's Navigation menu ▾ displays a drop-down list of all component folders located on your local hard drive within the Components directory (**Figure 4.5**).

Figure 4.5
The component browser
Navigation menu.

It's handy to store components you know you'll use often in the Components directory within SketchUp, so they'll be right in the Navigation menu's Favorites section. The Components directory is located here:

- On a Mac: *Your Hard Drive*/Library/Application Support/Google SketchUp 7/ SketchUp/Components

- On a Windows PC: C:\Program Files\Google\Google SketchUp 7\Components

If you have SketchUp models in folders in other locations, you can open those by choosing "Open a local collection" from the component browser's Details menu ▣. SketchUp will add the folder to the Favorites list in the Navigation menu ▾.

Once you've located the model(s) you'd like to import, click the icon, drag the model into the drawing window, and then click again to set the model in place.

Why Do Some Models Get All Flippity-Floppity?

Some SketchUp component files may be formatted with gluing planes that will assist or restrict the placement of the component file.

If a component has an assistive gluing plane assigned, you may notice that a component flip-flops around to align itself to the surface on which you're trying to place it.

If the gluing plane is restrictive, you may notice that SketchUp will only allow you to place the model on a particular type of surface. For example, some window and door components are set up such that they can only be placed on horizontal "ground" surfaces or vertical "wall" surfaces.

I'll provide a bit more information about creating components with gluing planes in Chapter 8, "Mastering Components." For now, just be aware that they exist, and that they might affect your ability to place components in your project.

GETTING MODELS FROM THE GOOGLE 3D WAREHOUSE

When I meet someone who's never heard of the Google 3D Warehouse, I'll often describe it as the "YouTube for 3D models." The Google 3D Warehouse (http://sketchup.google.com/3dwarehouse) is a freely accessible Web-based service that allows anyone to upload or download 3D models in SketchUp (.skp), Google Earth (.kmz), or Collada (.dae) file formats.

The Warehouse contains millions of 3D models that include just about everything (PG-rated, of course) you could ever imagine wanting to see in 3D. Amidst this vast sea of content in the Warehouse, you'll find the 3D georeferenced buildings that appear in Google Earth's 3D Buildings layer, as well as hundreds of manufacturer-specific product catalogs containing hundreds of thousands of real-world products. Of course, you'll also find loads of beautifully detailed models of the characters from Halo, *Battlestar Galactica*, *Transformers*, as well as everything you'd need to create 3D contingency plans for an apocalyptic zombie attack.

In much the same way that you might search YouTube for the music video of "I'm on a boat" and instead somehow end up watching the stop-motion LEGO version that some guy filmed in his living room, the open-source nature of the 3D Warehouse often makes it a bit of a hit-or-miss proposition when you're trying to find useful content for a project.

Finding What You're Looking For

Before getting into the specifics for downloading stuff from the 3D Warehouse, it's worthwhile to take a look at some of the best ways of finding what you're looking for in the first place.

Searching the Warehouse for models isn't much different than using Google to search for a Web site. The more specific you can be with your search word(s) or phrase, the better. For example, a generic search for the word "car" returns more than 25,000 models to browse through. However, typing a specific make and model (such as "Chevrolet Corvette") will whittle the results significantly (down to about 200).

If you really want to get fancy with your search results, check out the advanced search operators that Google has listed in the SketchUp Help center: http://sketchup.google.com/support/bin/answer.py?hl=en&answer=92457 (Google "3D Warehouse Advanced Search Operators"). I've listed some of my favorites in **Table 4.1**.

Table 4.1   Useful Advanced Search Operators

Operator	Definition	Example(s)
is:dynamic	Search for dynamic models only	is:dynamic
author	Used to specify the author's nickname	author:BlueMarbleProject
complexity	Search for models with a given level of complexity	Car complexity:low Car complexity:medium Car complexity:high
is:geo	Search for georeferenced items (marked with a location on Earth)	Dodger Stadium is:geo
near:	Search for items "near" the given location	near:Los Angeles, CA near:11755 Wilshire Blvd
filetype:	Search for models that contain the specified file type	filetype:skp filetype:kmz filetype:dae

Typing advanced search operators into the search bar is one way to quickly include common search filters and criteria, most of which are otherwise found in the dialog that comes up when you click the Advanced Search link next to the search bar (**Figure 4.6**).

Figure 4.6
The Advanced Search link and the 3D Warehouse's Advanced Search dialog.

Sourcing Dynamic Components

I use the "is:Dynamic" filter most often. Adding that to your search phrase will return only those models that have dynamic component (DC) options. For example, "French Door is:Dynamic" will return just a handful of models to choose from. For items such as windows, doors, and cabinets, you'll often find detailed dynamic components with configurable options for size, material, hardware, etc.

The "Ultimate Wood Outswing French Door" by Marvin Windows contains dynamic options, including 16 different available sizes that can be configured in 64 different ways. Often you'll also find dynamic components that include clickable interactions. The doors in this model, for example, will swing open and shut when you click them with the Interact tool 🖐.

NOTE Because of the way dynamic components are programmed, you'll typically need to import them directly into a project in order to get them to work as advertised. Downloading a dynamic component to your desktop and then opening it will not let you access its dynamic features.

Sourcing Products

The ability to source 3D models from real-world manufacturers' product catalogs is very useful for architects and designers who want to incorporate specific products into their designs. With over a billion page views since the 3D Warehouse site was introduced in 2007, manufacturers are realizing the benefits of uploading their catalogs to the Warehouse—letting designers and consumers visualize their products in 3D.

Collections are an organizational feature that manufacturers often use to replicate the experience consumers might have if they were to browse a traditional print catalog. For example, choose Collections from the drop-down menu to the right of the search bar, and then type in the name of a brand, or product line for your search (**Figure 4.7**). For example, "KraftMaid Cabinetry" or "Hayward Cabinets" (one of KraftMaid's product lines) will return specific catalog collections that you can browse through.

Searching for collections that contain a particular product type can be another effective way to locate specific products—for example, "KraftMaid Base Cabinets."

Figure 4.7 You can browse collections the way you might browse a manufacturer's product catalog.

Searching for models (by choosing Models from the drop-down) that correspond to a particular product name or SKU is probably the best option for narrowing your search to a single model. For example, "Hayward Sink Base Cabinet" or "JCB2488MTR" will definitely help you cut to the chase (**Figure 4.8**).

Figure 4.8 If you're going to search models for a specific product, try searching for the product's SKU code first.

Sourcing Georeferenced Content

Finding specific georeferenced models (that is, models that contain information about their specific geographic location on Earth) in the 3D Warehouse is another task for which search criteria can help speed the process.

If you're looking for buildings in a particular city, click the Collections radio button before searching for the city name—"Los Angeles, CA," for example. If you find more than one collection for a particular city, start with the one that contains the most models.

If you're searching for a specific building and you know its name ("Home Depot," for example) or the building address (such as "11755 Wilshire Blvd"), you can enter that info into the search bar and click the Models radio button.

Methods of Downloading

There are two main methods for downloading content from the 3D Warehouse: either by saving files to your computer's hard drive via your Web browser, or by directly importing them into your SketchUp project via the component browser or Get Models command.

Downloading from the Web

The 3D Warehouse is accessible online at http://sketchup.google.com/3dwarehouse. I use the Safari browser on the Mac, but Chrome, Firefox, and Internet Explorer all work in much the same way.

To download a file from the Warehouse, click the gigantic Download Model button, and then select the file format and/or version of SketchUp that you're using. When you click to download a file it will be saved automatically to whatever folder you've set as the default for your Web browser downloads. On my Mac I've got Safari set up to save files to the Downloads folder; on my PC I have Chrome set to download to my desktop.

When downloading from the Web, I'm typically downloading files that I eventually want to open on their own, rather than import into another project. For example, you'll often find entire models of rooms or buildings that have been uploaded for you to tinker with, such as the Kitchen design by KraftMaid that features their Putnam maple cabinetry line alongside a suite of Dacor appliances (**Figure 4.9**).

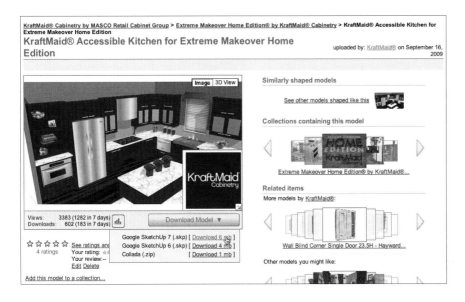

Figure 4.9 Files downloaded from the 3D Warehouse can be saved locally and opened directly in SketchUp.

Once I've downloaded a file and taken it for a spin, I'll typically copy and paste elements of the file into a project, and/or stash the file in a project folder for future reference.

NOTE If you download files from the 3D Warehouse, remember that you can save them and organize them in folders in the SketchUp application directory (see the previous section, "Using the Component Browser"). Any folders or files saved to the Components directory will automatically show up in your component browser Favorites list.

Downloading Directly into SketchUp

Without even opening your Web browser, you can download files directly into SketchUp via the component browser or via the Get Models command.

Via the component browser: The Search bar at the top of the component browser is linked directly to the 3D Warehouse. When you enter a search word or phrase, the results appear in the primary browser pane. Click the icon of the model to import it directly into your project (**Figure 4.10**).

Figure 4.10 Once you find a model, you can drag and drop it from the component browser into the drawing window.

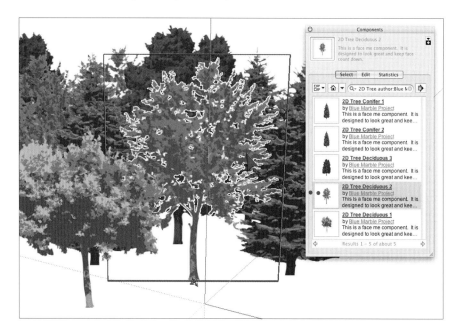

To save a model you've downloaded from the Warehouse to a folder in your local library, open the In Model library 🏠 in the primary pane. Then open the secondary pane 🐱 and navigate ▼ to a folder in which you want to save the downloaded component. Then drag and drop from the In Model pane above into the open folder in the secondary pane below (**Figure 4.11**).

Figure 4.11 To save a model for future use, drag and drop it from the In Model library to a folder in the secondary pane.

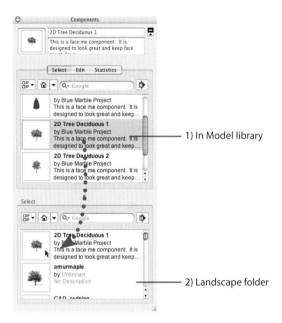

1) In Model library

2) Landscape folder

Playing Favorites

Once you figure out which search phrase to use to find the stuff you're looking for, you can save the search to your component browser Favorites list. Simply choose "Save to favorites" from the Details pop-up menu 🗗 in the component browser (**Figure 4.12**).

The search phrase will then show up in the Navigation ▾ menu drop-down list.

"Save as a local collection" is another option in the Details menu that works especially well for downloading entire catalogs to your desktop and automatically saving them to a folder in the SketchUp Components directory.

Commitment-phobes need not worry; the Remove From Favorites option is just as easy to use.

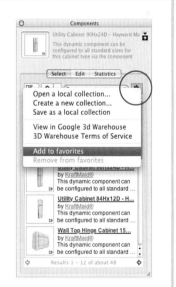

Figure 4.12 Save common searches as Favorites.

Via the Get Models command: The Get Models ⚙ command in the Google toolbar (View > Toolbars > Google) opens a mini Internet browser window within SketchUp (**Figure 4.13**). The search and download process is practically identical to downloading from the Web as described earlier; the difference is that when you click the Download button, you're asked whether you want to download the model directly into your SketchUp project (**Figure 4.14**). Clicking OK brings the model into your project; clicking No results in a dialog that lets you choose a folder on your hard drive. If you don't want that model after all, click Cancel.

Figure 4.13
The Get Models command launches the 3D Warehouse in a mini Web-browser window.

Figure 4.14
SketchUp gives you the option to download models directly into your SketchUp project.

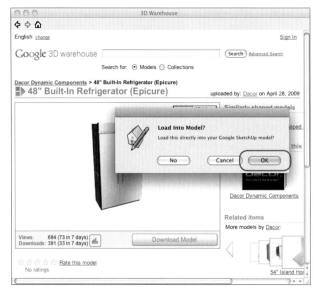

Creating Your Own Collections

Creating collections is a great way to catalog models on the 3D Warehouse for future use. For example, you might create a collection called "My Windows," "My Plants," "My Furniture," or any other type of model you regularly find yourself searching for. If you don't want people to know about your fetish for collecting *Star Wars* models, don't worry—for every collection you create within the 3D Warehouse, you have the option to make it private or to share it only with people you choose. You'll see a link below every image model that says "Add this model to a collection." Click the link to choose a collection from the drop-down list. Keep in mind that a model can be included in any number of collections.

When you're logged in to the 3D Warehouse you'll see a My Collections link at the top-right corner of the screen (**Figure 4.15**).

Figure 4.15
My Collections link.

📄 **NOTE** When you're logged in to the 3D Warehouse you can also access any models you've uploaded to the Warehouse, or any collections you've created from within SketchUp, by choosing the options for My Models or My Collections from the Navigation drop-down list in the component browser.

CREATING AN EASY-BAKE SITE MODEL

Environmental factors such as site location and context are important pieces of information that need to be taken into consideration for most architectural design projects. The Google "geo-trifecta" of SketchUp, Google Earth, and the 3D Warehouse is a powerful combo for all sorts of location-specific applications. SketchUp users are actively creating models for inclusion in Google Earth's 3D Buildings layer, and the 3D Warehouse is the portal through which those 3D Buildings are submitted. That's great news for designers, because it means that you can import any of those same geo-located models from the Warehouse directly into SketchUp to create a 3D model of your site that includes the surrounding buildings.

Taking Earth for a Spin

Google Earth is another amazing application, downloadable from http://earth.google. com (both free and pro versions are available). It's not hard to learn the basic navigation, and there's a tutorial available at http://earth.google.com/tour.html. To learn more about Google Earth, check out the "Google Earth for Everyone" full-length video training from School: http://www.go-2-school.com/products/view/9.

To create a site model:

1. Start up Google Earth and locate your project site (in this case, a parking lot adjacent to the Walt Disney Concert Hall in downtown Los Angeles, CA).

2. Turn on the Terrain layer and the 3D Buildings layer (**Figure 4.16**) to find out whether any of the buildings from that site have already been modeled.

Figure 4.16 Turn on the Terrain and 3D Buildings layers.

© 2009 Google, Map Data © 2009 Tele Atlas

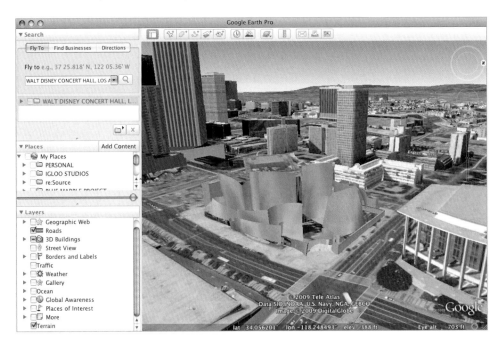

3. Reset the view in Google Earth (the shortcut is R) so that the north angle is pointing up toward the top of the screen and you are looking straight down at the site.

4. Turn off the 3D Buildings layer (but keep the Terrain layer turned on) so you can see the satellite imagery in Google Earth (**Figure 4.17**).

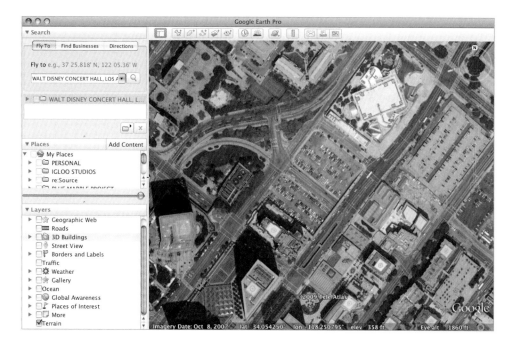

5. Switch over to SketchUp and import the satellite imagery of the location (**Figure 4.18**) using the Get Current View command in the Google toolbar (View > Toolbars > Google).

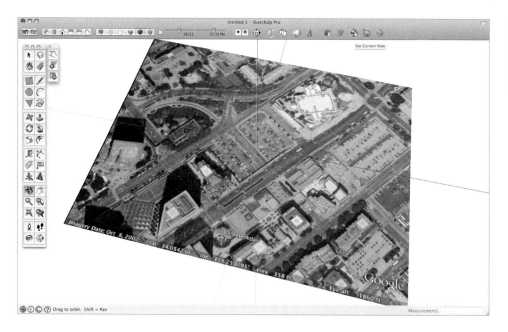

6.   Click the Toggle Terrain command ![toggle] to view the terrain in 3D.

7.   Use the Get Models command ![models] to search the 3D Warehouse and import specific buildings (such as the Walt Disney Concert Hall, as shown in **Figure 4.19a**).

Figure 4.19a
Use the Get Models command to find and import specific models.

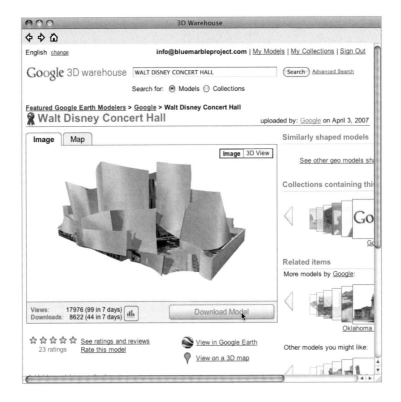

8.   Click the link to download the model, and then click OK to load the model directly into your project.

9.   You'll then see a pop-up window indicating that the location of your model building has a specific location associated with it that may be far away from the location of your model. Choose the option to "Preserve location" (**Figure 4.19b**) and the building will automatically land on the site in the model where it belongs (**Figure 4.19c**).

Figure 4.19b
If you choose the Preserve Location option SketchUp will automatically position the imported building for you, based on the model's embedded Geo-Reference data.

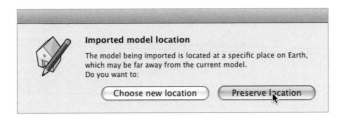

Figure 4.19c
A site model created by importing from Google Earth and the 3D Warehouse.

© 2009 Google, Map Data © 2009 Tele Atlas

Repeat steps 7–9 to import additional buildings. Remember that the advanced search modifier "near:" can help locate buildings nearby. For example, you could use the address for the Disney Concert Hall as the epicenter to search for additional buildings: "near:111 South Grand Avenue, Los Angeles, 90012."

Downloading Nearby Models

Searching the 3D Warehouse for familiar buildings or for buildings near a particular address are both ways to use the Get Models command to create site models. You can also search for models near a specific site using the Component Browser window.

1. Open the Component Browser window and choose Nearby Models from the Navigation drop-down menu (see **Figure 4.20**).

SketchUp automatically searches the 3D Warehouse for models whose geographic coordinates match the location of the site you have imported from Google Earth. Any available nearby buildings will appear in the Component Browser window.

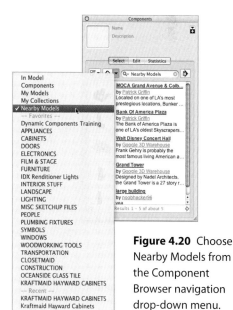

Figure 4.20 Choose Nearby Models from the Component Browser navigation drop-down menu.

2. Click the model preview icon to begin downloading the model (in this case, the "Grand Tower" building located just down the street from the Walt Disney Concert Hall (see **Figure 4.21**).

Figure 4.21 Clicking the model preview icon initiates the download process.

3. When prompted, choose to preserve the downloaded model's location. SketchUp will automatically download and position the model relative to the satellite image that was imported from Google Earth (see **Figure 4.22**).

Figure 4.22 The Grand Tower is just down the street from the Walt Disney Concert Hall.

No 3D for You!

You may find that nothing shows up on the 3D Buildings layer for your area in Google Earth—which means that no one has uploaded any models to the 3D Warehouse for it. So you're probably out of luck in terms of populating your current project, but you can help change that.

If you're interested in having 3D Models of the buildings in your city or town appear in Google Earth and the 3D Warehouse, check out Google's Cities in 3D program for information on how you may be able to help your local city government to get that ball rolling: http://sketchup.google.com/intl/en/3dwh/citiesin3d/index.html.

Cities around the world are using Google Earth as a means to promote tourism and commerce districts by creating 3D models of the buildings in their town, enabling potential new businesses, residents, and travelers to experience city amenities virtually. Amherst, Massachusetts (and the UMass campus) is one such city that has become quite an incredible success story of how a community's own citizens can collaborate on creating their own 3D city model for Google Earth (**Figure 4.23**). You can read more about their use of SketchUp, Google Earth, and the 3D Warehouse at: http://sketchup.google.com/3dwh/citiesin3d/amherst.html.

Figure 4.23
A 3D Google Earth model of Amherst City Center (Amherst, MA) with the College campus of UMass in the background.

© 2009 Google

You may find it helpful to contact a Professional 3D Geoweb Services company such as Blue Marble Project (info@bluemarbleproject.com) to assist in creating 3D models or to simply help consult on, or manage the process.

SIZE MATTERS

The models on the 3D Warehouse are created by experts and novices alike. As such, the precision and care with which the components have been created varies widely. Among the most common issues with content downloaded from the Warehouse is the size of the file, both in terms of the object's relative size in the model, and also the byte size of the file. You won't run into very many problems with relative size or byte size if you stick to searching for manufacturer catalogs and Geo content, but you don't want to miss out on the other 95 percent of the content in the 3D Warehouse. So search away, and see what you come up with. If you end up importing a 3-foot-long car, all is not lost. You've got some options.

Scaling Your Components

The Scale tool: The Scale tool 🔲 is probably the first tool that comes to mind when you need to scale an object that comes in at the wrong size.

In this example we'll use a model of a car that you can download from the 3D Warehouse. Using the Get Models command 🔲, search for and download the model "Car Model (Not to Scale)" in the Real World Google SketchUp Chapter 4 collection.

When using the Scale tool to size a component, you can eyeball it, enter a specific scale factor in the Measurements box in the bottom-right corner, or enter an exact size in the direction of the axis about which you are scaling.

For example, click the center-front scale handle. While scaling the model out along the green axis, press and hold the Shift key to constrain on center the proportions of the model, and then click to initially scale the model up to an arbitrary size. Then type 182.5" and press Enter to scale the car to its exact, proper length (**Figure 4.24**).

> **NOTE** With dynamic components, you may find that some of the scale handles are turned off. In most cases that means the model is already at the correct scale and handles are turned off to prevent you from screwing up the model. If you're using SketchUp Pro and you feel like you need to scale a DC, you could try turning the scale handles on by editing the dynamic component attributes. If the component gets all messed up, don't say I didn't warn you. You may want to do a Save-As before tinkering with a DC so that if something goes wrong, you won't have to download it again.

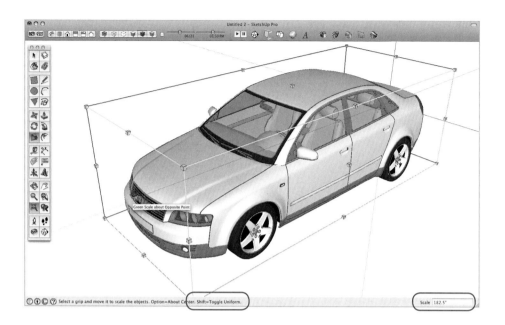

Figure 4.24 The Scale tool can be used to scale an object based on a known exact overall dimension along the red, green, or blue axis.

The Tape Measure tool: Among the Tape Measure tool's <span></span> many uses is its ability to scale components within the model based on a known exact dimension. For example:

1. Re-import the same car model that we used in the previous example.

2. Right-click the component and choose Edit Component (**Figure 4.25**).

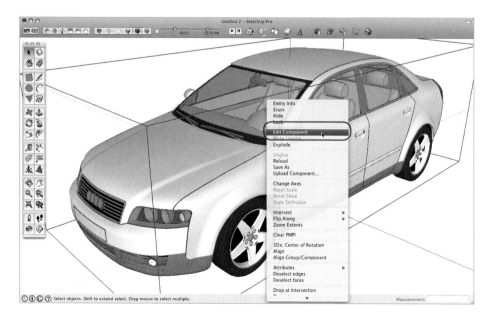

Figure 4.25 Edit Component.

3. Use the Tape Measure tool ![tape measure icon] to measure lengthwise from one endpoint to another endpoint (**Figure 4.26**). Tip: Click an endpoint on the frontmost part of the model, then press the left arrow key to lock the green axis, and then orbit around and click an endpoint on the backmost part of the model.

Figure 4.26 Using the Tape Measure tool.

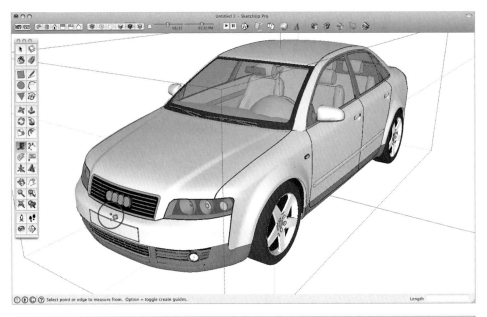

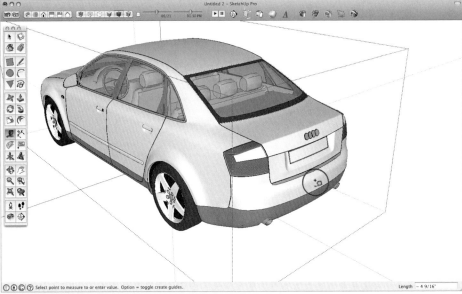

4. In the Measurements dialog you'll see where SketchUp is telling you that the model is ~4' 7 ¹⁄₁₆". At this point you can tell SketchUp what that distance should be. Type in 182.5" and press Enter (**Figure 4.27**).

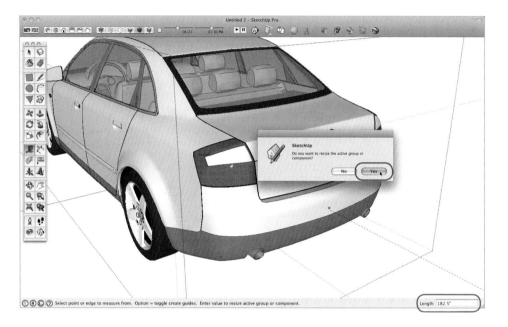

Figure 4.27 Enter a new value for the length.

5. When SketchUp asks if you want to change the size of the active component, click Yes (Figure 4.27).

6. Zoom out using the Zoom Extents tool.

7. The last step is to close up the component wrapper. The easiest way is to take the Select tool (press the spacebar as a shortcut) and then press the Esc (escape) key.

NOTE An important difference between using the Scale tool and using the Tape Measure tool is that scaling an object with the Scale tool may change the position of the bottom of the component in the blue axis (vertical) direction, whereas the Tape Measure tool scale option will keep the bottom of the component in the same spot.

Reducing File Size

Polygon count and image-based texture maps are two of the most significant contributing factors to file size. A model's polygon count can also tax your computer's graphics card and potentially bog down SketchUp's performance. It doesn't make sense to let imported components hog your system resources if they're just in your project as window dressing. It does make sense to choose models that are just detailed enough for your purpose.

Take the car model that you just resized, for example. It's a beautiful model, but the amount of detail would likely be overkill for most situations.

The 3D Warehouse shows that the model is about a 7 MB file. With the model already downloaded, go to Window > Components > In Model Library. Then select the car component in the list, click the Statistics tab, and then choose the Expand check box. In the Statistics pane for the components you'll see that there are over 130,000 entities contained in just this one model (**Figure 4.28**). That's not so great unless you're working on an ad and the model of this car is the only thing you'll be working on.

Figure 4.28
The 7 MB file of this car model contains over 130,000 entities.

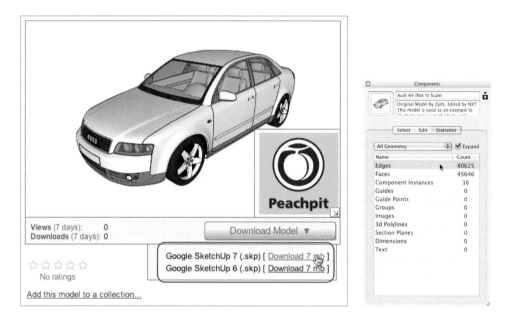

Compare those statistics against a model of a Ford Escape that you can find in the Real World Google SketchUp 7 Chapter 4 collection in the 3D Warehouse, which comes in at 1 MB, and contains about 11,000 entities (**Figure 4.29**). Even though the model of the Escape is textured, it is still a significantly smaller file. For projects where it would be necessary to place a few cars around—either in a garage, curbside, or in a small parking lot—I'd much rather go with the lower-poly, textured model of the Escape.

If you had to put cars all over the place to depict a busy road, intersection, or large parking lot, your best bet would be something from Google's collection of low-poly vehicles, which include cars like the sedan in **Figure 4.30** (also in the collection for this chapter, or you can search for "Sedan author:google"), which comes in at a mere 64 Kb and has been modeled with just over 1200 entities.

Ford Escape

Image | 3D View

Views: 1163 (45 in 7 days)
Downloads: 517 (23 in 7 days)

Download Model ▼

Google SketchUp 7 (.skp) [Download 1 mb]
Google SketchUp 6 (.skp) [Download 1 mb]

☆ ☆ ☆ ☆ ☆   See ratings and
7 ratings   Rate this model

Add this model to a collection...

Figure 4.29 The textured model of this Ford Escape contains over 11,000 entities and weighs in at around 1 MB.

Sedan

Image | 3D View

Views: 4358 (33 in 7 days)
Downloads: 7257 (86 in 7 days)

Download Model ▼

Google SketchUp 5 (.skp) [Download 64 kb]

☆ ☆ ☆ ☆ ☆   See ratings and reviews
6 ratings   Rate this model

Add this model to a collection...

Figure 4.30 The sedan model is optimized for use in projects where you might need to put a lot of cars in your project.

NOTE "Max-Polys" is an advanced search operator that can help refine search results based on a models polygon count. If you're looking for a component that you'll need to copy many times, this is a good filter to use. Try looking for components with a maximum of 1000 polygons and then increase that number if you're having trouble locating a suitable model. For example, "car max-polys:1000."

One of the best file-size savers is to use low-poly, 2D components in lieu of high-poly 3D components. You'll most often find this to be an acceptable option when adding landscape components (such as trees, bushes, etc.) and people to your models. Add "2D" to your search phrase for these types of components and you'll be off to a good start. Some of the best trees I've ever used can be found by searching for "SetTree3D author:pepe." These tree models use an exceptional blend of low-poly, textured, "face-me" components (see Chapter 8, "Mastering Components") while adding depth to the various elements of the tree to lend more realism.

Too Much Junk in the Trunk

Polygon count issues are one thing, and downloading a component that simply has more elements than you need is another common problem. Paste in Place is a command you can use to quickly extract the parts you need to keep, and dump the rest.

1. Open a new file and then choose Get Models ![icon]. Search for the "Kraftmaid Extreme Makeover Home Edition" and download the model of the Riojas family's accessible kitchen by Kraftmaid.

2. Right-click the component and choose Edit Component (**Figure 4.31**).

Figure 4.31
Edit Component.

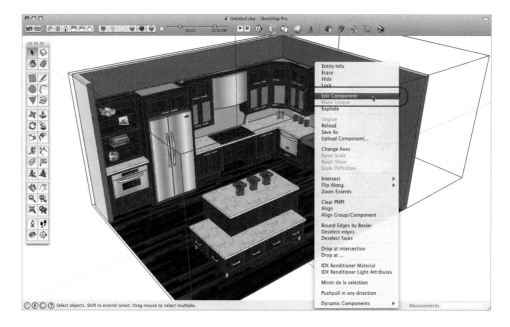

3. Select the kitchen island, and then press Command+X to cut the island and place it on to the Clipboard (**Figure 4.32**).

Figure 4.32
Cut the island.

4. Press the Esc key to close the component.

5. Choose Edit > Paste in Place (my recommended custom shortcut is Option+ Shift+V) to paste the island back into the model—outside of the component that contains the rest of the kitchen (**Figure 4.33**).

Figure 4.33
Paste in Place.

NOTE If you want to save all of the components from the kitchen to a local folder so that you'll have access to them offline: Click the In Model icon in the component browser 🏠. Then choose "Save as a local collection" from the Details menu 🔁.

6. Take the Eraser tool (keyboard shortcut E) 🧽 and click the kitchen to leave the island unto itself (**Figure 4.34**).

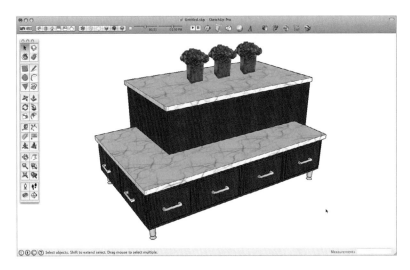

Figure 4.34 Erase the kitchen.

NOTE The Purge Unused option in the Model Info window purges all In Model libraries of unused components, layers, materials, and styles. To purge only the unused components, go to the component browser and navigate to the In Model library 🏠. Then choose the option for Purge Unused from the Details menu 🔁. Similar options can be found in the Layers, Materials, and Styles windows.

7. To remove the other components that would otherwise still be embedded in the file, choose Window > Model Info > Statistics > Purge Unused.

OTHER COMPONENT RESOURCES

There are other great online resources for getting your hands on professional-quality SketchUp components. The following sites offer samples from their component collections that can be downloaded from the 3D Warehouse.

- **Form Fonts: www.formfonts.com** Form Fonts is a subscription-based site with thousands of professional-quality 2D models, 3D models, and texture maps. When 3D Warehouse searches turn up empty, I'll often turn to Form Fonts. I've had an account on this site for nearly four years and find it an invaluable resource for delivering projects on tight deadlines.

- **Entourage Arts: www.entouragearts.com** This site sells a number of CD-ROM volumes with 2D NPR (non-photorealistic) components of people and landscape elements. Each component comes in SKP, PNG, and MCD format. The files can be used in SketchUp, Piranesi, and Photoshop to create renderings with a softer, more hand-drawn aesthetic.

CHAPTER FIVE

Importing CAD Files

The ability to transport information seamlessly between any of the various 3D and 2D design and drafting programs is at best a dream, albeit one that is likely shared by many of us. For the time being, the interoperability between SketchUp and other CAD applications still involves some shenanigans.

As the great debate about CAD software rages on, and battles for CAD supremacy are waged between Autodesk and its enemies, I've managed to find my little corner of Zen amidst the tumult.

I came to realize after having installed a bazillion modeling, design, drafting, and rendering applications, that I like using software the way I used to use analog mixed media. In my old art bin I used to have Conté crayons and charcoal sticks on the top shelf, sketching and technical pencils on the second tier, Rapidographs below that, and a jumble of watercolor stuff, Prismacolor pencils, eraser shields, and various Exacto blades scattered in the bottom of the bin. And that was just the stuff in the bin—not including all the other stuff I had around my drafting table. There was a time for using each and all of those different media—either for design sketches, presentation renderings, or working drawings.

Nowadays I tend to try using SketchUp for just about everything—except for creating working drawings, which are still created in AutoCAD, Revit, or Vectorworks, where the drafting tools are more effective and efficient for creating the kinds of documents that are typically required by local building departments and builders. Photoshop, Illustrator, Flash, After Effects, Final Cut, Cinema 4D, Piranesi, and about a dozen other applications round out the list of digital tools we often use to get things done.

In my digital art bin, SketchUp is the tool of choice for visualizing and communicating ideas in three dimensions, which makes it an incredibly useful tool throughout all stages of the design and building process. When combined with the companion program Layout, SketchUp is inching closer to offering a viable standalone replacement software for other CAD drafting tools. Together they can pretty much get the job done for smaller-scale projects, such as finish carpentry projects, set designs, and kitchen and bath projects—but for projects that require full-scale construction documents, such as ground-up commercial or residential projects, SketchUp probably won't meet all your needs.

Working with CAD data in SketchUp presents a number of challenges, such as getting the files in good shape, managing layers, and working with curves and contours—all of which I'll discuss in this chapter. There's also the issue of exporting CAD files from SketchUp, but we'll get to that a bit later in Chapter 10.

CHOOSING CAD IMPORT OPTIONS

NOTE Even if you're using a program for drafting other than AutoCAD, you can probably export your drawings in AutoCAD format (DWG or DXF). If your drafting program has an option to export to SketchUp's SKP format, just use that instead and skip this section.

Opening a non-native CAD file in SketchUp is an easy process, but you can avoid some headaches if you take a little care when bringing in the file. Let's look at each of the import options that SketchUp provides.

To import a CAD file, select Import from the File menu. Then choose the option in the File Format drop-down menu for "AutoCAD Files (*.dwg, *.dxf)" (**Figure 5.1**).

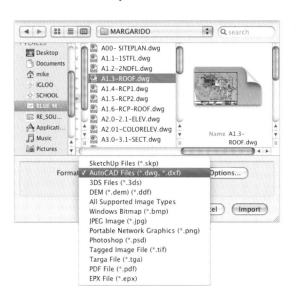

Figure 5.1
Importing AutoCAD files.

Avoiding Stickiness

If you're using a template such as "Plan View - Feet and Inches," which opens new files beginning with an empty drawing space, the first CAD file you import will come in as a bunch of loose, sticky lines. As soon as you get those lines into SketchUp, I suggest grouping them immediately.

If there's already something in the model (like Sang, the guy who's standing at the origin in the Architectural templates), SketchUp will import a CAD file as a component and the component wrapper will keep it from sticking to anything else in the model.

In the Import dialog, choose the CAD file you want to import by browsing for it, and then click the Options button. In the Options dialog, make sure the scale is set to Inches and that all three check boxes are checked, so that "Preserve drawing origin," "Merge coplanar faces," and "Orient faces consistently" are all enabled (**Figure 5.2**). Click OK, and then click Import.

If your import was successful, you should see an Import Results dialog that shows you some statistics of your model (**Figure 5.3**).

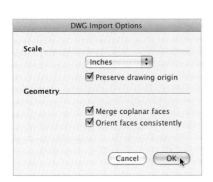

Figure 5.2 Recommended import settings.

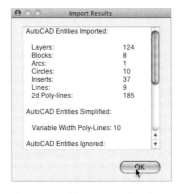

Figure 5.3 The Import Results dialog details the data SketchUp was able to successfully translate from your CAD files.

Scale

The Scale drop-down menu is a bit of a misnomer as it's not really asking about scale, or about the units of your SketchUp model—rather, it's asking for the units that the *CAD file* was drawn in. When SketchUp imports a CAD file, it switches the default units to match what you have specified in SketchUp (under Model Info > Units). In the United States, most CAD programs (and SketchUp) are typically set up with the default units in inches, for architectural design.

If you import a CAD file and don't pick the correct scale units, you might get an error message like the one in **Figure 5.4**—in which case, try again and pick a different one.

Figure 5.4 An error message you might get when importing a CAD file into SketchUp. This one typically suggests a scale/ units issue.

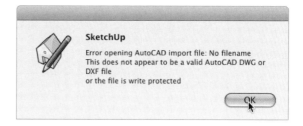

Preserve Drawing Origin

For smaller-scale projects it's a good idea to preserve the drawing origin. Often during a project, the design changes and project files need to be updated frequently (both in CAD and in SketchUp). When the drawing origin is preserved during the initial and subsequent CAD file imports, the drawings will be imported on top of each other in reference to the same origin—making it a lot easier to notice the differences between each version.

For larger files, such as site plans or surveys, the drawing origin may represent a GPS coordinate or surveyor stake that lies far away from the project site. If that's the case, it's probably better to discard the drawing origin by deselecting the "Preserve Drawing Origin" option. The import will result in the CAD file landing closer to the SketchUp model origin. Since surveys and as-built drawings typically only have to be imported once, at the beginning of a project, the drawing origin is less important because you'll rarely need to re-import revised versions of those kinds of files.

Orient Faces Consistently

The option to "Orient faces consistently" is most useful when importing 3D CAD files, but I tend to just leave it checked for all CAD imports.

The orientation/direction of a face is an important attribute to be aware of and maintain throughout a project. The direction of a face is visually represented by the default face colors blue (inside) and white (outside), as shown in **Figure 5.5**.

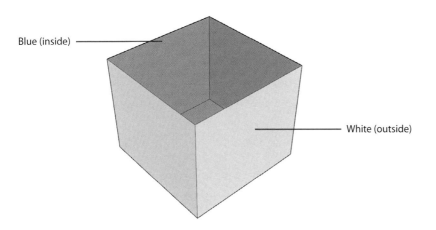

Blue (inside)

White (outside)

Figure 5.5 Default face colors visually illustrate the orientation and direction of a face.

If you import a CAD file into SketchUp and you notice that despite having checked the option to orient faces consistently, some or all of the faces in your model are blue (turned inside-out), here are some ways you can fix that.

Reverse Faces

The Reverse Faces command is located in the context menu and appears whenever you right-click a face. Reverse Faces flips the direction of a face from white to blue or vice versa (**Figure 5.6**). The process goes a bit faster if you preselect multiple faces before using the Reverse Faces command.

NOTE The Reverse Faces option will not appear if you right-click a group or component. You must be in Edit Group, or Edit Component mode and then right-click a face to access this option.

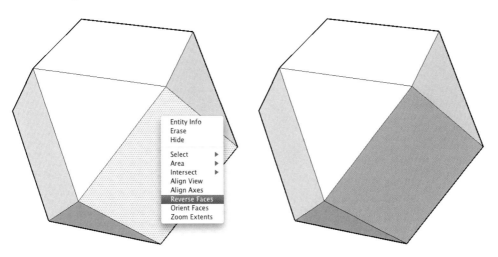

Figure 5.6 Before and after using the Reverse Faces command to flip the orientation of a single face.

Orient Faces

The Orient Faces command is also located in the context menu and appears whenever you right-click a face. Orient Faces causes SketchUp to reevaluate all faces connected to the one you right-click. SketchUp will orient the connected faces so that they correspond to the orientation of the face you clicked (**Figure 5.7**).

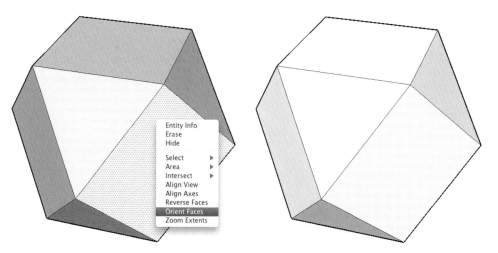

Figure 5.7 Before and after using the Orient Faces command to flip the orientation of a bunch of faces.

In other words, if you right-click one face that has the white side facing out, then all the faces of that object will be oriented so that the white side is facing out.

Hidden Geometry

If you import a curved surface and notice that only some parts of the surface are inside out, and the above options aren't working to fix the problem, you can turn on Hidden Geometry (View > Hidden Geometry) and then use the Reverse Faces command to properly orient the inside-out parts individually.

Can't I Just Paint It?

If this section has you thinking about having seen a blue-and-white jumbled mess of faces at some point in a past project, and you decided at the time to "fix" the model by using the Paint Bucket tool to apply a uniform material to all the surfaces…well, that just hid the problem; it didn't get rid of it.

While you may think the faces look OK once they've been painted in SketchUp, you'll often experience issues when exporting from SketchUp to other modeling and rendering applications. For example, materials applied to blue faces in SketchUp have a tendency to render backwards in some applications. In other applications, materials applied to blue faces are dumped during the export/import process, so blue faces are rendered black. One of the more technical reasons for all this is that other 3D modeling programs respect surface "Normals"—which are defined by a vector that sticks out tangent to the orientation of a face. The direction of the Normal vector determines the direction of the face, which often affects the way textures and materials are rendered. SketchUp is cool because you don't really have to know about all that—you just need to get the blue and white colors sorted out.

The good news is that even after you've painted a model, you can still easily view the surfaces based on the default blue/white colors using the Monochrome Face Style display mode (View > Face Style > Monochrome) . Then use Reverse Faces or Orient Faces to fix anything that may be inside-out.

WORKING WITH 2D CAD FILES IN SKETCHUP

In many of the firms at which I've worked or consulted over the past six years, the process of creating 3D models in SketchUp begins by referencing a given set of 2D plan and elevation drawings that were created in some other CAD application. This section outlines a few of the procedures and techniques that you can use to create accurate 3D models in short order.

To work along with the examples in this section, you can copy over to your hard drive the DWG file Sample CAD File.dwg from the DVD included with this book. There is also a SketchUp file of the same model in the 3D Warehouse; search for "Working With CAD Example author:Blue Marble Project," which you can use if you can't or don't want to import the DWG file.

Prepping Your Files in CAD

The file Sample CAD File.dwg (included with the sample files on the companion DVD) is an example of a CAD file already optimized for import into SketchUp.

For the purpose of this book, I'll focus on the SketchUp side of the how-to process. If, however, in addition to using SketchUp, you also happen to be a draftsperson working in CAD, the following tips are intended to help you better optimize CAD files prior to importing them into SketchUp.

Save As: For starters, it's typically a good idea to save a copy of your CAD file. I typically keep a folder of files called CAD Files in the folder with my SketchUp models. In this folder I keep a record of the CAD files that I've created specifically for importing into SketchUp.

DWG Format: When saving your CAD files, if you have a choice, you're better off saving them as DWG files, as opposed to DXFs. DWG files translate a bit better into SketchUp.

No Notes: CAD file text and notations won't translate into SketchUp, so you can turn off, freeze, or delete stuff on the text, symbol, and annotation layers.

Explode/Embed: SketchUp will read only those entities native to a drawing. Referenced drawings won't show up, so explode/embed any referenced entities in the drawing.

Flatten: If you've created 2D plan and elevation drawings that you're going to import into CAD, check to make sure that the drawings have been flattened. Edges and endpoints that are slightly off plane can cause problems in SketchUp.

Units: As mentioned earlier in this chapter, it's a good idea to note the default unit settings in CAD, as you'll be asked about them during the import process.

Layers: I'm about to go out on a fragile limb in the next section (by telling you that your CAD layering system is rendered useless in SketchUp), but for those of you who are determined to keep continuity between your layers in CAD and your layers in SketchUp, I'd suggest parsing out your CAD file into multiple files that each contain layers that do not overlap/interfere with each other. Say you're designing a house, and you've got all your walls on a layer (i.e., A_WALL_FULL). You can do a Save As (call it Project X_Walls.dwg) Then freeze/hide the walls layer, delete *everything* else, purge the drawing, and then unhide the walls. In some cases you may be able to keep a couple of layers together in the same drawing (maybe windows and doors, or appliances and fixtures). Then import the files one at a time and line them all up in SketchUp. Importing the layers as separate files will preserve the autonomy of the entities within each layer.

Managing Layers

When the CAD file is imported into SketchUp, the layers from that file come over right along with it. However, layers function differently in CAD than they do in SketchUp. For example, in AutoCAD you're able to draw two lines right on top of each other and separate them on different layers. One of the lines might represent the face of a wall and be on a layer called something like A_WALL_FULL; the other edge might represent a cabinet and be on a layer called A_FIXT_CASE. In CAD, even though the lines are parallel with each other, those lines will stay autonomous, and you'll be able to control the visibility of one line or the other by turning on or off their respective layers. That all changes as soon as you import that CAD File into SketchUp.

SketchUp isn't a 2D drafting tool—it's a three-dimensional modeling program. The ability to draw a bunch of autonomous, overlapping edges in a 3-Dimensional environment doesn't really help someone create a 3D model more efficiently. If SketchUp sees two or more edges that were hanging out in the same spot in CAD, it will go ahead and merge those edges into one. Furthermore, if the edges were on separate layers in CAD, SketchUp will decide which of those layers to put the newly merged edge on.

I've seen some pretty elaborate systems that people have developed for keeping their layers consistent in SketchUp and CAD. In my experience, however, it's not worth it. My suggestion: Once you get the CAD files into SketchUp, simply merge the entire drawing into a single layer and call that layer "CAD Stuff." Then use the information you've imported as a reference for creating your 3D model.

Before we get to the 3D modeling part, let's take a minute to get the layers sorted out. As mentioned, you can either import the CAD example file from this book's DVD before starting this exercise, or you can download Working With CAD Example.skp from the 3D Warehouse.

1. Start by opening the Layers window (Window > Layers) as shown in **Figure 5.8**.

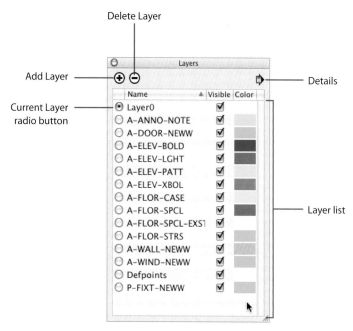

Figure 5.8 The Layers window.

2. Click Add and create a new layer called "CAD STUFF" (**Figure 5.9**). Make this new layer the current layer by clicking the radio button next to the layer name.

3. Select all the other layers (use the Shift or Command key to select multiple layers).

4. Click Delete. When prompted, tell SketchUp to "Move all the layer contents onto the current layer" (**Figure 5.10**).

5. Make Layer 0 the current layer again by clicking the radio button next to Layer 0 (**Figure 5.11**). Note: It's generally a good idea to keep Layer 0 as the current layer at all times. The process of moving contents from deleted layers is one of the few times that it can be useful to temporarily change the current layer status.

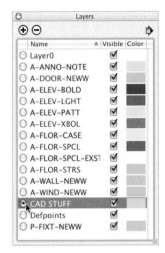

Figure 5.9 Click the Add Layer button to create a new layer.

Figure 5.10 When you delete a layer, SketchUp gives you options for what you want to do with the contents of the layers you're deleting. In this case, since CAD STUFF is the current layer, you'll want to choose the option Move to Current.

Figure 5.11 Clicking the radio button next to a layer will make it the current Layer.

6. Ensure that the edges in the model are grouped. Select all (Command+A) and then choose Edit > Make Group (Command+G).

7. Save the changes you've made to this file before continuing with the next section.

I'm not saying this is the only way to work with your CAD layers in SketchUp, but in my experience, it's the least frustrating. If you just can't fathom a world where your

CAD layering system doesn't exist, you're certainly welcome to try getting them to work in SketchUp. My best advice though, would be to take a deep breath and let go.

Drawing Walls

Now let's look at a tried-and-true method for creating walls. I have seen and used dozens of methods for working with CAD files over the years. This one may seem a bit convoluted and may take a little getting used to, but I guarantee it will produce more consistent and more efficient results than any other.

NOTE I repeat: Before continuing, make sure that the edges that were imported from the CAD file are grouped (see step 6 in the previous section).

1. Continuing with the same file as in the previous section, start by using the Rectangle tool (recommended shortcut: N)  to draw a rectangle on the ground atop one of the walls that runs parallel to the axes (**Figure 5.12**). Note: It is not recommended that you snap to any of the endpoints or edges in the CAD drawing during this step.

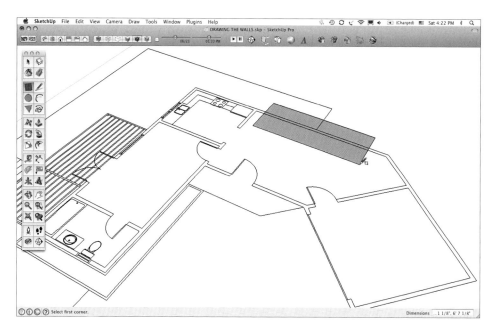

Figure 5.12 Use the Rectangle tool to draw the first wall section.

2. Push/Pull (recommended shortcut: Q)  the rectangle up to a height of 9 feet, then push/pull the sides of the wall and infer the edges of the CAD file below to get the correct width and length dimensions (**Figure 5.13** on the next page).

Figure 5.13 Use the Push/Pull tool to draw the first wall segment.

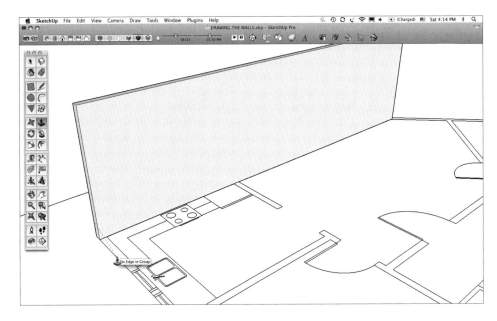

3. Once you've got the first wall segment in place, take the Move tool (M) and toggle the Move/Copy function (press the Ctrl key [PC] or Option key [Mac]).

4. Click and let go on one of the inside vertical edges and start moving a copy of the edge over along the axis direction that runs parallel to the length of the wall (**Figure 5.14**).

Figure 5.14 Use Move/Copy to start copying the edge over.

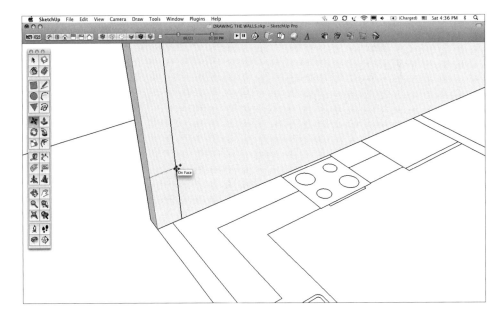

5. While moving the edge along the axis direction, press and hold Shift to lock the axis inference. Keep Shift held down and click the endpoint in the plan below to set the copied edge down in the correct place (**Figure 5.15**).

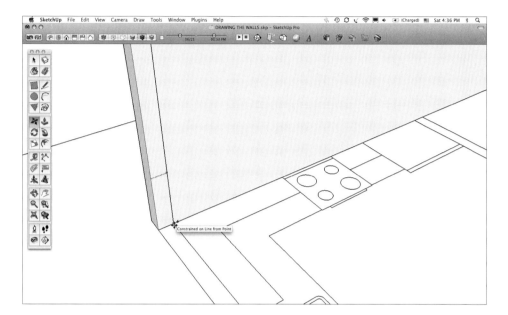

Figure 5.15 Lock the axes inference and then infer the endpoint in the plan below.

6. Use Push/Pull to pull out the next wall section. Be sure to infer the outside edge of the building in the CAD plan below (**Figure 5.16**).

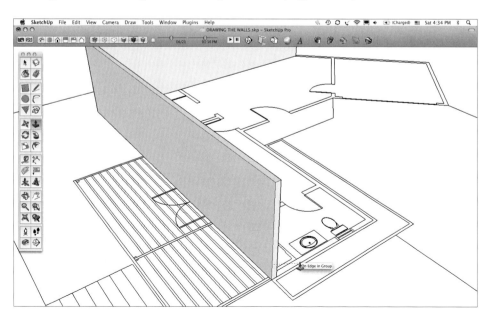

Figure 5.16 Push/Pull the next wall segment.

7. Repeat this process until the exterior walls have been modeled (**Figure 5.17**).

Figure 5.17 Keep going until you've drawn the exterior walls that are aligned to the axes.

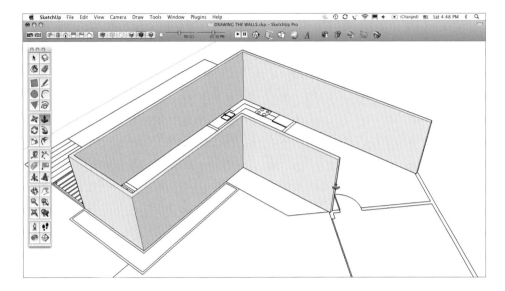

8. If a building, or part of a building, is drawn at an angle (as is the case with this example), use the Axes tool (recommended shortcut: Shift+A) to align the axes to the building (**Figure 5.18**). The Axes tool requires three clicks: 1) origin, 2) red axis, 3) blue axis.

Figure 5.18 Align the model axes to the building.

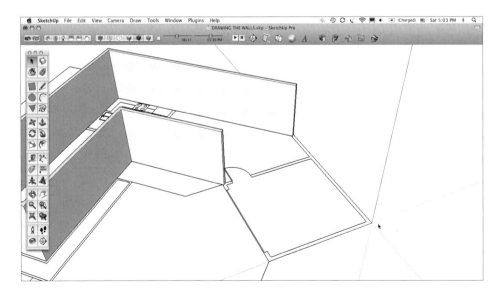

9. Start modeling the angled exterior walls. By following the same process outlined above in Steps 1–7.

10. When you get to the angled wall intersections, go ahead and fully overlap the walls through the corners (**Figure 5.19**).

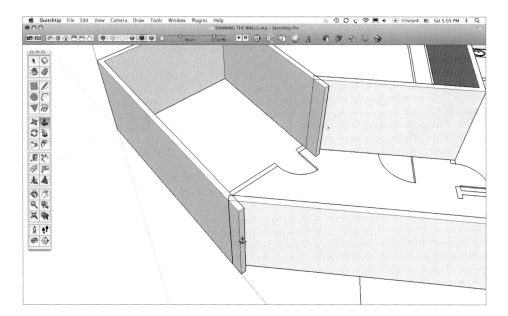

Figure 5.19 Push/Pull the angled walls through the corner intersections.

NOTE You should generally try to avoid rotating the building, especially if you plan on being able to leverage the CAD import option for Preserve Drawing Origin.

11. Take the Select tool (recommended shortcut: V) and triple-click the walls to select them. Note: Use Shift+triple-click if needed to select all of the walls.

12. Right-click the walls and choose Intersect > Intersect Selected (**Figure 5.20**).

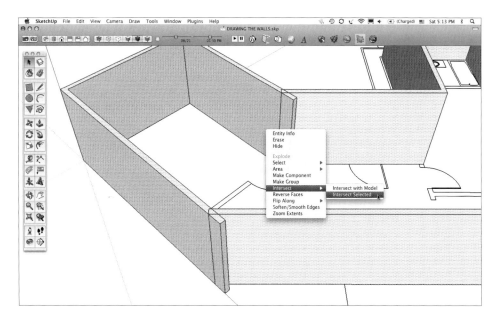

Figure 5.20 Select the walls and then choose Intersect Selected.

13. Use the Eraser tool (E) 🧽 to clean up the intersections by erasing the extra stuff you don't need (**Figure 5.21**).

Figure 5.21 Erase the extra stuff.

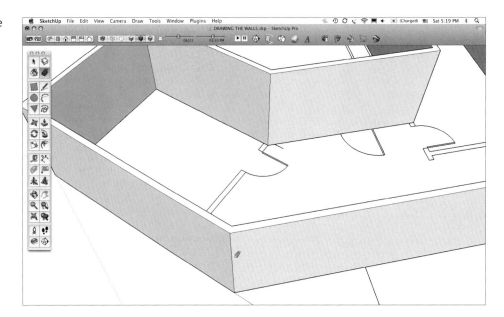

14. Once the exterior walls have been modeled, reset the model axes by right-clicking either of the axes (off in white space, away from the model) and choose Reset (**Figure 5.22**).

Figure 5.22 Reset the axes.

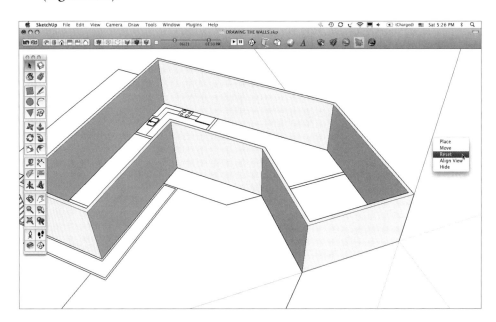

15. Use the Select tool (V) and triple-click the walls to select them. Right-click the walls and choose Make Group (PC shortcut: Ctrl+G, or Mac shortcut: Command+G; **Figure 5.23**).

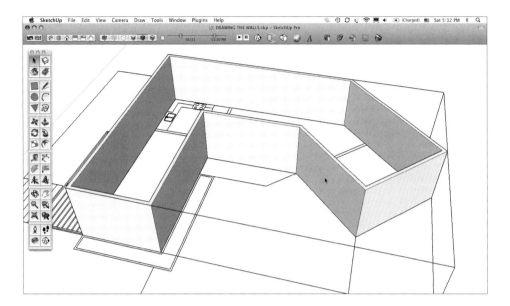

Figure 5.23
Group the walls.

16. Create a new layer called "Exterior Walls." Right-click the walls and choose Entity Info. Choose the Exterior Walls layer from the Layer drop-down menu in the Entity Info dialog to put the Exterior Walls group on that layer (**Figure 5.24**).

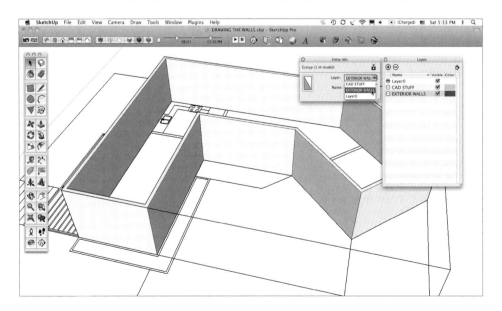

Figure 5.24 Add a new layer for the Exterior Walls and put the group on it.

17. Repeat the same steps for drawing the Interior Walls. Once the interior walls are drawn, group them separately and place them on a new layer called "Interior Walls" (**Figure 5.25**).

Figure 5.25 Model the Interior Walls and place them on a new layer.

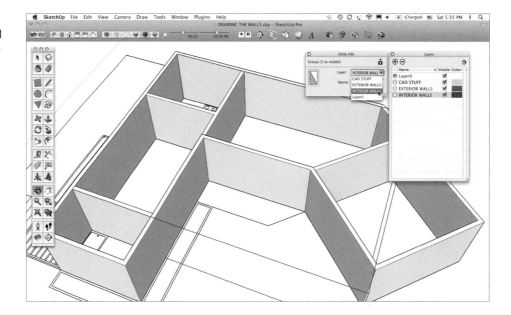

Drawing Windows and Doors

For the next part of this example we'll focus on working through the windows and doors. As with the previous example of drawing the walls, there are probably dozens of ways you could go about this. The following steps are a reliable way to create accurate window and door openings in reference to imported CAD plans.

Windows

Let's start with the windows. Having drawn the walls the way we did—by pulling wall sections through the window and door openings—we're now in a position to simply punch out the windows and doors.

1. Right-click the Exterior Walls group and choose Edit Group from the context menu.

2. Take the Tape Measure tool (recommended shortcut: D) and click the bottom edge of the west wall (be sure to look for a Red "On Edge" inference dot) to start

NOTE Keep in mind as you work through this example that your exterior walls and interior walls are in different groups. Be sure that you are in Edit Group mode before working on the doors and windows for either section of the model.

pulling a guide line up from the bottom edge. Then type 36 and press Enter to set the guide at a height that marks the windowsill (**Figure 5.26**).

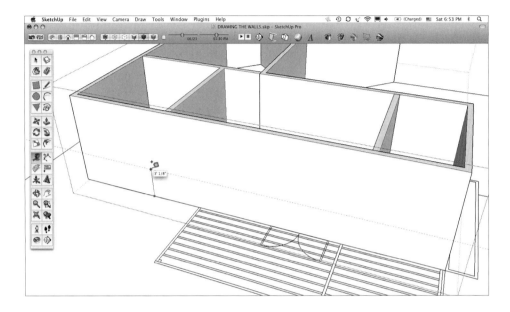

Figure 5.26 The Tape Measure tool creates guides parallel to an edge when you click anywhere along an edge where you see the red "On Edge" inference dot.

3. Use the Tape Measure tool 🖋 again to set the Header height at 7 feet.

4. Take the Rectangle tool (N) ▦ and draw a rectangle that infers the guides for the sill and header heights (**Figure 5.27**). Don't worry about the width; we'll get to that in a second.

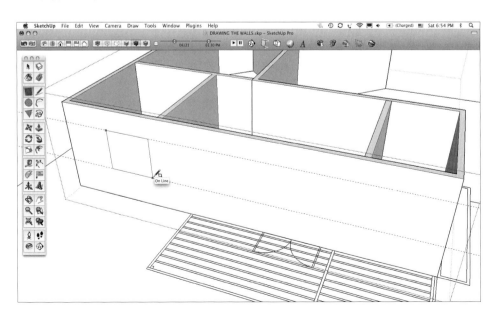

Figure 5.27 With the guides in place you can draw a rectangle that infers the established sill and header heights.

5. Push/Pull (Q) 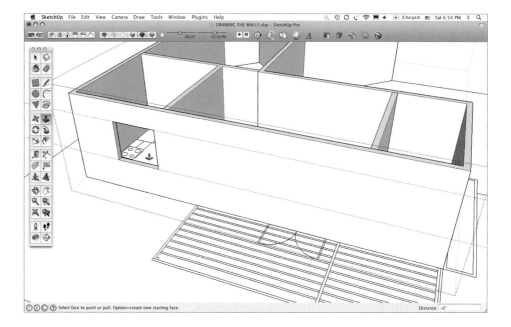 the new rectangle to the back face of the wall to create an opening (**Figure 5.28**).

Figure 5.28 Use Push/Pull to punch a window opening through the wall.

6. Toggle on X-Ray view mode (recommended shortcut: X) . The command icon is located in the Face Style toolbar, and the command is also located under View > Face Style > X-Ray.

7. Push/Pull (Q) the jamb and then infer the corresponding edge for the window in the plan below (**Figure 5.29**).

8. Orbit around so that you can Push/Pull the other jamb and again infer the edge for the window in the plan below (**Figure 5.30**).

9. Repeat these steps as necessary for the other windows in the model.

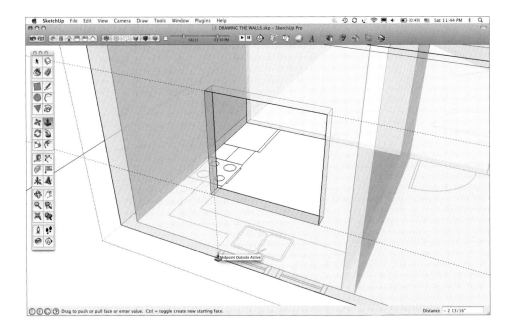

Figure 5.29 X-Ray mode is a great face style to use for inferring information in the CAD plan below.

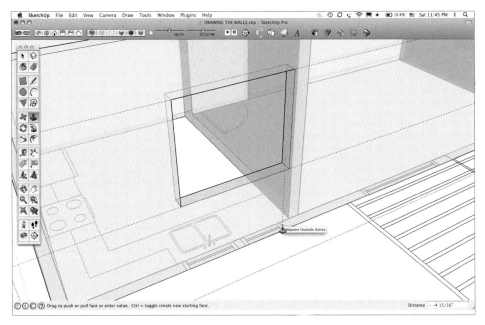

Figure 5.30 Push/Pull both sides of the window opening so that they correspond to the plan below.

Doors

It's entirely possible to use the process described earlier to model the door openings, but I want to show an even easier option for the doors. The following process for drawing the door openings assumes you've got precise CAD files to work from. Step 3 of this example asks you to trace over the CAD plan and infer specific endpoints. If those points are off by even the slightest of margins, this process falls short—in which case you can fall back on the process described previously for drawing the window openings.

1. Toggle off X-Ray view mode (X) ⬡ .

2. Orbit ✤ around so that you're looking underneath the walls.

3. Take the Rectangle tool (N) ▮ and trace over the door opening (**Figure 5.31**). Be sure to infer from endpoint to endpoint.

Figure 5.31 Trace the door opening with the Rectangle tool.

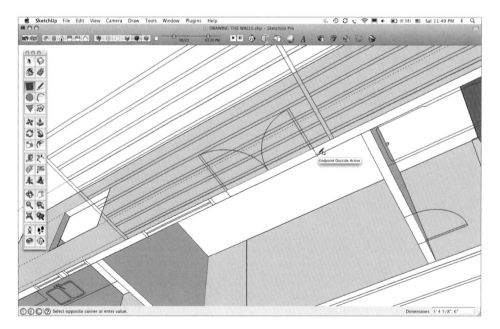

4. Push/Pull (Q) 🠹 the bottom of the door up, then type in a height value of 7' and press Enter (**Figure 5.32** on the next page).

5. Repeat these steps as necessary for the other doors in the model. Again, remember that you'll need to make sure you're in Edit Group mode for the correct group depending on whether you're trying to add doors to the Exterior Walls group or the Interior Walls group. (Edit Group shortcut: Select tool [V] then double-click; Close Group shortcut: Select Tool [V] then press the Escape key.)

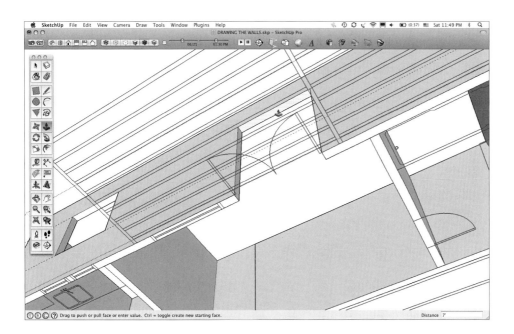

Figure 5.32 Push the face up and enter the dimension for the header height to create an accurate door opening.

NOTE When you double-click a face with the Push/Pull tool, it will repeat the same distance and direction as the previous push/pull. You can use that trick to save a little time by modeling all the doors that have a similar header height, one right after the other.

6. Once you've finished modeling the door and window openings you can Zoom Out, close up any open groups, and clean up any dashed guide lines in the model by choosing Delete Guides from the Edit menu (**Figure 5.33**).

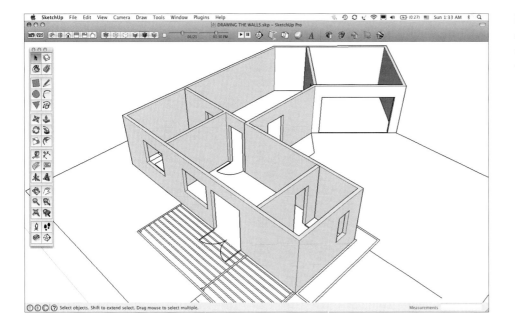

Figure 5.33 Zoom out, close up the group, and delete the guides.

At this point, keep in mind that the 3D Warehouse is chock-full of doors and windows ready for you to download and plop right into your model. Marvin Windows has a great collection of dynamic components that work well with this example.

If integrating SketchUp and CAD in your workflow is at the top of your list of things to figure out, you should check out the Google SketchUp Pro Series: *SketchUp + CAD Training* DVD by School. The DVD takes the information from this chapter a few steps further by illustrating methods for referencing elevation drawings, methods for modeling the roof, trellis, landscape, and hardscape areas, as well as material applications and furniture placement.

You can purchase the *SketchUp + CAD* DVD from the School Web site at www.go-2-school.com/products/view/10.

Modeling Complex Shapes

Complex geometrical shapes that have been drawn in CAD might take more time than it's worth to redraw from scratch.

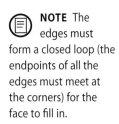

NOTE The Make Faces script requires you to download and install the Progress Bar script (progressbar.rb), also available on the Smustard Web site.

Here's a method you can use for modeling some of the more non-rectilinear portions of an imported CAD file.

For this example you'll want to download and install the Make Faces Ruby script (makefaces.rb): www.smustard.com/script/MakeFaces.

1. Assuming your CAD drawing is a group/component, take the Select tool and double-click it to go into Edit Group/Edit Component mode.

2. Select the edges that define the outline of the shape.

3. Copy the edges to the clipboard (Edit > Copy).

4. Close the group/component (Escape key).

5. Paste in Place outside the group (Edit > Paste in Place).

NOTE The edges must form a closed loop (the endpoints of all the edges must meet at the corners) for the face to fill in.

6. Use the Make Faces Ruby script (Tools > Make Faces) to get the surface to fill in.

If the 2D shape of an object consists of a number of curved lines, you may want to consider employing some of the methods outlined in the following section for working with imported curved lines and contours.

WORKING WITH CONTOURS

In the previous chapter we looked at a method for creating quick and dirty site models by importing the satellite imagery and topography from Google Earth. Another commonly used method for creating terrain models involves importing contour line drawings that, you guessed it, were drawn in CAD. The following process illustrates a method for creating terrain models from 3D contour line drawings. Nowadays most surveyors can send 3D contours if you ask for them.

Lost in Translation

SketchUp doesn't do curves. Splines, polysplines, nurbs—all that good stuff gets translated into straight-line segments—lots of them! Most surveys I've come across include contour lines drawn in CAD as polyspline curves. When those curves are imported into SketchUp, the resulting contours, when translated, are comprised of thousands of tiny line segments (**Figure 5.34** on the next page). Working in a file with that many edges is problematic enough; things get really lame if you try to create terrain surfaces in SketchUp from contour edges that are made up of tons of segments.

Simplify Contours (SimplifyContours.rb) is a great Ruby script for reducing the number of segments of curved polylines that have been imported into SketchUp from CAD. You can download the script from the SketchUp Web site at http://sketchup. google.com/download/rubyscripts.html.

Once installed, the Simplify Contours command will show up in the Plugins menu. To use the script, just preselect one (or more) contour lines and then choose the Simplify Contours command (**Figure 5.35**). When prompted, enter a degree angle. (I've found that an angle between 5–10 degrees works well, depending on the level of precision you need to retain in the contours.) The higher the degree angle you choose, the more simplified (and less accurate) the lines will become.

Figure 5.34
Contour lines with
tons of edge seg-
ments result in con-
tour surfaces with
tons of faces.

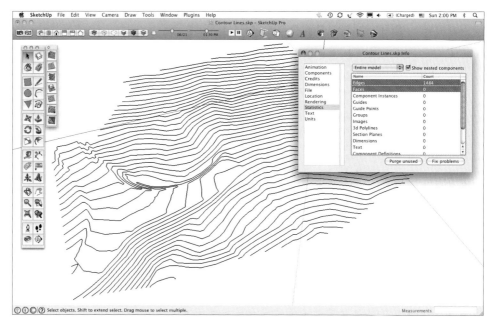

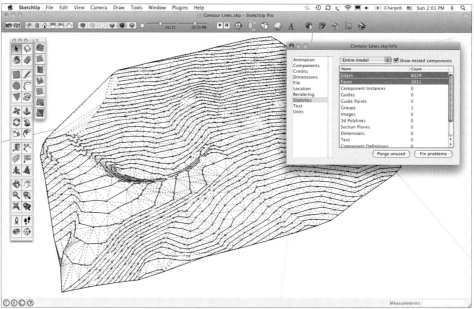

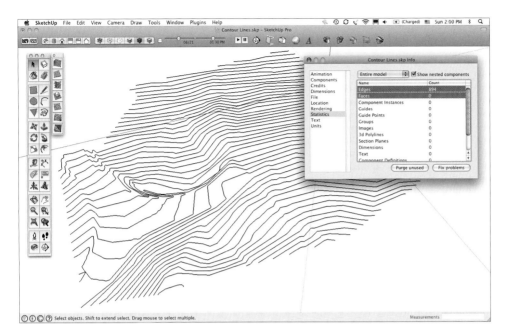

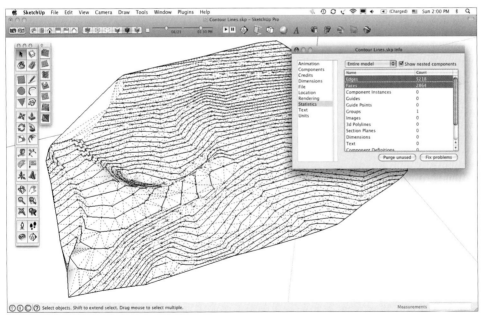

Figure 5.35
Simplified contour lines can be turned into surfaces with far fewer edges and faces.

The trickiest part about using the Simplify Contours command is that it can be a bit finicky. The contour lines need to form a single, continuous loop in order for the script to work. Errors will occur with this script (namely, SketchUp will delete your contour lines entirely) when either loops or crisscrosses are present.

Loops: The contours should be a single polyline drawn as either an open-ended contour or a single closed loop. If the contour contains one or more loops (**Figure 5.36**), the entire contour line will disappear when you run the Simplify Contours Ruby script. Loops are sometimes inadvertently created when SketchUp translates imported polyspline curves that were originally drawn in CAD.

Figure 5.36 Fix any lines that loop back onto each other.

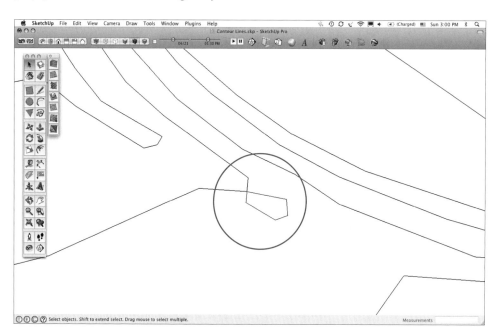

Crisscrosses: If the contours are divided into segments, the segments need to meet each other at the endpoints. If contour lines cross through each other (**Figure 5.37**), the entire contour line will disappear when you run the Simplify Contours Ruby script.

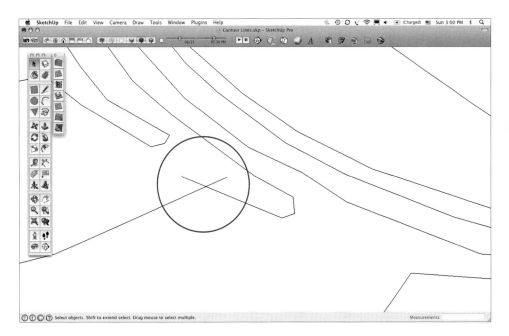

Figure 5.37 Fix any lines that overlap or cross through each other.

NOTE You can use another script called StrayLines (LabelStrayLines.rb) to locate the open endpoints of any overlapping edges. StrayLines can be downloaded from www.smustard.com/script/StrayLines.

Once the contours have been simplified, you can use the Sandbox tools (**Figure 5.38**) to turn them into a terrain surface. To follow along with the next part of this example, make sure that the Sandbox Tools extension is turned on (Window > Preferences > Extensions > Sandbox Tools), at which point you should be able to open the Sandbox toolbar (View > Toolbars > Sandbox).

Figure 5.38 The Sandbox toolbar.

Once you've selected all the contour lines (Mac: Command+A; PC: Ctrl+A), you can then choose the From Contours tool and SketchUp will create a terrain surface by triangulating the endpoints of the contour lines. The surface is automatically created as a new group.

NOTE Choose Edit > View Hidden Geometry to view and edit the individual edges and faces that make up the terrain.

For more information about the basics of using the Sandbox tools, check out the video tutorial *The SketchUp Show*, Episode 17: "Sandbox Part Deux," included on this book's DVD or online at www.go-2-school.com/Real-World-Google-SketchUp-7.

WORKING WITH 3D CAD FILES

More and more companies are finding new ways to use SketchUp to complement work done in other 3D modeling applications. For example, architectural design firms often face major design revisions late in a project or during construction, at which point a highly detailed 3D model may have already been drawn in another CAD application. In such cases it's often more efficient to use SketchUp to quickly visualize and evaluate alternative design scenarios prior to, or in lieu of, making time-consuming changes in CAD.

Manufacturing companies often use 3D programs like Solidworks or Autodesk Inventor for product design as well as the creation of engineering and manufacturing specs. The models created in those programs, however, can't provide the marketing benefit companies receive by distributing 3D product information via the 3D Warehouse.

The process of importing 3D CAD files is typically a bit more straightforward than that of importing 2D files. Because the model imports in 3D, there may not be much work to do on the 3D modeling side of things. However, some interesting things often happen in the process of importing CAD files. The most common issue is that when models are saved in DXF format from whatever program they were modeled in the first place, the surfaces are wildly triangulated. When the files are imported into SketchUp, there are often tons of extra visible edges in the model.

Making It Look Good

You can follow along with this example by downloading the model "Eames Molded Plywood Dining Chair author:SmartFurniture" from the 3D Warehouse.

You'll also want to download and install the Delete Coplanar Edges Ruby script ([CASF]DelCopEdges.rb) from the Ruby Library Depot (www.crai.archi.fr/RubyLibraryDepot/Ruby/en_geo_page.htm).

This model of an Eames chair illustrates some common issues with importing 3D CAD files into SketchUp—not the least of which is how fugly they look.

The process for getting this thing to look good in SketchUp is twofold: smooth out the normals, and get rid of the unnecessary coplanar edges.

Normal edges define an angle (between 0 and 180 degrees) between two faces. Coplanar edges are drawn between two faces that lie in the same plane. Checking both boxes in the Soften/Smooth dialog would smooth out everything. While that's useful for some things, in this case it's a shortcut that would leave us with a bunch of unnecessary geometry taking up file size. Better just to use the slider to smooth the normal edges and then delete the coplanar ones.

1. Using the Select tool (V) ▸, triple-click the model until you've selected all the edges and faces of the back of the chair (**Figure 5.39**).

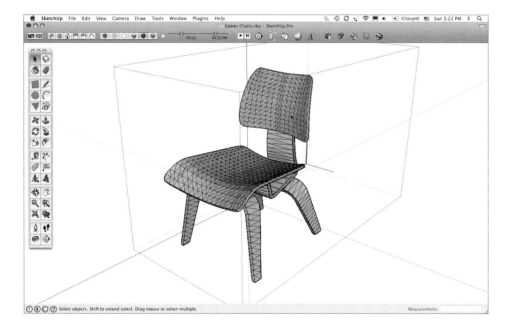

Figure 5.39 Triple-click with the Select tool to select all edges and faces on the back of the chair.

Model courtesy of SmartFurniture.com

2. Right-click the selection and choose Soften/Smooth Edges from the context menu.

3. Check the box for Smooth Normals, and then move the slider over to about 45 degrees (**Figure 5.40** on the next page).

Figure 5.40 Smooth edges with normal angles less than or equal to 45 degrees.

Model courtesy of SmartFurniture.com

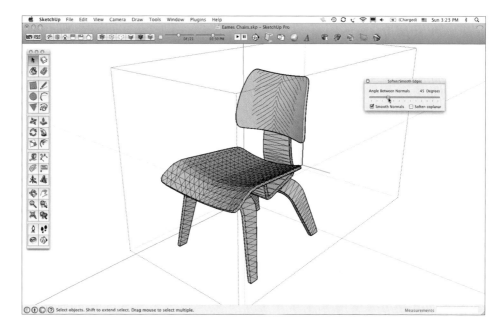

4. Right-click the selection again and choose Delete Coplanar Edges from the context menu (**Figure 5.41**).

Figure 5.41 Delete the coplanar edges.

Model courtesy of SmartFurniture.com

NOTE The Delete Coplanar Edges script is pretty reliable, but in some cases you may see faces disappear. If needed, you can manually erase the coplanar edges with the Eraser tool 🖋 instead.

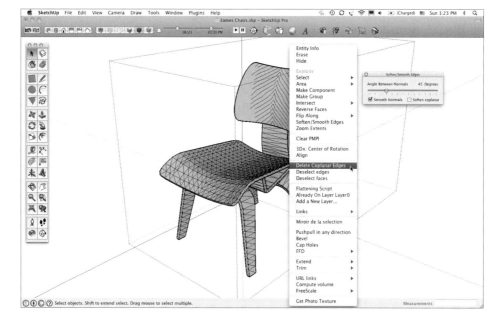

5. Repeat these steps until all pieces of the chair are smoothed out (**Figure 5.42**).

Figure 5.42 The smoothed-out chair looks better and contains less excess coplanar geometry.

Model courtesy of SmartFurniture.com

Teeny Tiny Bits

When you're working with CAD files (3D CAD files in particular), you may notice that the teeny tiny bits are tough to work with. At the extremes of the size spectrum (really small or really big), SketchUp is a bit finicky. Some of that has to do with the Units settings and some of it has to do with SketchUp's limitations and tolerances.

If you're having trouble working with tiny geometry that you've imported into SketchUp, try adjusting the Units settings in the Model Info window. Choose a setting with the highest tolerance. For example, set the units to Decimal Inches with a tolerance of 0.000000", and uncheck Length Snapping.

If that still doesn't get the job done, another option would be to use the scale tool to scale up the geometry by a factor of 10 or even 100. SketchUp's tolerances should then be suitable for working on the oversized objects. Once you're done you can scale the geometry back down by a factor of .1 or .01, depending on the factor you used to scale up.

Additional Resources

By now you should have a pretty decent understanding of the many ways you can begin to incorporate a variety of CAD file types and formats into your workflows. Working with CAD files is one of the more complicated topics when it comes to using SketchUp professionally, and one that generates a lot of questions. For more information on this subject be sure and check out the video tutorials that were included on the DVD that came with this book.

You might also want to look into the following resources:

- *The SketchUp Show,* Episode 20: "Working with CAD" (www.go-2-school.com/Real-World-Google-SketchUp-7)

- *Google SketchUp Pro Series - SketchUp + CAD* Instructional DVD (http://www.go-2-school.com/products/view/10)

- *Google SketchUp for Site Design: A Guide for Modeling Site Plans, Terrain and Architecture* by Daniel Tal (Wiley, 2009)

CHAPTER SIX

Importing Images

There's truly something awesome about the process of taking a 2D image and manipulating it in 3D. For the most part, it's just fun, but the ability to effectively import images into SketchUp provides a tremendous advantage for designers. That statement holds especially true for those skilled in traditional, hand-drawn media. As you'll see later in this chapter, SketchUp can provide a wonderful bridge between hand-drawn imagery and 3D computer modeling.

In addition, SketchUp's ability to import digital photographs, such as a picture of an old wooden door or a shiny new stainless steel appliance, can help lend a tremendous amount of realism to your model.

SketchUp's image import options also provide users with a way to leverage the vast hoards of digital photos that can be found and downloaded via Google Image Search and Google's Street View imagery database.

Regardless of the type of image you're planning to import, the process starts from the File > Import menu options (**Figure 6.1** on the next page). From the image import dialog you are given three options for importing an image into SketchUp: 1) Use As Image, 2) Use As Texture, and 3) Use As New Matched Photo.

Figure 6.1 Image import options.

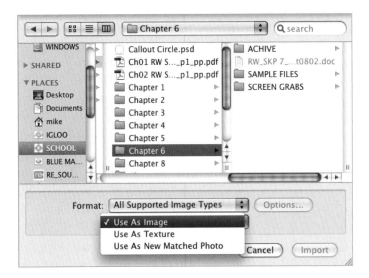

Before diving into the particulars of the actual image import options, I have some information to share about optimizing your images and saving them in an appropriate image file format.

Choosing an Image File Format

SketchUp supports the import of a wide variety of image file formats, including JPEG, TIFF, PNG, BMP, PDF (Mac only), TGA, and GIF. So are there any differences between these formats, and if so, what considerations should be taken into account when trying to decide which format to import?

Alpha Channel Transparency

In addition to the Red, Green, and Blue color channels that combine to define the color of the pixels in an image, the alpha channel stores information about the transparency value of each pixel in an image. PNG, TIFF, PSD, and PDF image formats will retain alpha channels. Say, for example, that you've edited an image of a tree in Photoshop to crop out the background. If you save the file in a format that retains the alpha channel, SketchUp will be able to interpret the background as being transparent; otherwise, the background will show up as white (**Figure 6.2**).

One potential downside to consider when deciding whether to import images with transparent backgrounds—any image file with transparent pixels (whether in PNG,

PSD, TIFF or PDF format) applied as a texture to a face in SketchUp will not receive shadows.

Figure 6.2 The image on the left is a TIFF that can retain a transparent background even when imported into SketchUp. The image on the right is a JPEG—a format that converts transparent backgrounds to solid white.

Image File Size

When you import an image file into SketchUp, your SketchUp file will increase in size by the same amount as the file size of the image. TIFF files and PSD files are uncompressed file formats. On the one hand, they look great, and if you're working with layered PSD or TIFF files in Photoshop, you don't have to flatten the images before importing them into SketchUp. On the other hand, saving your image as a compressed file format (such as JPEG or PNG) before importing into SketchUp will generally result in much smaller SketchUp file sizes.

The Versatility of PNGs

You'll probably find that most image-editing applications have an option for saving files as PNG (Portable Network Graphic) format. The PNG format is a compressed file format, it looks great, and it retains alpha channel transparency.

In Photoshop, for example, you can use the option Save for Web and Mobile Devices to save PNG images that retain transparency (**Figure 6.3** on the next page). This is a great option in situations where you've had to crop an image to create a transparent background—or for reducing the file size of your images.

  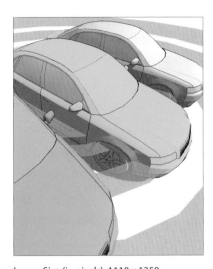

Image Size (in pixels): 1110 x 1350
File Size (in kilobytes): 6.500

Image Size (in pixels): 1110 x 1350
File Size (in kilobytes): 556

Image Size (in pixels): 1110 x 1350
File Size (in kilobytes): 612

Figure 6.3 A TIFF file on the left, PNG in the middle, and JPEG on the right. You can see that the PNG file is much smaller than the TIFF, looks crisp, and also has a transparent background.

IMPORTING AN IMAGE AS AN IMAGE OBJECT

This import option results in creating image objects that are unique in that they are unlike any other kind of SketchUp entity. Despite having a protective wrapper around them (they resist stickiness), they are not defined as groups or components. They have faces, but the edges that define the face are not visible. They are textured and yet the textures don't appear in the In Model material library. They simply are what they are: image objects. The following examples are intended to highlight scenarios in which this image import option can be most effectively utilized.

Some of the files you'll need to follow along with the examples in this section can be copied from "Chapter 6_Importing Images" on the companion DVD or downloaded from the "Real World Google SketchUp 7 - Sample Files" Picasa album at "http://picasaweb.google.com/tadrosio/RealWorldGoogleSketchUp7SampleFiles."

Gluing Image Objects—Signage

A useful feature of imported image objects is that they will automatically "glue" to an existing face in the model if you import an image directly onto it. The gluing action A) keeps the image aligned and attached to the plane of the face that the image is imported onto and B) keeps the image from "Z-fighting" (**see Figure 6.4**) with any textures that may have been applied to the existing face. Both features make this option a good choice for importing images of posters, artwork, logos, signage, architectural elements, etc.

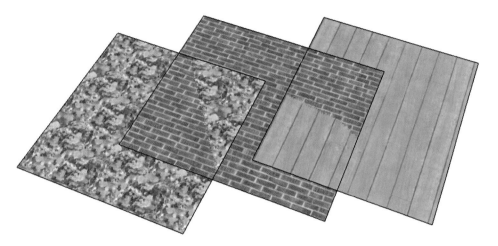

Figure 6.4 *Z-fighting* refers to the fluttering effect that appears when two faces with different textures lie parallel to each other in the same plane.

Art.com is a great Web site for finding downloadable images of artwork and posters and getting dimensions for the framed pieces for personal, noncommercial use. In this example I'll use an image of one of my own framed sketches. You can copy the image for this example from the accompanying DVD or from the Real World Google SketchUp 7 Sample Files Picasa album online at http://picasaweb.google.com/tadrosio/ RealWorldGoogleSketchUp7SampleFiles. Note that actual dimensions for this frame are 27 inches wide by 39 inches high.

1. Start by downloading the sample file for this example (titled Framed Art_27x39.jpg) from the companion DVD, or from the Real World Google SketchUp 7 Sample Files Picasa album (picasaweb.google.com/tadrosio/ RealWorldGoogleSketchUp7SampleFiles).

2. Draw an 8-foot cube in SketchUp. (Optional: For illustration purposes, I've added a brick texture to the front face of the box and a 2D person for scale; **Figure 6.5** on the next page).

Figure 6.5 An 8-foot cube with a brick texture.

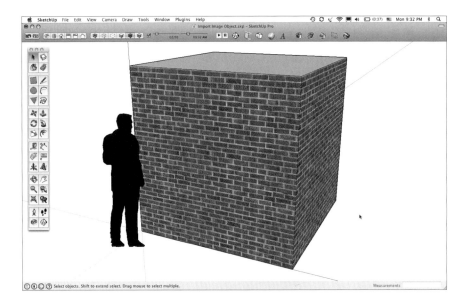

3. Go to File > Import. Choose the option for "All Supported Image Types" from the File Format drop-down menu and choose the option Use As Image. Navigate to the image file and choose Import.

4. Once imported, the image will be attached to the cursor (**Figure 6.6**).

Figure 6.6 Enter a width or height dimension during the import process to size the image appropriately.

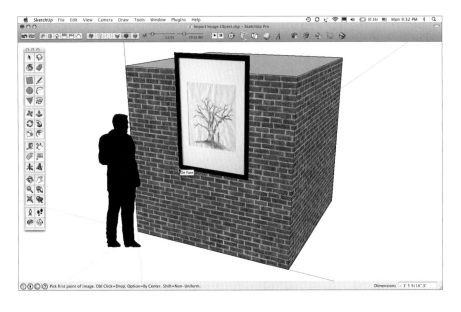

5. Click once to set the insertion point, move the cursor out to size the image, and then click a second time to set the image in place (**Figure 6.7**).

NOTE If you know the overall dimension (height or width) you can type in the dimensions as you're importing the image. If you know the height (in this case 39"), stretch it vertically and type in the dimensions; if you know the width (in this case 27"), stretch it horizontally and type in the dimensions.

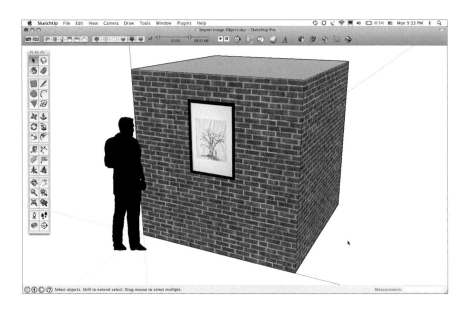

Figure 6.7 When image objects are imported onto an existing face, the image is glued to that face. The gluing behavior will eliminate any Z-fighting that typically occurs when two parallel faces with different textures are placed on top of each other.

If you try to move the image around you'll see that it's glued to the face that you imported it onto. Likewise, if you try to move or Push/Pull the face of the box, you'll notice that the image moves with it. If you ever need to detach the image from the face, right-click it and choose Unglue from the context menu.

Placing Free-Floating Images—Backgrounds

The previous example illustrates an option for importing an image object directly onto a face—in which case the image will be glued to the face on which it is imported.

Another option is to simply import the image into the model as a free-floating object. A common scenario for utilizing this option would be the creation of a backdrop or background image.

JC Backings is a company in Hollywood that rents out large-scale background images for use on film and stage sets. Its Web site (www.jcbackings.com) is full of all kinds of great background images that can be pulled into SketchUp. Whether or not you're a film and stage pro, this workflow process is valuable for creating models that require an accurate representation of a background.

NOTE After you unglue the image object, you'll have to move it an inch or two off the face in order to keep the textures from Z-fighting. There is no option to Re-glue, so once you Unglue, you would either have to Undo back, or reimport the image.

1. Start by going to the JC Backings Web site, and search for image #CT-641 (**Figure 6.8**).

Figure 6.8 Search for the background image #CT-641 from the JC Backings Web site.

NOTE JC Backings is an example of a professional site that film and stage folks might check out to search for specific background images. For generic imagery you could substitute Google Images (http://images.google.com/) in Step 1 and search for and download images of just about anything.

2. Right-click the image and choose Save Image As to save the image to your computer's hard drive (**Figure 6.9**).

3. Go to File > Import and choose the options All Supported Image Formats and Use As Image. Then navigate to the file and choose Import.

4. Click once to set the insertion point of the image, and then scale the image up and click a second time to set the image in place.

   The real-world dimensions for this image are listed on the JC Backings Web site. In this case, we know that it is 14 feet tall in real life. So when you're sizing the image initially, you can move the cursor along the vertical edge of the image and type in 14' and press Enter to set the image at the correct size (**Figure 6.10**).

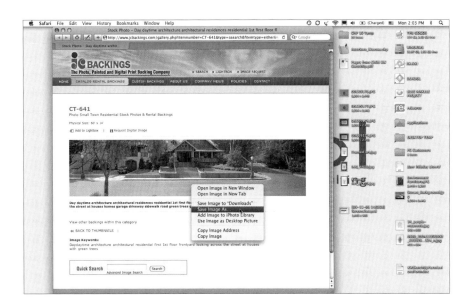

Figure 6.9 Right-click the image and save it to your desktop.

Image © JC Backings

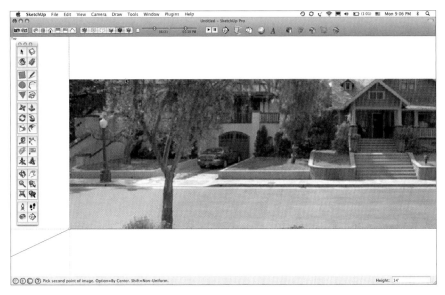

Figure 6.10 Click once to set the insertion point for the image, and then type in a dimension while sizing it.

Image © JC Backings

5. At this point we could reasonably assume that if we sized the height dimension correctly (at 14'), the width should end up equal to 60' (per the dimensions listed on the JC Backings Web site). However, if you use the Dimension tool (Shift+D) to verify that assumption, you'd see that the image is actually measuring out at around 60'6½"—so it looks like somehow the aspect ratio of this image got tossed around a bit (**Figure 6.11** on the next page).

NOTE Another way to import files as image objects is to drag the image files from a file browser window into your SketchUp drawing window.

Figure 6.11 Double-check the aspect ratio of images down-loaded from the Web.

Image © JC Backings

6. Type in 60' and press Enter while using the Scale tool (S) to scale the model horizontally and fix the proportions of the backdrop image to correspond to its actual real-world size (**Figure 6.12**).

Figure 6.12 Use the Scale tool to fix any issues with aspect ratio.

Image © JC Backings

7. Use the Rotate tool (R) to tilt the image up. Start with a click-drag along the bottom edge of the image to set the axis of rotation, then click anywhere on the image to start tilting it up, and click a third time to set the angle of rotation. For accuracy, type 90 and press Enter (**Figure 6.13**).

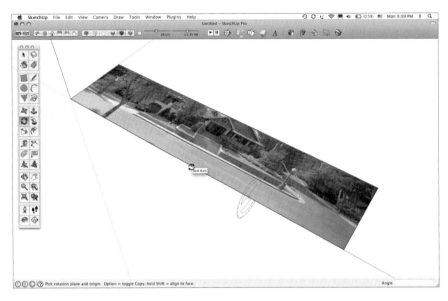

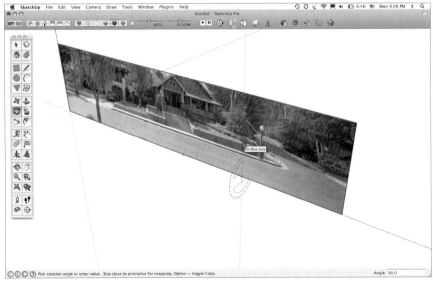

Figure 6.13 Use the Rotate tool to tilt the image up.

Image © JC Backings

8. The Move tool (M) is an obvious choice for getting the image positioned in the right place in the model. Remember too, though, that the Move tool also works for rotating the image. When you hover over the image with the Move tool, you'll see little red crosshairs. If you hover over the crosshairs, the Move tool will turn into a Rotate tool, at which point you can click to start rotating the image about its center along either of the axes (**Figure 6.14**).

Figure 6.14 The Move tool is useful for moving and rotating images.

Image © JC Backings

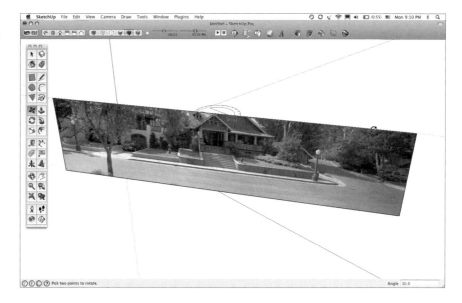

Plans and Elevations

The process described in the previous section can be taken yet a step further. A common scenario for this next example is when you're working with hand-drawn imagery such as plans and elevations, especially those that are drawn to scale. This example shows a process you can use to take a 2D image of a Kitchen Elevation that was drawn at 1 inch to one-quarter inch scale and turn it into a 3D model.

The sample files for this example can be copied from the companion DVD—or you can download them from the Picasa Web album at http://picasaweb.google.com/tadrosio/RealWorldGoogleSketchUp7SampleFiles.

1. Go to File > Import. Choose the option for All Supported Image Types from the File Format drop-down menu, and choose Use As Image. Navigate to Kitchen_Elev.jpg and choose Import.

2. Click once to set the insertion point of the image, scale the image up, and click a second time to set the image in place (**Figure 6.15**). Don't worry about the image scale quite yet; we'll get to that in Step 9.

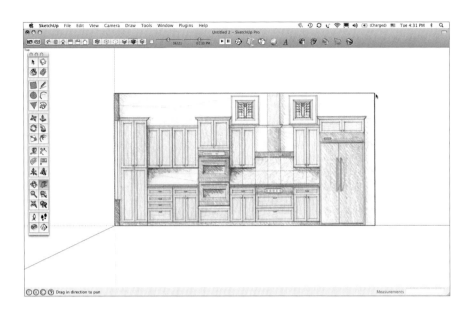

Figure 6.15 Place Kitchen_Elev.jpg into the model as an image object.

3. Use the Rotate tool (R) 🔄 to tilt the image up. Start with a click-drag along the bottom edge of the image to set the axis of rotation, then click anywhere on the image to start tilting it up, and click a third time to set the angle of rotation. For accuracy, type 90 and press Enter (**Figure 6.16**).

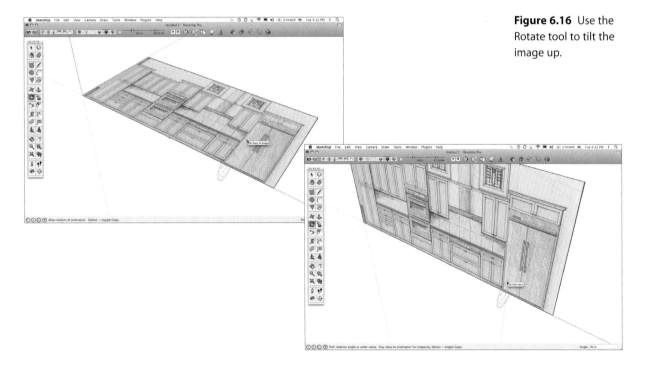

Figure 6.16 Use the Rotate tool to tilt the image up.

4. Right-click the image and choose Explode.

5. With the Select tool (V) ▶, double-click the image to select the face as well as the edges. Then right-click and choose Make Group (**Figure 6.17**).

Figure 6.17 After exploding the image, select the face and edges and group them.

NOTE When you explode an image object, you will then have the ability to edit the face and the edges that define that face. The image is also converted into a projected texture.

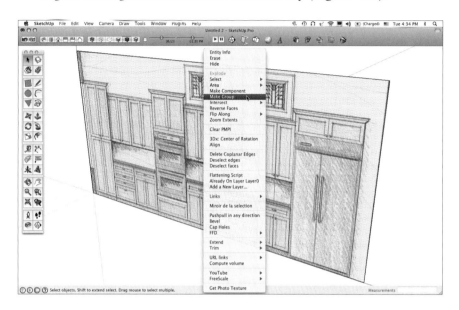

6. Then double-click the image again with the Select tool to go into Edit Group mode (**Figure 6.18**).

Figure 6.18 When you're in Edit Group mode you should see a dashed black bounding box around the image.

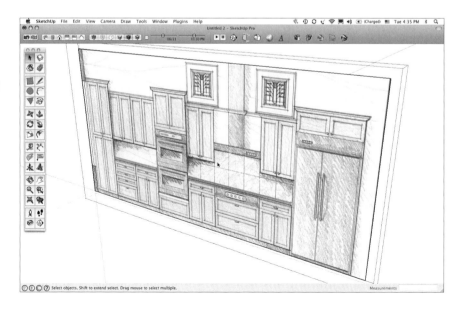

In the previous example we looked at scaling an image during import. That option works well when you happen to know the overall dimension of an image. In this case, we instead know that the counter top is 36" tall. That's not a dimension we could have used to scale the image from the onset, but we can use that dimension now, by scaling the image with the Tape Measure tool.

7. Take the Tape Measure tool (D) 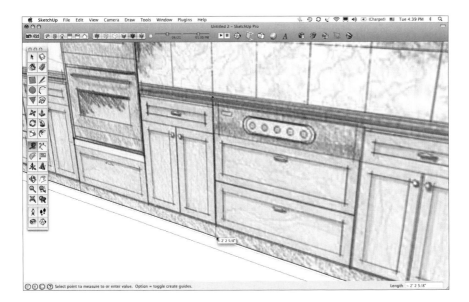 and click once at the top of the counter, then click at the bottom of the counter, and then type in the dimension for the distance that should be between the two points. In this case, enter 36 (**Figure 6.19**).

Figure 6.19 Use the Tape Measure tool to scale the group based on the known dimension of the image.

8. When SketchUp asks, "Do you want to resize the active group or component?" click Yes.

9. Now that the image has been scaled, you can use the drawing tools to trace the outline of the cabinetry. Start by using the Rectangle tool (N) to trace over a section of the base cabinets (**Figure 6.20**).

Figure 6.20 Trace over the base cabinets with the Rectangle tool.

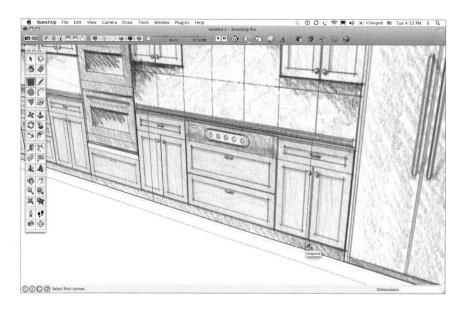

10. Using the Push/Pull tool (Q) , pull out the base cabinet section (**Figure 6.21**). Enter 24 to set the dimension of the base cabinets 24 inches deep.

Figure 6.21 Pull the base cabinets out 24 inches.

11. Adjust the size of the base cabinets by Push/Pulling the top, bottom, or either of the side faces.

12. Use the Rectangle tool (N) to draw rectangles on the top of the counter for the tall cabinets and built-in appliances.

13. Push/Pull (Q) the rectangles up from the counter (**Figure 6.22**). Adjust the dimensions on the sides if necessary.

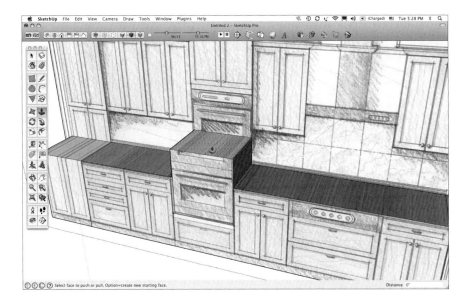

Figure 6.22 Pull the Tall cabinets up from the counter and gauge the height of the top of the cabinet based on the image texture.

14. Trace over the wall cabinets with the Rectangle tool (N).

15. Then take the Push/Pull Tool (Q) and pull those out 12 inches (**Figure 6.23**).

16. At this point you may want to save the work you've done in this example because we'll reference this model again later in the book.

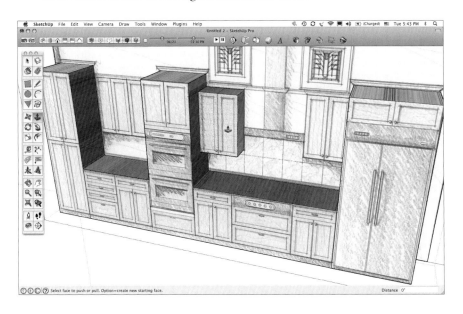

Figure 6.23 Pull the wall cabinets out 12 inches.

Figure 6.24
Imported images of hand-sketched designs can be combined with sketchy styles for 3D conceptual design presentations.

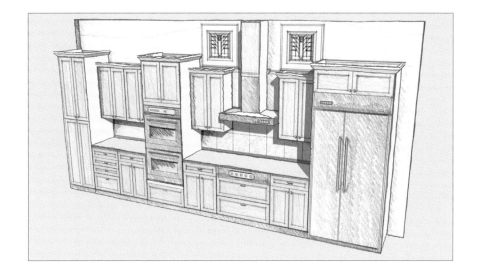

If you want to take this model a bit further, you could use the Follow-Me tool ↻ to model the crown molding around the tops of the upper cabinets. And you can check out the section "Sampling Onscreen Colors" in Chapter 7 for more information on how to get rid of the streaky textures on the sides of the cabinets. In the real world, depending on the phase of the project or the type of information you need to communicate, you could either leave the sketchy texture stuff in there and call it a wrap (**Figure 6.24**), or you could download a bunch of 3D cabinets and appliances from the 3D Warehouse to flesh out the design with actual products (**Figure 6.25**).

Figure 6.25 Replace the sketchy textures with real-world products from the 3D Warehouse for detailed design drawings.

Importing PDFs

Plans and elevations are commonly transferred in PDF format. If you're hoping to import a PDF into SketchUp, you'll first want to determine what kind of PDFs you've got. They actually come in two different varieties: raster format and vector format.

Rasterized PDFs aren't much different than a bunch of JPEGs, so whether you import those directly or save them out as JPEGS and then import—the results are pretty much the same.

Remember too, that direct import of the PDF format is only supported on the Mac OS. So if you're working on a Windows PC, you'd have to use Acrobat (or equivalent) to export the pages of your PDF file as a series of JPEGs or TIFFs and then import those instead.

Vector-Based PDFs are more commonly exported from CAD programs—and they're a whole different story. Vector lines are far more accurate than their rasterized counterparts, and in most cases you can extract the edges and endpoints from the PDFs.

To extract the vector line work you first need to open the PDF in Adobe Illustrator, at which point you would then be able to edit and manipulate the edges. Illustrator also has an option to export the vector line work as a DWG file. After exporting as a DWG file from Illustrator, you could then import the DWG file into SketchUp and utilize the processes outlined in Chapter 5.

Mac users: If you forgo the Illustrator workaround (or simply don't have Illustrator) and end up importing a vector-based PDF directly into SketchUp, the file will automatically be converted into a raster graphic with a transparent background—at which point you can use the method outlined in the previous section to turn the image into a 3D model.

Importing an Image as a Texture

This section explores various ways to utilize the image import option Use As Texture. As the name suggests, this option is the most effective way to import an image directly onto a face in the model and have that image automatically behave as a *tiled* texture. It's also a great way to add detail to a model without actually having to model everything in 3D.

Projected Versus Tiled Textures

Before getting into the specifics for importing texture images into SketchUp, it's important to understand the difference between the two fundamentally different types of SketchUp textures: those that are *projected*, and those that are not (referred to simply as *tiled* textures).

The difference between these two textures is evident in the ways in which they are displayed when applied to different kinds of surfaces.

Tiled textures. You can think of tiled textures as behaving kind of like wrapping paper. Whatever the pattern is—brick, wood, tile, or birthday balloons—it doesn't matter; the image will keep repeating on and on in all directions to fill whatever face the texture is applied to. When the texture gets to an edge, it will simply wrap around the corner and keep repeating to fill the next face, and so on. Tiled textures work really well for walls and boxes but aren't all that great for texturing curved or complex curved surfaces like spheres or terrain models.

Projected textures. You can think of projected textures as behaving kind of like a video projector. Projected textures are similar to tiled textures in the sense that the patterns repeat over and over in all directions to fill whatever face the texture is applied to. However, instead of wrapping around corners, a projected texture will stay aligned in reference to the face on which it was originally placed. In essence, the face to which a projected texture is applied will function similar to an actual real-world projector, in the sense that the texture can be projected from that face onto any other surface in the model. Projected textures work great for curved and complex curved surfaces like spheres, cyc walls (curved walls typically used as film or photography backdrops), and terrain models (**Figures 6.26** and **6.27**).

Figure 6.26
Comparison of tiled (left) versus projected (right) textures on a box.

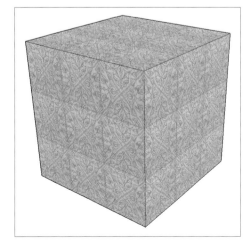 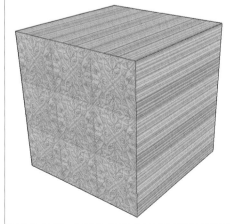

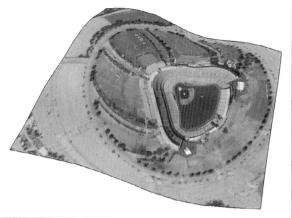

Figure 6.27 Comparison of tiled (left) versus projected (right) textures on a terrain. © 2009 Google

To toggle a texture back and forth from projected to tiled, right-click any textured face and choose Texture > Projected from the context menu. A check mark indicates that a texture is projected; no check mark means it's tiled.

Creating and Importing Cropped Textures

Generally speaking, I tend to encounter two main scenarios where it makes sense to crack open Photoshop and edit an image before importing it into SketchUp: 1) I need to crop an image down to the part that I intend to use in SketchUp; 2) I want to use a portion of an image and create a pattern that will tile as a seamless texture.

Since I've only got so many pages, this section will look at the first, and less involved of the two scenarios, which deals with basic cropping techniques and the import of cropped images into SketchUp.

The sample files for this example can be copied from the companion DVD, or you can download them from the Picasa Web album at http://picasaweb.google.com/tadrosio/RealWorldGoogleSketchUp7SampleFiles.

1. Start by opening the image Thailand.jpg in an image editing program such as Photoshop.

2. Using the Crop tool (C), select a region around the door in the middle of the screen (**Figure 6.28** on the next page).

Figure 6.28 Drag a region around the door using the Crop tool.

NOTE If you don't have access to an image editing program like Photoshop or Gimp, you can skip ahead to Step 6 and use the cropped version of the image titled Thailand_ Cropped.jpg.

3. Check the box for Perspective correction (**Figure 6.29**).

Figure 6.29 Check the Crop tool option for Perspective correction.

4. Drag the corners of the crop selection to align to the corners of the doorway (**Figure 6.30**).

5. Drag the center point until you feel it snap to the center of the cropped area and then press Enter to crop the image and correct the perspective distortion.

You should end up with an image that looks like **Figure 6.31**, which you can then save as Thailand_Cropped.jpg.

Figure 6.31 The resulting cropped image.

6. Now head over into SketchUp and start by drawing an 8-foot cube.

7. Go to File > Import. Choose the option for All Supported Image Types from the File Format drop-down menu, and choose the option Use As Image. Navigate to the image file Thailand_Cropped.jpg and choose Import.

8. Click once on a face to set the insertion point of the image, and then scale the image up and click a second time to set the image in place (**Figure 6.32** on the next page).

Figure 6.32 The Use As Texture option allows you to place a tileable image texture directly onto a face.

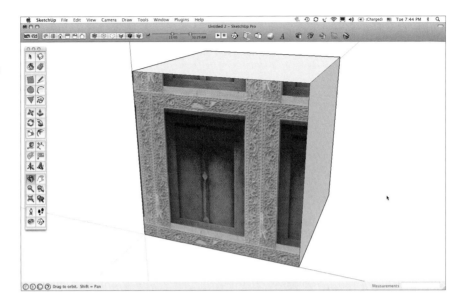

9. To correct the size and position of the texture, right-click the texture and choose the context menu option Texture > Position Texture.

10. Then right-click the image a second time and make sure that the option Fixed Pins is checked (**Figure 6.33**).

There are two different pushpin modes for positioning textures: Fixed Pin mode and Free Pin mode. You can check or uncheck the Fixed Pins option to toggle between the two modes. For cropped images, you're better off using the Fixed Pin mode.

Figure 6.33 While in Texture Position mode, right-click and make sure Fixed Pins is the active pushpin mode.

Why Do My High-Resolution Images Look So Crummy?

In Chapter 1, "Setting Your SketchUp 7 Preferences," we looked at the Open GL setting (Window > Preferences > Open GL tab) for Use Max Textures Size.

By default, that option is left unchecked, and as such, SketchUp will downsample any imported image to a maximum width resolution of 1024 pixels wide. With the Use Max Texture Size option checked on, SketchUp will display the maximum resolution allowable based on your computer's graphics capabilities. Note: this option will only improve the visual quality of images that you've imported with a fairly high native resolution. Many of the images you download from the Web will be low resolution, and no matter what you do those kinds of images will look grainy when you zoom in close to them in SketchUp.

While your textures may look a heck of a lot better with the Max Texture Size option turned on, the trade-off of performance degradation may not be worth it for day-to-day use. If SketchUp slows considerably you can go back, turn the preserve Max Texture Size option off, and reserve its use for renderings and presentations.

11. In Fixed Pin mode you'll notice that the pushpins are all different colors (**Figure 6.34**). You can click and drag the pins to the corners of the face to get the texture to fit perfectly. The most effective way to manipulate the pushpins is to position them in the order: Red, then Green, then Blue (RGB).

The Red pushpin allows you to move the image, the Green pushpin lets you rotate or scale the image, and with the Blue pushpin you can shear the image or scale it vertically.

Figure 6.34 Align the pushpins to the corners of the box. Go in the order R, G, B.

NOTE If you make a mistake, don't use Edit > Undo (Cmd+Z)! The texture position process has its own special Undo/Redo options that show up if you right-click while in Position Texture mode. There is also an option for Reset, which will restore the image to the original state it was in when you first imported it onto the face.

12. Right-click and choose Done to exit the Texture Position mode.

13. Save your work: We'll keep working with this file in the next section.

If the proportions of the size of the texture relative to the size of the face are working for you, great—if not, you're free to change the size of the box or go back into Texture Position mode and change the size of the texture.

There are a couple options for changing the size of the box/texture:

- The image texture is a tiled texture, so if you Push/Pull, or Move the end of the box to make it longer, the texture will continue to repeat (**Figure 6.35**).

Figure 6.35 If you Push/Pull the end of the box, the textures will keep tiling.

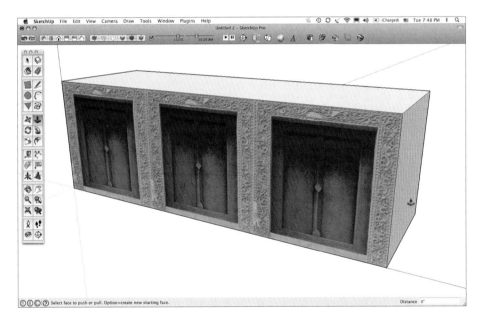

- If you use the Scale tool to change the size of the box, the texture will scale relative to the size of the face (**Figure 6.36**). Then if you Push/Pull or Move the end of the box, the texture will repeat and keep whatever proportions you scaled it to.

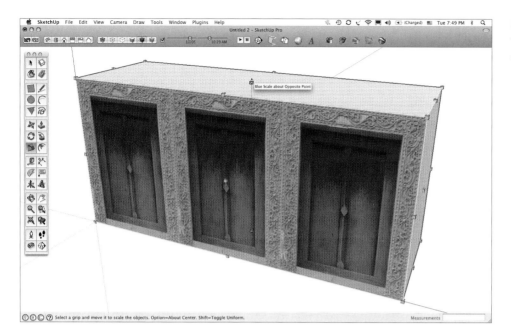

Figure 6.36 Scaling the entire box also scales the textures.

Seamless Textures

To check out a couple of methods for creating seamless textures for wood flooring, bathroom tile, kitchen countertops, and organic landscape material, check out *The SketchUp Show,* Episode 40: "ImageSynth & SketchUp," and Episode 41: "Creating Tileable Textures" video tutorials included in this book's companion DVD and online at www.go-2-school. com//Real-World-Google-SketchUp-7.

Imagesynth (www.luxology.com/whatismodo/imageSynth/) and Filter Forge (www. filterforge.com/features/) are two great Photoshop plug-ins that are useful for creating seamless textures. If creating seamless textures isn't the kind of thing you're into, all is not lost; you can cut to the chase by downloading seamless image textures from Web sites like Form Fonts (www.formfonts.com) and Filter Forge (www.filterforge.com/filters).

Working with Perspective Photos in SketchUp

The previous example dealt with images that were first cropped nicely, and then imported into SketchUp. In this example we'll look at ways of working with and cropping perspective images directly in SketchUp.

The sample files for this example can be copied from the companion DVD, or you can download them from the Picasa Web album at http://picasaweb.google.com/tadrosio/RealWorldGoogleSketchUp7SampleFiles.

1. Go to File > Import. Choose the option for All Supported Image Types from the File Format drop-down menu, and choose the option Use As Image. Navigate to the image file Brick_Wall.jpg and choose Import.

2. Click once on a face to set the insertion point of the image, and then scale the image up and click a second time to set the image in place (**Figure 6.37**).

Figure 6.37
Perspective photos can also be placed on faces as textures, and then cropped directly in SketchUp.

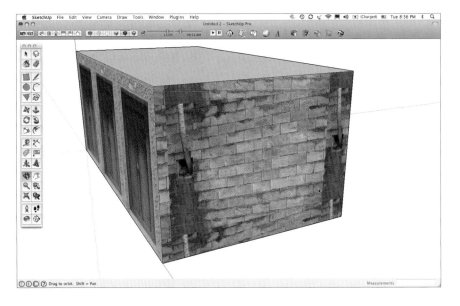

3. Right-click on the image and choose Texture > Position Texture.

4. Right-click again and uncheck Fixed Pins to toggle into Free Pin mode (**Figure 6.38**). In Free Pin mode you'll notice that the pushpins are all colored the same yellowish color.

5. The goal for this next step is to place the pushpins such that they define the bound of the portion of the image that you want to use for your texture. In this case we want to be somewhat particular about the tops and sides of the region of brick we define so that the cropped texture can repeat seamlessly.

To manipulate the position of the pins, click and release to pluck the pin out from the image, move it over, and then click a second time to stick the pin back into the texture (**Figure 6.39**).

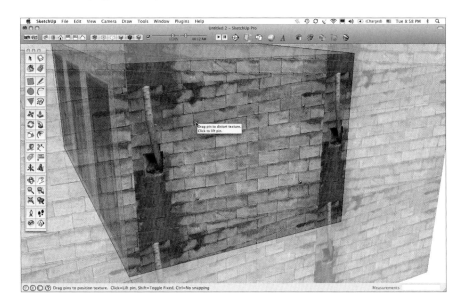

Figure 6.39 Place the pins at the corners of the area that you want to use as a texture.

6. The next step requires you to click and drag each of the pushpins to the corresponding corners of the face. Midway through the process, the image may start to look real funky, but once you've placed all four pins, the texture should fit nicely on the face (**Figure 6.40**).

Figure 6.40 Drag the pins to the corners of the box to get the texture to fit perfectly on the face.

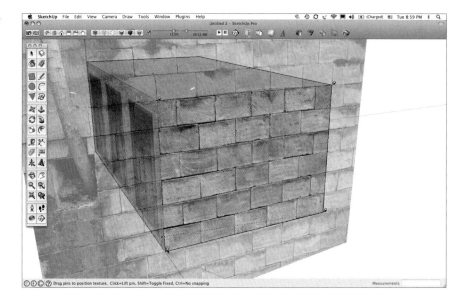

7. Right-click and choose Done to exit the Texture Position mode.

8. Right-click again and choose Make Unique Texture from the context menu. This option saves a cropped version of the texture so you don't have to do the pushpin thing again.

9. Take the Paint Bucket tool (P), and then press and hold Alt while clicking on the texture to sample it. Then let go of Alt and click to paint the brick texture around to the other faces (**Figure 6.41**). Images imported directly as textures behave as *tileable* textures, so you'll see the brick wrap nicely around the corners of the box.

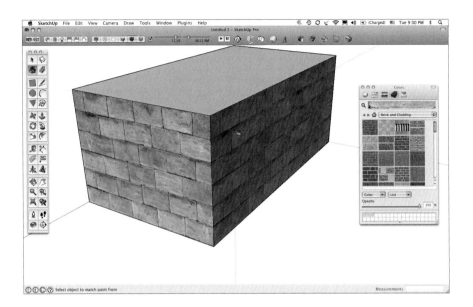

Figure 6.41 Use the Paint Bucket tool to sample and paint the unique texture onto the remaining sides of the box.

I've included an additional image of Spanish roofing tiles among the sample files. You can use that image to practice working with the procedures outlined in this section (**Figure 6.42**).

Figure 6.42 A roofing texture can be applied to finish off this model.

Importing Street View Imagery as a Photo Texture

In addition to the myriad options for importing imagery into SketchUp we've explored so far, Google has gone a step further in terms of creating photo-textured models of real-world buildings by allowing you to directly import imagery from the Google Maps Street View.

Since Street View imagery, is by its nature linked to a specific location, the option for importing Street View imagery can leverage any kind of location-based information that you may have assigned to your SketchUp model.

The following example takes a look at the interconnectedness between SketchUp, Google Earth, and SketchUp's new Get Photo Texture tools.

1. Launch Google Earth and search for the Peachpit Press office by searching for "1249 8th Street, 94710."

2. Zoom in to the Peachpit Press building and press R to reset the view (**Figure 6.43**).

Figure 6.43 Search for the Peachpit Press office in Google Earth.

© 2009 Google, Map Data © 2009 Tele Atlas

3. Go back to SketchUp and click the Get Current View button ⬤ to import the site into SketchUp (**Figure 6.44**).

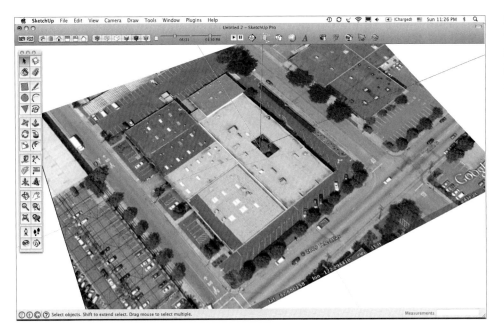

Figure 6.44 Import the current view from Google Earth into SketchUp.

© 2009 Google, Map Data © 2009 Tele Atlas

4. Use the Pencil tool (L) ✎ to trace an outline that matches the footprint of the building and then use the Push-Pull tool (Q) ⬆ to pull the box up 18 feet (**Figure 6.45**).

Figure 6.45 Draw an 18-foot-tall box aligned to the footprint of the Peachpit Press building.

© 2009 Google, Map Data © 2009 Tele Atlas

NOTE You can also open the Photo Textures window via the Window menu.

5. Right-click the west side of the building and choose Get Photo Texture from the Context menu.

    The Photo Textures dialog (**Figure 6.46**) automatically shows available street view imagery for the face that you right-click. You can click and drag the bottom-left corner of the window to make it bigger, and you can use the street view window or the map to navigate and pan around to find the best street view of the building. In some cases, the best view might be off to the side a bit, where you can see past any trees, cars, or signs that might block your view.

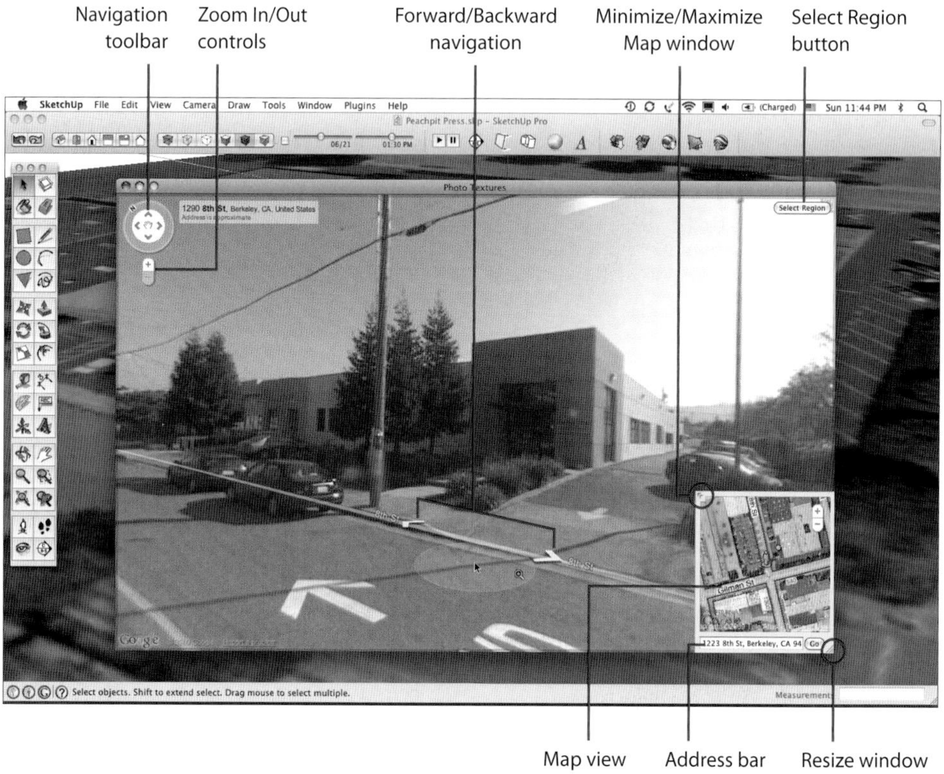

Figure 4.46 The Photo Textures dialog.

© 2009 Google

Navigation toolbar · Zoom In/Out controls · Forward/Backward navigation · Minimize/Maximize Map window · Select Region button

Map view · Address bar · Resize window

6. Click the Select Region button and then drag the blue push pins to choose the part of the image that you want to use as a photo texture (**Figure 6.47**).

7. Click the Grab button to apply the Street View image to the face of the building. You can then minimize or close the Photo Texture dialog to see how the model looks with the texture applied (**Figure 6.48**).

Figure 6.48 Click Grab to apply the Photo Texture to the model.

NOTE You can use the Paint Bucket tool to sample the black-and-white satellite image from the terrain and paint it onto the roof to use as a reference for modeling the parapet wall bordering the roof.

Depending on the results from Step 7, you can edit the building and the applied textures (using the methods described earlier in this chapter).

8. Model the parapet wall based on the information available from the Street View and satellite images (**Figure 6.49**).

   The street view image that was imported in Step 7 provides a relatively unobstructed view of the southwest corner of the building; however, the trees in the view are blocking a large portion of the rest of the west elevation. To solve these kinds of problems, you can break a face up into different pieces and import different photo textures for each face.

9. Use the Pencil tool (L) ✎ to draw a vertical line down the west face of the building between the green and white stuccoed areas, dividing the face into two parts (**Figure 6.49**).

10. Right-click the northern section of the face with the texture of the trees blocking the elevation and choose Get Photo Texture from the context menu. Then navigate in Street view to find an unobstructed view of that section of the building and repeat Steps 6 and 7 (**Figure 6.49**).

Figure 6.49 Grab an unobstructed photo texture of the northern section of the west elevation.

© 2009 Google, Map Data © 2009 Tele Atlas

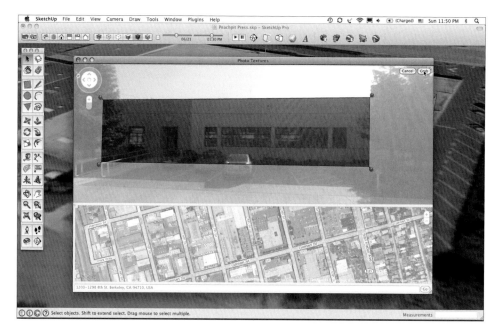

11. [Optional] At this point feel free to continue importing additional photo textures onto other faces of the building (**Figure 6.50**).

Figure 6.50 The completed SketchUp model.

12. [Optional] Once you've finished modeling the building you can use the Place Model tool 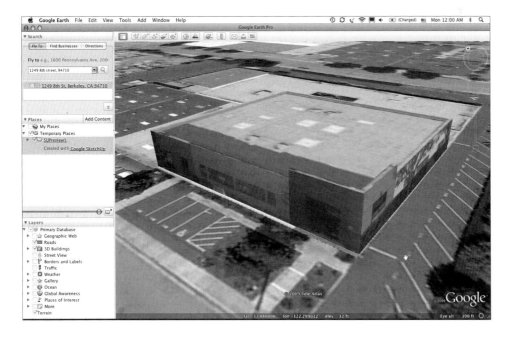 to export the textured building to Google Earth and view your model in context (**Figure 6.51**).

Figure 6.51 The finished SketchUp model in Google Earth.

© 2009 Google, Map Data © 2009 Tele Atlas

Here are few tips for getting the most out of Get Photo Textures:

- The Photo Textures dialog allows you to minimize the map window, thus maximizing the Street View window, so you can get textures of larger buildings.

- Get Photo Textures works regardless of whether you've imported a site from Google Earth. You can type an address into the search bar at the bottom of the dialog to search for and import Street View images *from anywhere* in the world and bring those images *into any SketchUp model*.

- You can right-click any face in your model and grab a photo texture for that face regardless of the size, scale, or shape of the face. SketchUp will create a clipping mask in the Photo Textures dialog that mimics the outline of any irregularly shaped faces.

Realism Redefined

Adding photos of real-world products and materials to your model can lend an aesthetic realism to your model that may allow you to forgo the time-consuming process of creating additional photorealistic renderings with one of the SketchUp rendering plug-ins or a third-party rendering application.

Figure 6.52 is an image of a SketchUp model I worked on for a developer where I textured just about everything in the model—from the floors to the cabinets to the furniture to the coat rack—with various photos that we had taken of the real materials and products that he wanted to use in the project. In addition to the ability to tour through the 3D, textured model in real time, we were able to export dozens of images from the SketchUp model in a matter of minutes without having to "render" the model in another application.

Figure 6.52 A more realistic look can be achieved by importing photo textures throughout a model.

IMPORTING AN IMAGE AS A MATCHED PHOTO

It's often said that a picture is worth a thousand words, in which case perhaps it would be even more valuable to turn a picture into a 3D model. The concept of using computers to convert 2D imagery into 3D models is technically referred to as photogammetry, and has been around since the mid-19th century. The applications for modern-day photogammetry are fairly widespread. Truly automated photogammetry is a complex process that often involves the use of advanced software and a ridiculous amount of computing power.

Nowadays, slightly more hands-on programs like SketchUp and PhotoSynth provide free and relatively easy-to-use tools for turning boring pictures into interactive 3D experiences.

SketchUp's photogrammetric tools are accessed via the image import option Use As New Matched Photo. For most users, these tools generally serve two main functions:

- Creating a 3D model of a building or object from a photograph

- Aligning a 3D model to a photo of a background scene to establish the perspective and alignment prior to exporting an image of the model for use in a composite rendering

The next example illustrates the process of creating a 3D object (such as a building, piece of furniture, etc). I cover the basic steps here; for some of the more involved steps, I've listed some additional resources at the end of this section.

The sample files for this example can be copied from the companion DVD, or you can download them from the Crate & Barrel Web site (www.crateandbarrel.com).

1. Choose File > Import. Choose the option All Supported Image Types from the File Format drop-down menu, and choose Use As New Match Photo. Navigate to the file Abbott_1.jpg and choose Import.

2. The Match Photo interface includes a number of adjustable widgets and options that we'll look at, but first let's take a quick tour of the drawing window interface and the photomatch dialog (**Figures 6.53** and **6.54** on the next page).

📄 **NOTE** It's possible to import multiple images through the Match Photo process. For example, you might have a second image that showed the opposite view of an object. In cases where you plan to use multiple images, you will want to choose a position for the model origin that is common between the photos, such as either the bottom-left or bottom-right corner.

Scene Tab for returning to
Match Photo view

Dashed Perspective
alignment guides

"X" boxes

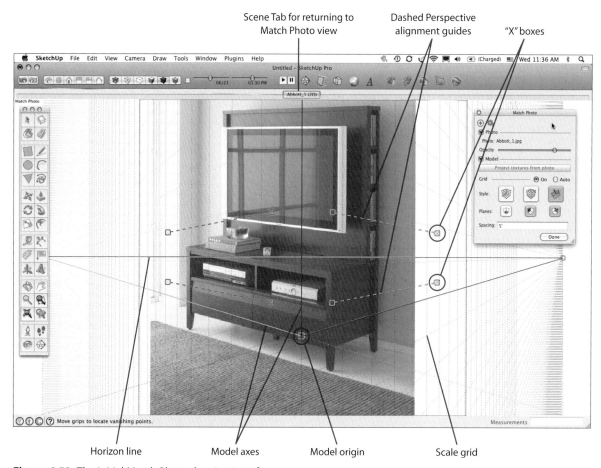

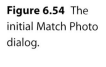

Horizon line　　Model axes　　Model origin　　Scale grid

Figure 6.53　The initial Match Photo drawing interface.　Photo: Steven McDonald

Figure 6.54　The
initial Match Photo
dialog.

New Match Photo
Image Visibility toggle

Edit Match Photo

Image Opacity slider

Model Visibility toggle
Project Textures button

Grid Visibility toggle

Grid Style options

Grid Plane Visibility options

Grid spacing

Done button

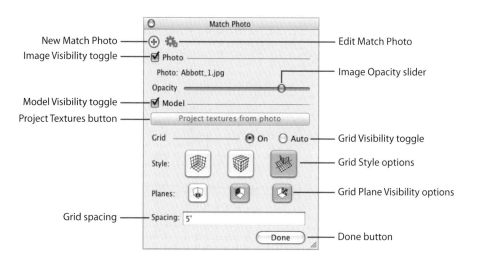

3. Click and drag the yellow origin box to drag the model origin over to the bottom-front corner of the console (**Figure 6.55**).

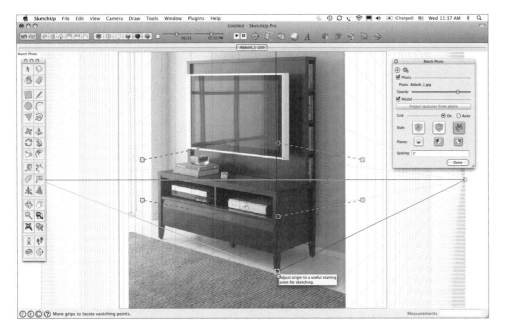

Figure 6.55 Drag the yellow box to set the model origin.

Photo: Steven McDonald

4. Click and drag the large "X" boxes to align the perspective bars to the perspective references in the image (**Figure 6.56**). If needed, you can zoom in and out.

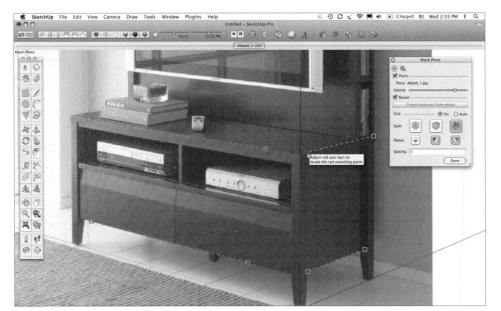

Figure 6.56 Drag the big "X" boxes to align the perspective bars.

Photo: Steven McDonald

NOTE When aligning the perspective bars, it is important to try to align the bars to something level. Trying to align to sloped ground planes, roof lines, or sloped ceilings won't work.

5. Set the grid spacing in the Photo Match dialog. The spacing could be something general, such as 24", or it could be something specific to the dimension of the object that you're trying to model. In this case, we know that the furniture piece is 60" tall, so we'll use that.

> **NOTE** Depending on the kind of image you're working with, you may want to tinker with the grid style and grid plane display modes. The goal is to choose a grid style that will help you to determine the scale of the model you're trying to build. The first button generally works well for interior images and the third button works well for exterior images.

6. Click and drag either of the axes (preferably the blue axis) to alter the grid scale until the spacing of one 60" grid square lines up to the height of the object in the image (**Figure 6.57**).

Figure 6.57 Drag the axes to match the grid spacing to a known dimension in the image.

Photo: Steven McDonald

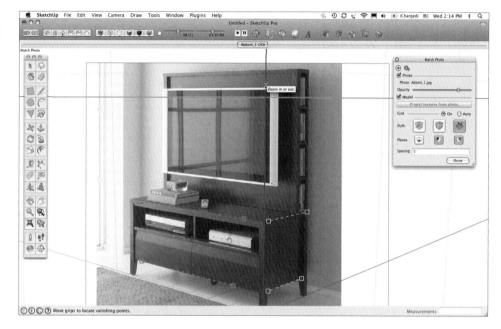

> **NOTE** If you accidentally/prematurely exit the Match Photo setup, you can either right-click the background image and choose the option Edit Match Photo, or you can click the Edit icon (looks like gears) in the Match Photo dialog. Another note: If you inadvertently orbit the model, the image will disappear. You can click the scene tab at the top of the drawing window to return to the Match Photo view and restore the background image.

7. Click Done to exit the Match Photo setup so that you can begin modeling.

8. Start by drawing the base of the console with the Rectangle tool (**Figure 6.58**). In cases where you don't have a complete set of measurements, you can get an acceptable level of accuracy simply by referencing the image. In this case, you can enter the exact Depth and Width dimensions for a more accurate model: type 20,52 and press Enter.

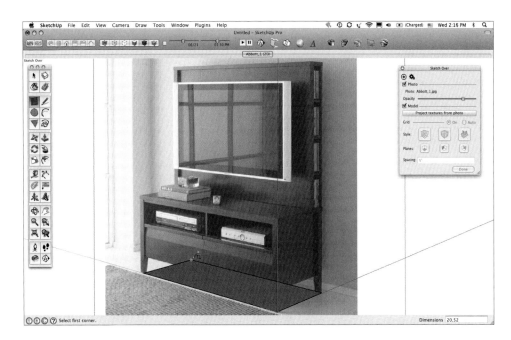

Figure 6.58 Draw the base with the Rectangle tool.

Photo: Steven McDonald

9. Push/Pull the base up to the height of the console. Again, you can either approximate by referencing the image or enter the exact known height for the console: type **62** and press Enter (**Figure 6.59**).

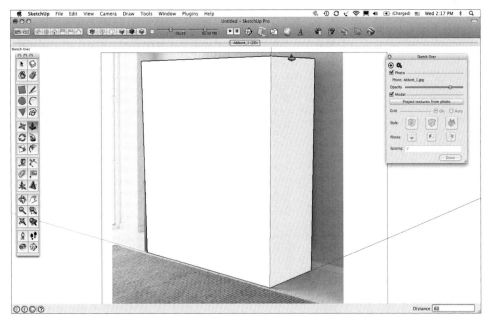

Figure 6.59 Pull the base up to the appropriate height.

Photo: Steven McDonald

10. Click the button "Project textures from photo" to apply the Match Photo image of the console to the box (**Figure 6.60**).

Figure 6.60 Use "Project textures from photo."

Photo: Steven McDonald

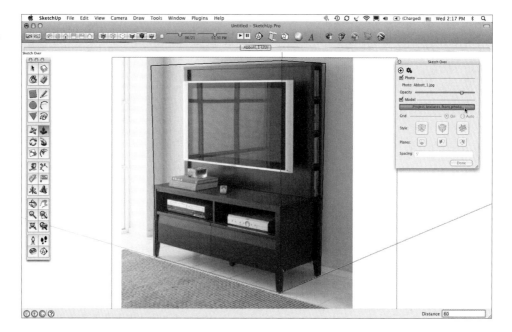

11. Since the model and the textures are dimensionally proportionate, you can now use the image textures as a guide for fleshing out the rest of the details (**Figure 6.61**).

Figure 6.61 Use the textures as a reference for modeling the details.   Photo: Steven McDonald

12. Click the scene tab and reproject textures if necessary. You can also use Texture Position tools illustrated in previous sections of this chapter to fine-tune the textures (**Figure 6.62**).

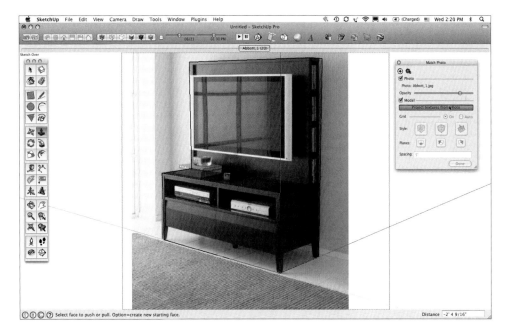

Figure 6.62 If the textures degrade while you're modeling the details, you can click the scene tab at the top of the page and then reproject the textures.

Photo: Steven McDonald

NOTE Reprojecting the Match Photo image will overwrite the textures for the entire model. You can select a specific face(s) before reprojecting the image in order to overwrite the texture for a specific face.

Match Photo is a great tool for applying textures to multiple faces of a model at the same time, but it's better to use Match Photo option to figure out the size and shape of the model. Since Match Photo textures are projected onto a face, you'll often notice that they look OK from the angle that the image was taken, but from other views, the textures might look rather streaky (**Figure 6.63** on the next page). After having used Match Photo to figure out the geometry for the model, you can import images that were taken from head-on angles using the option Use As Texture to replace the streaky textures with better-looking ones. Additional views of the console are provided with the sample files for this chapter, in case you want to give that a shot (**Figure 6.64** on the next page). I uploaded a fully textured model (**Figure 6.65** on the next page) to the 3D Warehouse as a reference for you to download and mess around with. Search for "Abbott 52" Media Console."

Figure 6.63 Match Photo textures may look good from the angle that the picture was taken but look streaky from other angles.

Photo: Steven McDonald

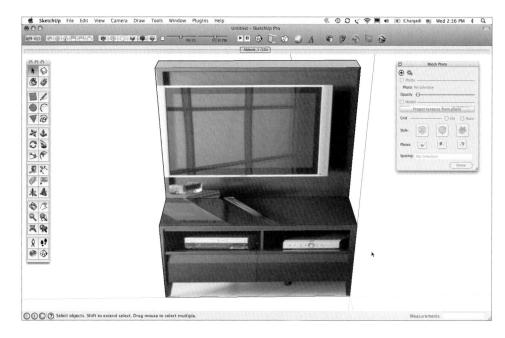

Figure 6.64 You can replace streaky textures by importing texture images taken from straight-on angles.

Photo: Steven McDonald

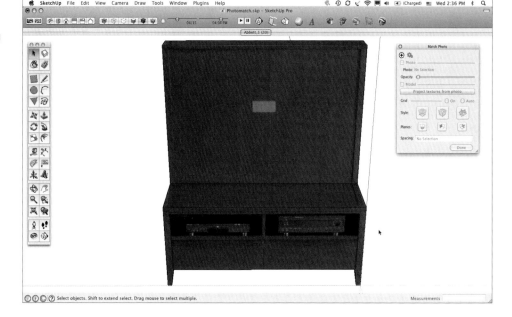

Figure 6.65 You can download the completed model from the 3D Warehouse. Search for "Abbott 52" Media Console."

Additional Resources

There are a wide variety of applications for the image import option for Match Photo. For more information, you may want to check these resources. (Unless otherwise noted, all are available at www.go-2-school.com/Real-World-Google-SketchUp-7.)

- *The SketchUp Show,* Episode 23: "Remodel Your Garage"

- *The SketchUp Show,* Episode 27: "Photomatch for Components"

- *The SketchUp Show,* Episode 34: "Photomatch and Compositing"

- *The SketchUp Show,* Episode 47: "Using Photomatch to Design a Kitchen"

- *School Series Google SketchUp Level 2* instructional DVD
  www.go-2-school.com/products/view/6

CHAPTER SEVEN

Mastering Materials

Chapter 6 covered the details of the options for importing images into SketchUp. Just about every option and example outlined in Chapter 6 eventually led to some kind of tutorial for working with textures in SketchUp.

This chapter expands on the image importing options from Chapter 6 and takes a look at the various options for creating and editing materials and textures using SketchUp's Materials browser. We'll also explore options for creating and organizing entire SketchUp material libraries.

As you'll see in this chapter, there's certainly no shortage of downloadable images from the Internet that can be used straight out of the gate as SketchUp materials. Just keep in mind that SketchUp is primarily a 3D computer-modeling program, not an image editor. This chapter explores ways of turning just about any image into a SketchUp material, as well as the available options for editing those images in SketchUp. However, the options for editing images in SketchUp are somewhat limited, so you'll probably want to keep Photoshop close by for those times when you need to do extensive image editing work.

MATERIALS AND TEXTURES

The terms *textures* and *materials* will be used often in this chapter. The term *texture* refers specifically to those materials with an image-based texture map.

The broader category of *materials* includes textures as well as any flat colors. As you'll see in this chapter, you can define color values for your SketchUp materials by entering numeric RGB, HSB, CYMK, and/or grayscale values.

Conceptually speaking, all textures are materials, but not all materials are textures.

You can open SketchUp's Materials browser window via the Window menu (Window > Materials) or by simply selecting the Paint Bucket tool (which will automatically launch the Materials browser window).

The tools and options within the Materials browser allow you to create, edit, size, colorize, and organize your SketchUp materials. Based on the operating system you're using, the Materials browser may look and function a bit differently. Take a minute to familiarize yourself with the Mac (**Figures 7.1**) or Windows (**Figures 7.2** on page 156) version of the Materials browser window.

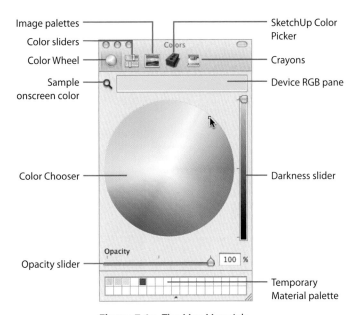

Image palettes
Color sliders
Color Wheel
Sample onscreen color
Color Chooser
Opacity slider

SketchUp Color Picker
Crayons
Device RGB pane
Darkness slider
Temporary Material palette

Figure 7.1a The Mac Materials browser window, Color Wheel tab.

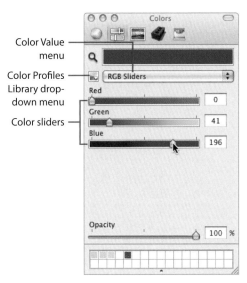

Color Value menu
Color Profiles Library drop-down menu
Color sliders

Figure 7.1b The Mac Materials browser window, Color Sliders tab.

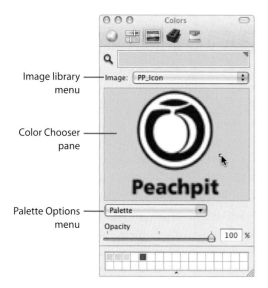

Image library menu

Color Chooser pane

Palette Options menu

Figure 7.1c The Mac Materials browser window, Image Palettes tab.

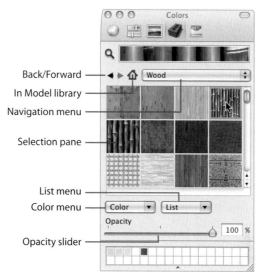

Back/Forward

In Model library

Navigation menu

Selection pane

List menu

Color menu

Opacity slider

Figure 7.1d The Mac Materials browser window, Color Picker tab.

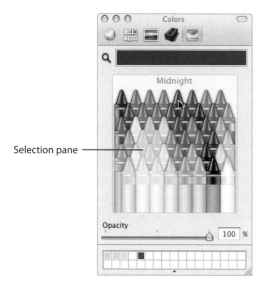

Selection pane

Figure 7.1e The Mac Materials browser window, Crayons tab.

Figure 7.2a
The Select tab controls for the Windows Materials browser window.

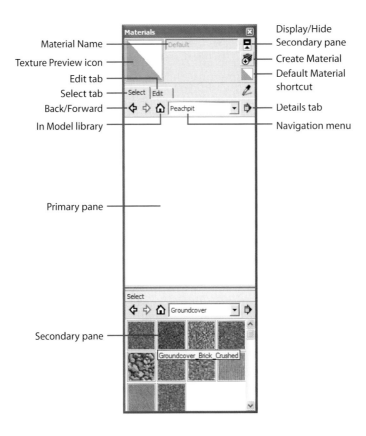

Material Name
Texture Preview icon
Edit tab
Select tab
Back/Forward
In Model library

Display/Hide
Secondary pane
Create Material
Default Material
shortcut

Primary pane

Details tab
Navigation menu

Secondary pane

Figure 7.2b
The Edit tab controls for the Windows Materials browser window.

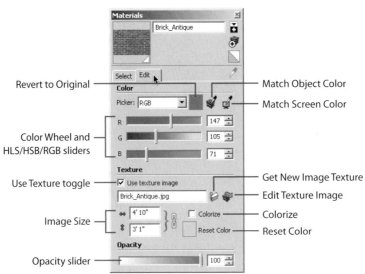

Revert to Original

Color Wheel and
HLS/HSB/RGB sliders

Use Texture toggle

Image Size

Opacity slider

Match Object Color
Match Screen Color

Get New Image Texture
Edit Texture Image
Colorize
Reset Color

CREATING AND MANAGING YOUR MATERIAL LIBRARIES

Having organized content libraries—whether components, styles, or materials—makes you far more efficient when using SketchUp in a professional workflow. If you've ever stumbled around for a component or material while presenting to a client or working with a co-worker, you know as well as anyone that disorganized libraries are time wasters that can make you look like a fumbling hack. This section explores the options available for creating and managing custom material libraries in SketchUp.

The Materials browser includes a fairly long list of material libraries to choose from, including wood, tile, roofing, groundcover, etc. However, I find it useful to create additional libraries for specific projects (e.g., Kitchen Remodel), material types (e.g., Sustainable Finishes), and specific manufacturers (e.g., Oceanside Glass Tile).

Depending on whether you work on the Mac or Windows platform, the options for creating and managing your material libraries are different enough that in some of the sections below I've separated the instructions into two parts so you can follow whichever one is relevant to you.

Disclaimer: Technically speaking, the term *library* refers to the entirety of your SketchUp materials. The materials library subfolders are referred to specifically as *collections* on a PC and *lists* on a Mac. To simplify things, I refer to all material folders (both the entire materials library as well as the collections/lists) as *libraries*. This section illustrates the options for creating sublibraries for categorizing your materials within the SketchUp Materials browser.

Creating a New Library from Scratch

The option to create a new material library from scratch is useful for setting up a library for new material types (e.g., Sustainable Materials) that will eventually be pooled together from any number of existing libraries.

PC Options:

1. Choose "Open or create a collection" from the Details menu ⬚ .

2. When prompted, navigate to the SketchUp 7 Materials directory, My Computer\C:\Program Files\Google\Google SketchUp7, and then choose the option Make New Folder.

3. Give the new material library a name (e.g., Peachpit). By default, once the new library is created, it will open in the primary pane (**Figure 7.3**).

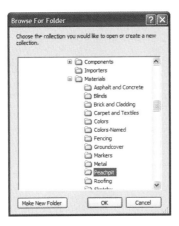

Figure 7.3
Name the folder for your new collection.

4. Click the Secondary Pane button ⊡ and navigate to an existing library in the secondary pane from which you want to copy over a material (e.g., Wood; **Figure 7.4**).

5. Drag and drop the material from the existing library in the secondary pane to the new library in the primary pane (**Figure 7.5**).

Figure 7.4
Navigate to an existing collection in the secondary pane.

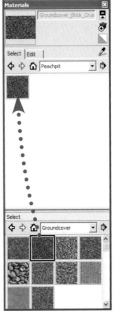

Figure 7.5
Drag and drop from an existing collection to the new collection.

Mac Options:

1. From the Color Picker tab in the Materials dialog, choose New from the List menu (**Figure 7.6**), give the new library a name (e.g., Peachpit), and then click OK.

Note: By default, the new library will automatically be saved as a folder in the SketchUp 7 materials directory located under Macintosh HD/Library/Application Support/Google SketchUp 7/SketchUp/Materials.

Figure 7.6 Choose New from the List menu.

2. Click the little round button at the bottom of the Materials browser to pull down the temporary palette.

3. Navigate to an existing library from which you want to copy over materials for your new library.

4. Drag a material from any of the existing libraries to the temporary palette below (**Figure 7.7**).

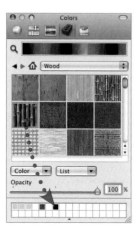

Figure 7.7 Copy a material to the temporary palette.

5. Navigate to the new material library, and then drag and drop the material up from the temporary palette into the new library (**Figure 7.8**).

Figure 7.8 Drag and drop the material from the temporary palette to the new material library.

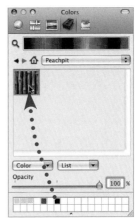

Aside from a general aversion to redundancy, I haven't found a particular downside to putting copies of materials in a couple of different libraries (e.g., a project library as well as a typological library). If anything, it makes it more intuitive to be able to find a material in whichever library you might happen to look for it.

6. If for whatever reason you want to remove a material from one of the libraries (to avoid redundancy), right-click the material and choose Delete from the context menu.

Duplicating an Existing Library

The option to duplicate an existing library is a quick way to save a copy of your In Model library. You can use this option to create material libraries based on particular projects or by manufacturer (by downloading materials from the 3D Warehouse into a new SketchUp model).

There are a number of colors and textures available to download from the 3D Warehouse. Plus, you'll find that textures from any of the 3D models downloaded from the 3D Warehouse will show up in the In Model material library.

1. Start a new SketchUp file.

2. Click the Get Models icon to access the 3D Warehouse and search for the textures that were uploaded by Oceanside Glass Tile (**Figure 7.9**).

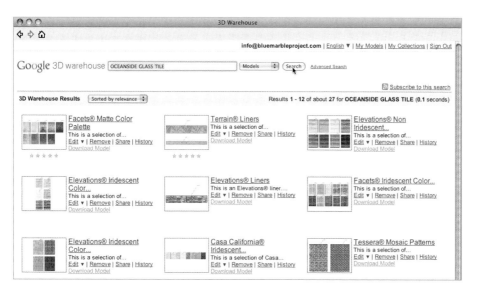

Figure 7.9 Search the Google 3D Warehouse for textures (such as Oceanside Glass Tile).

3. Download as many of the texture files as you wish directly into your SketchUp model. You could potentially download their entire catalog.

4. Open the Materials browser and navigate to the In Model library ⌂ , where you'll see all of the materials that were imported along with the files from the 3D Warehouse (**Figure 7.10**).

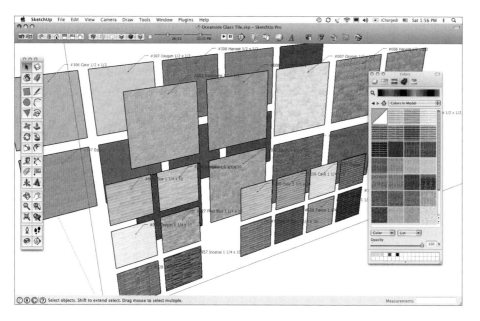

Figure 7.10 Navigate to the In Model materials library.

5. **On a PC:** Choose Save Collection As from the Details menu (**Figure 7.11**).

   On a Mac: Choose Duplicate from the List drop-down menu (**Figure 7.12**).

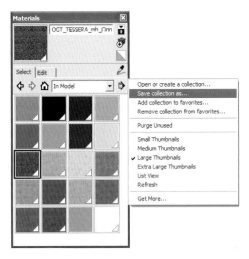

Figure 7.11 PC: Create a new material library that contains the In Model materials.

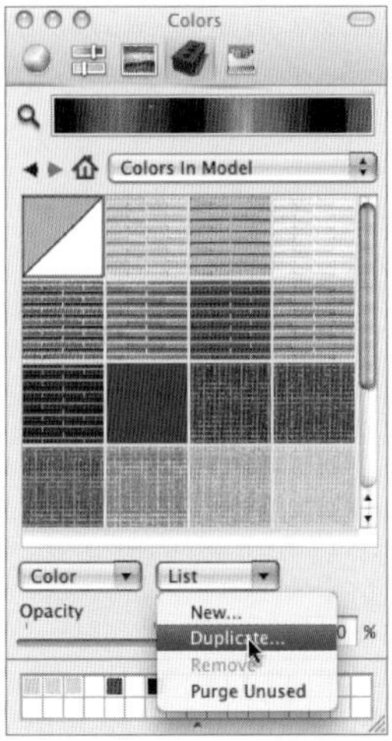

Figure 7.12 Mac: Create a new material library that contains the In Model materials.

6. Give the library a name (e.g., Oceanside Glass Tile).

7. **Mac only:** Navigate to the new library and then right-click the default (white/blue) material and choose Remove.

CREATING NEW MATERIALS

The options for creating new materials enable you to specify an exact color value for your material or import seamless image textures for use as SketchUp materials. This section explores options for creating new materials—both simple colors as well as image textures.

Creating a New Color

Creating a new color is one of the more basic options, since it doesn't involve having to specify any image texture properties. This option is most commonly used in situations where you need to create a specific color based on a given set of RGB values—such as needing to match a Pantone color, the color scheme for a corporate identity, or a paint sample from Home Depot.

To start, open a new file and click the Paint Bucket tool to launch the Materials browser.

On a PC:

1. Click the Create Material icon 🎨 and give the new color a name.

2. Choose a color from the color wheel or specify an exact color value using the RGB, CMYK, HSB, or grayscale color sliders.

3. Optional: Set the default opacity for the texture.

4. Click OK.

On a Mac:

1. Click the Color Wheel to choose a color or click the Color Sliders tab to specify an exact color value from the RGB, CMYK, HSB, or grayscale color sliders.

2. Click over to the Color Chooser tab and then drag the color from the Device RGB pane down into the In Model library.

3. Optional: Right-click the texture and choose Edit.

4. Optional: Set the default opacity for the texture and then close the material.

NOTE When setting a material's opacity, keep in mind that any material with opacity equal to or less than 70% will allow light to pass through. A material with opacity greater than 70% will cast a shadow.

Bonus Packs

SketchUp's default material library includes a decent selection of both textures and colors from which to choose. However, you can download a Bonus Material pack from the SketchUp Web site that includes hundreds of additional materials to choose from: http://sketchup.google.com/download/bonuspacks6.html.

The trick with the Bonus Material pack is that it was created for SketchUp version 6, so, by default, the installer file for the Bonus Material pack will add the bonus materials to your SketchUp 6 Materials folder. If you've only ever installed SketchUp 7, the installer will create a new SketchUp 6 Materials directory in which to place the SKM files. After installing the bonus pack, you can copy the SKM files to your SketchUp 7 Materials folder (see earlier in this section for the Materials folder locations).

Sampling Onscreen Colors

Sampling onscreen colors is an efficient way to create new materials that fit in with a given set of textures.

When I need to replace a streaky projected texture or patch a section of a face with a texture that isn't working out (which happens a lot when using the match photo option), I'll often sample an onscreen color to use in the model.

In Chapter 6 you saw an option for creating a model of a kitchen based on a hand-sketched image that was imported and then exploded. The result was a projected texture that created streaky textures on the sides of the cabinets that were pulled out from the image.

1. Download the Streaky Sketchy Kitchen model from the 3D Warehouse to your computer's hard drive and then open the file in SketchUp (**Figure 7.13**).

    Note: Do *not* import the Streaky Sketchy Kitchen file directly via the Get Models command.

2. Click the Paint Bucket tool to open the Materials browser.

3. **PC:** Create a new color material (it can be any color to start out). Then edit the material and use the Sample Onscreen Color tool to sample the off-white color of the cabinets.

    Mac: Use the magnifying glass in the Materials browser to sample the off-white, onscreen color of the cabinets.

Figure 7.13
Download Streaky Sketchy Kitchen from the 3D Warehouse and open the file in SketchUp.

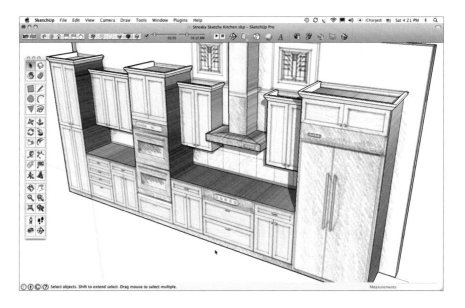

4. Paint the sides of the cabinets with the sampled color (**Figure 7.14**).

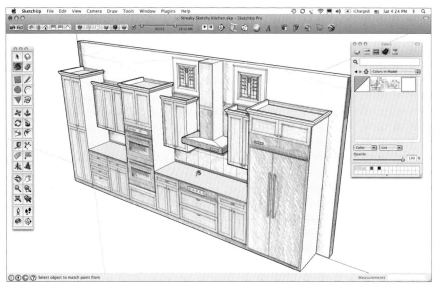

Figure 7.14
Replace the streaky textures with the sampled color.

Creating a New Texture

Chapter 6 illustrated processes for importing images directly onto a surface as a texture (a process that inherently leads to an immediate use of the texture in the model). This section explores options for creating a new texture by defining an image for it. Perhaps you'll want to use the new texture right away, perhaps not. Either way, it will be saved in a library, ready to go.

In terms of the differences between the two options—that's pretty much it. Chapter 6 looked at the option to import images as textures using the Import option; this chapter looks at ways to do it via the Materials browser.

For this example you can use just about any image file. Ideally, you'll want to use an image file that will tile seamlessly. For more information about creating seamless tileable images for use as SketchUp textures, check out Episode 41 of *The SketchUp Show,* "Tileable Textures" and Episode 40, "ImageSynth and SketchUp," at www.go-2-school.com/Real-World-Google-SketchUp-7.

ImageSynth is a Photoshop plug-in for creating seamless, tileable images. You can download the plug-in and find out more information about it at the imageSynth Web site, www.luxology.com/imageSynth.

NOTE One advantage to creating textures via the Materials browser is that you're able to specify both the width and height of the image texture, irrespective of the original image file aspect ratio.

Filter Forge is another Photoshop plug-in useful for creating seamless, tileable images. In addition to being able to download a free trial version of the plug-in from the Filter Forge Web site (www.filterforge.com), you can also search for and download thousands of free tileable images created by other Filter Forge users.

The following example illustrates a process of creating SketchUp textures using images from the Web that are already set up to tile seamlessly.

1. From the Filters section of the Filter Forge Web site (www.filterforge.com/filters), search for Slate Flooring.

2. Click the Slate Flooring texture by Crapadilla to get to the texture preview page.

3. Right-click the image preview and choose Save Image As from the context menu (**Figure 7.15**). Then save the image as Dark Gray Slate.jpg to a folder on your computer's hard drive.

Figure 7.15
Filterforge.com is a great Web site for downloading seamlessly tileable images for use in SketchUp.

On a PC:

4. Click the Create Material button and give the new texture a name (e.g., Horiz_Slate).

5. Toggle on the Use Texture Image option and then click the "Browse for Material Image File" icon .

6. Navigate to the location where the image file Dark Gray Slate.jpg has been saved, click the image file, and choose Open.

7. Optional: Set the default opacity for the texture.

8. Click OK.

On a Mac:

4. Choose New Texture from the Color drop-down menu (**Figure 7.16**).

5. When prompted, choose the image file Dark Gray Slate.jpg.

6. When prompted, give the texture a name (such as Dark Gray Slate) and a default size (in this case, 4' × 4') and click OK (**Figure 7.17**).

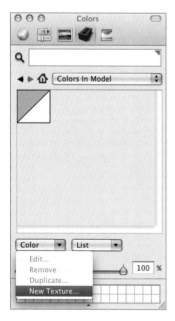

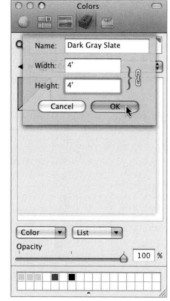

Figure 7.16 Choose New Texture from the Color drop-down menu.

Figure 7.17 Give the new material a name and assign a default texture size.

The material is now located in the In Model library, where you can either use the material in a project, add it to an existing library (e.g., Stone), or create a new material library for it.

To reiterate, I'll typically use the preceding process to create materials for a particular library. When I want to create a material for a project, I'll use the "Import as texture" option discussed in Chapter 6.

Ruby Script: Mass Material Importer

The Mass Material Importer Ruby script (massmaterialimporter.rb) is a great tool for creating new materials *en masse*. You can download the script from the Materials—Render section of the Ruby Library Depot (www.crai.archi.fr/RubyLibraryDepot/Ruby/en_ren_page.htm).

1. Gather up whatever cropped images you want to import into SketchUp and put them into a folder on your desktop.

2. Name the image files based on what you want the SketchUp material names to be.

   When choosing material names for SketchUp, it's best to use simple text names with underscores between words, and use lowercase file extensions—for example, 2x2_Bath_Tile_Green.jpg. If you put spaces or symbols (such as apostrophes) in the filenames or otherwise break from the suggested conventions, you may run into trouble when exporting your SketchUp model to other modeling/rendering applications.

3. Choose the Import Materials script from the Plugins menu.

4. When prompted, navigate to the folder on your desktop that contains the texture images, choose any one of the files from the folder, and then choose Open.

5. Each of the images is automatically imported as a 10" × 10" texture, after which you can edit each material (see the following section) and resize them according to their actual, real-world size. It may come in handy to include some kind of a reference to the real-world texture size/scale in the image texture/material filename so that you can reference the filename when defining the size.

6. Once you've imported a bunch of materials, you can duplicate the In Model library and save the imported materials for future use.

EDITING SKETCHUP MATERIALS

SketchUp includes a bunch of options for editing new and existing materials. When editing existing materials, it's a good idea to edit materials located in the In Model library—that way you'll still have the original version of the material to revert back to if you change your mind or if things go wayward during the editing process.

On a Mac you can get a material to appear in the In Model library by simply painting it onto a face in the model using the Paint Bucket tool.

On a PC you have the additional option of dragging any material from a library in the secondary pane into the In Model library in the primary pane (or vice versa).

New materials are automatically added to the In Model library, so before editing those you might want to either duplicate the material or drag a copy of it into an existing library so that you have a version of the material to fall back on if you change your mind about the edits.

To get into Edit Material mode, you can do any of the following:

* Double-click a material in the In Model library.

* Right-click a material in the In Model library and choose Edit from the context menu.

* PC Option: Select the material and then click the Edit tab.

* Mac Option: Select the material and then choose Edit from the Color menu.

Editing Colors

While in Edit Material mode, you can use the color wheel or color sliders to alter the value of a basic color material.

You can also use the color options to colorize an image texture. For example, if you're using a brick texture in a model and the client asks you to make the bricks a bit more yellow, you can colorize the texture to alter the overall color. The results you'll get from this process are akin to adding a color filter to an image in Photoshop.

Editing Texture Images

If I encounter a situation for which the SketchUp material editing options just don't cut it, that's when I choose "Edit texture image in external editor" from the Edit section of the Materials browser. This option extracts the image file from the material and opens it directly in Photoshop (or whichever image-editing application you chose in the Preferences > Applications pane).

Once in Photoshop, you can use the more advanced image editing options available for cropping and touching up your image textures.

As soon as you're done editing the image texture, you can save the changes in Photoshop and close the image file. SketchUp will automatically update the material in your model.

NOTE If you accidentally click another material while you're in Edit Material mode, you will inherit the color/texture and scale properties. If that happens, just close the material and click Undo.

NOTE You'll notice that one of the benefits of editing the In Model texture is that you're able to see how the edits affect the material in real time, while looking at the material as it's applied to faces in the model.

NOTE If you already have an image texture applied to a face in the model, you can right-click the texture and choose Edit Texture Image from the context menu in order to open the texture image in your chosen image-editing application.

Swapping Black-and-White Satellite Imagery from Google Earth with Color Imagery

The process of swapping a colored satellite photo to replace the standard black-and-white imagery imported from Google Earth is a rather involved process that requires you to use a number of different material editing options.

You'll need to have Google Earth (free or Pro) installed in order to follow along with the beginning part of this example. If you don't have Google Earth, you can skip to the second section "Resizing an Image Texture" and copy the sample files from the included DVD. The sample files are also available for download from the 3D Warehouse (search for Dodger Stadium Site) and the Real World Google SketchUp 7 Picasa album online at picasaweb.google.com/tadrosio/RealWorldGoogleSketchUp7SampleFiles.

Importing Site Imagery from Google Earth

We'll start this exercise in Google Earth.

1. Launch Google Earth and navigate to a site of your choosing. I'll use the site for Dodger stadium in this example. To locate this site in Google Earth, simply type `Dodger Stadium` into the search tab and press Enter.

2. In Google Earth, press the keyboard shortcut R to reset the view so that North is pointing up and the tilt is reset to be looking straight down.

3. From the View menu, turn off the Navigation toolbar and turn off the status bar.

4. Clear the search results pane to remove any place marks that might be obstructing the view, and turn off any unnecessary Google Earth layers such as the 3D buildings layer, Geographic Web, etc. that may be cluttering the view of the satellite image (**Figure 7.18**).

NOTE Keep the Terrain layer turned on so that SketchUp can import the satellite image in 3D.

5. Save the Google Earth view as an image file using the option File > Save > Save Image. With Google Earth Free, the maximum allowable resolution is based on your screen resolution; in Google Earth Pro, you can save an image up to a maximum image resolution of 4800 pixels wide.

6. Save the Color version of the Satellite image to your desktop or pictures folder and give it an easily recognizable name—for example, Dodger Stadium Sat Image. jpg.

7. Start a new file in SketchUp and import the site location from Google Earth using the Get Current View tool 🌐 located in the Google toolbar (View > Toolbars > Google).

Resizing an Image Texture

When you import a satellite image from Google Earth into SketchUp, the image texture is given a default size of 1" × 1"—despite the fact that in real life the area represented by the image is likely much larger.

This same scale mismatch often happens when importing images directly as textures. In Chapter 6, you looked at options for scaling an image at the moment it is imported, but if you're not careful you may end up with textures that have odd default sizes. This section explores options for editing the default texture size to make it easier to swap out different images for your textures.

1. Right-click the satellite image that you imported from Google Earth and choose Unlock from the context menu (**Figure 7.19** on the next page).

2. From the View menu, turn on Hidden Geometry.

Figure 7.19 Choose Unlock from the context menu.

© 2009 Google

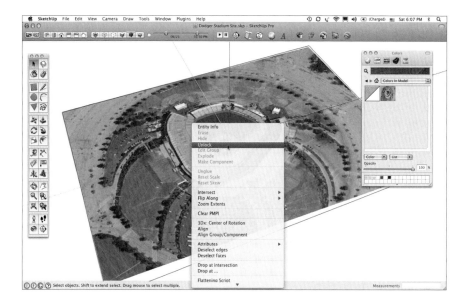

3. Take the Tape Measure tool and measure the actual width of the satellite image that was imported from Google Earth. Make sure you are measuring the flat, 2D version of the image that is on the Google Earth Snaps layer, not the 3D version on the Google Earth Terrain layer (**Figure 7.20**).

4. Highlight the dimension in the Measurements dialog and copy the value using Ctrl+C (PC) or Cmd+C (Mac).

Figure 7.20 Measure the width of the image, and then copy the dimension from the Measurements dialog.

© 2009 Google

5. Open the material library (Windows > Materials) and navigate to the In Model library.

6. Select the material for the black-and-white satellite image imported from Google Earth.

PC: After selecting the material, click the Edit tab (**Figure 7.21**).

Mac: Right-click the material and choose Edit from the context menu (**Figure 7.22**).

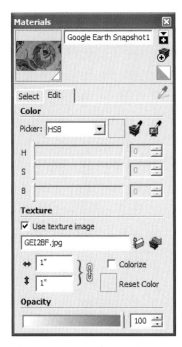

Figure 7.21 PC: Choose the satellite image material and then click the Edit tab.

Figure 7.22 Mac: Right-click the satellite image material and choose Edit from the context menu.

7. Unlock the aspect ratio by clicking the chain-link icon, paste the width dimension into the space with the horizontal arrows, and then press Enter.

The material will stretch horizontally, which is to be expected, so don't freak out (**Figure 7.23** on the next page).

Figure 7.23 Paste the width dimension of the image into the corresponding texture size field and press Enter.

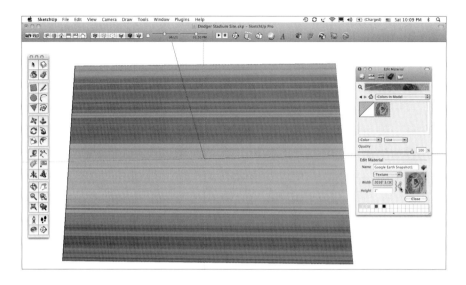

8. **PC:** Click back over into the Select tab to save the changes.

   Mac: Click the Close button in the material editor to save the changes.

9. Measure the height of the Google Earth image in the model with the Tape Measure tool.

10. Repeat steps 4–8, but this time, when you get to Step 7, enter the dimension into the field with the vertical arrows (**Figure 7.24**).

    This time the texture will grow vertically and the surface will look like a big gray square.

Figure 7.24 Paste the height dimension of the image into the corresponding texture size field and press Enter.

Swapping a Texture Image

1. Go into Edit Texture mode for the black-and-white satellite image texture.

2. Reload the color version of the satellite image to replace the black-and-white image.

   PC: Click the Load Texture icon (**Figure 7.25**).

   Mac: Choose Load from the Texture drop-down menu (**Figure 7.26**).

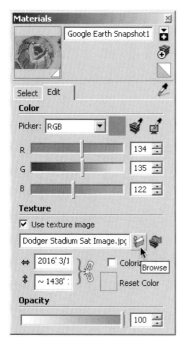

Figure 7.25 PC: Click the Load Texture icon.

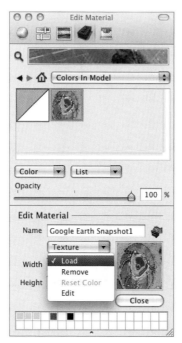

Figure 7.26 Mac: Choose Load from the Texture drop-down menu.

3. Choose the Dodger Stadium Sat Image.jpg file from the location you saved it to.

4. Mac users only: Click Close to save the changes.

Positioning Textures

The image texture has been properly sized, and you've swapped out the black-and-white image for the color version—but as a result of all that, the position of the texture has been thrown a bit out of whack. This section details the process of getting the image back in line with the geometry.

1. Right-click the satellite image and choose Edit Group.

2. Right-click the image again and choose Texture > Reset Position.

3. Right-click the image again and choose Texture > Position.

4. Use the Fixed Pin mode to align the texture to the corners of the surface. You can position the pins in the order of the color wheel—Red, Green, Blue, and then Yellow (**Figure 7.27**).

Figure 7.27 Use the fixed pins in the order Red, Green, Blue, Yellow to position the texture on the face.

© 2009 Google

5. Right-click the image and choose Done to exit the Position Texture mode.

6. Right-click the texture and choose Projected.

7. Take the Select tool (V) ▸ and press Esc to close the group containing the 2D version of the satellite image.

Sampling Image Textures

This section shows how to sample the aligned, projected texture from the 2D version of the site, and paint it onto the 3D terrain.

1. Take the Paint Bucket tool 🪣 and press and hold the Alt key (PC) or Option key (Mac). You'll see the Paint Bucket tool icon turn into an eyedropper that you can use to sample the projected texture and load it into the paint bucket.

2. Click the Toggle Terrain tool 🗺 in the Google Toolbar to toggle from the 2D version of the terrain to the 3D version (**Figure 7.28**).

> **NOTE** If the Terrain layer is turned on in Google Earth, there are actually two different objects imported onto two different layers when you use the Get Current View command to import satellite imagery from Google Earth into SketchUp: a flat 2D version of the terrain that is located on the Google Earth Snaps layer, and a 3D version containing the topographic data from Google Earth that is located on the Google Earth Terrain layer. The Toggle Terrain tool essentially toggles the visibility of one layer or the other. Theoretically, you could turn on both layers simultaneously via the Layers window.

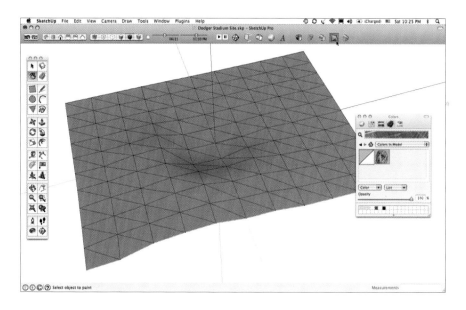

Figure 7.28 Use the Toggle Terrain tool to turn off the layer containing the 2D version of the terrain and turn on the layer containing the 3D version of the terrain.

3. Right-click the 3D terrain and choose Unlock from the context menu.

4. Right-click again and choose Edit Group.

5. From the Edit menu, turn off Hidden Geometry.

6. Paint the projected texture onto the 3D terrain with the Paint Bucket tool 🪣.

7. Close the 3D terrain group (**Figure 7.29**).

Figure 7.29
The completed 3D terrain with a colored satellite image.

© 2009 Google

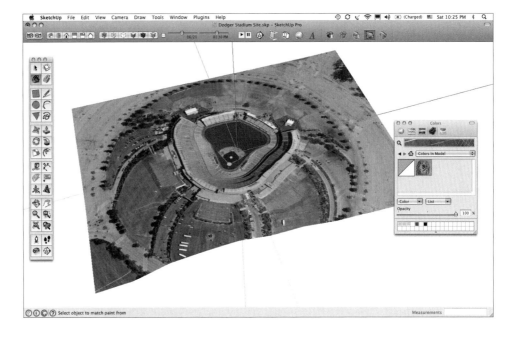

Additional Resources

For more information about some of the Materials browser options discussed in this chapter, check out Episode 53 of *The SketchUp Show,* "Import Satellite Imagery and Terrain from Google Earth in Color!" online at www.go-2-school.com/Real-World-Google-SketchUp-7.

There's also a recording available at the same URL of Q&A Webinar that I hosted on May 5, 2009, during which I discussed, in a fair amount of detail, the various tools and options for the Mac Materials browser.

In addition to downloading images and materials from the Google 3D Warehouse and sites like Filter Forge, you might also want to check out the expansive library of materials available from the Form Fonts Web site (www.formfonts.com).

CHAPTER EIGHT

Mastering Components

In earlier chapters you learned about SketchUp's "sticky" behavior—that is, the tendency in SketchUp for overlapping edges and faces to automatically join together. You've also seen how groups and components effectively separate geometry in the model and keep objects from sticking together.

Both groups and components share the function of being able to effectively isolate and protect objects from other geometry in the model—but that's about where the similarities end. The benefits of creating a group are effectively limited to:

- Allowing you to quickly separate otherwise loose entities into their own autonomous objects—for example, separating the edges and faces that make up the walls of a building from those that make up the roof.

- Allowing you to gather up a bunch of scattered objects so that you can quickly select them—for example, grouping all of the chairs around a table (and perhaps even grouping them together with the table) so that you can quickly select and move the items together as a set.

Components, on the other hand, present a whole other level of functionality, especially given the functionality introduced in SketchUp version 7 to create dynamic components.

This chapter explores some of the more advanced functionality for creating components and looks at some of the most effective ways to use components to save time and increase productivity in SketchUp.

CREATING BASIC COMPONENTS

To answer the all-too-familiar question, "When should I create a component versus when I should create a group?" my answer would be that you consider the following general rules of thumb:

- Any time you draw an object that you plan to create copies of, make it a component first. Then place copies (a.k.a. instances) of that component around the model.

- If you're ever in doubt about which option to use, just make it a component. Making something a component gives you more options for what you can do with it later.

As you'll see, working in this way lays the groundwork for being able to more efficiently revise your model later on. If the repeated elements in your project are modeled as components, then you'll only have to revise one of the component instances, as opposed to having to edit each copy individually.

Once the "must create components" mindset sinks in, you'll get better about planning out your SketchUp modeling work as a process of creating and assembling the various parts and pieces of a project, perhaps even to the extent that your SketchUp models are built in a way that closely mimics the way that your project would be built and assembled in the real world.

Let's begin this section by creating a simple bookcase component.

1. Start a new file and draw a box 36" wide by 14" deep and 52" tall. Note the relation of the box to the axes in **Figure 8.1**.

2. Triple-click the box with the Select tool (V) ▸ to select all of the edges and faces.

3. Right-click the box and choose Make Component from the context menu to bring up the Component dialog (recommended shortcut: Shift+G; **Figure 8.2**).

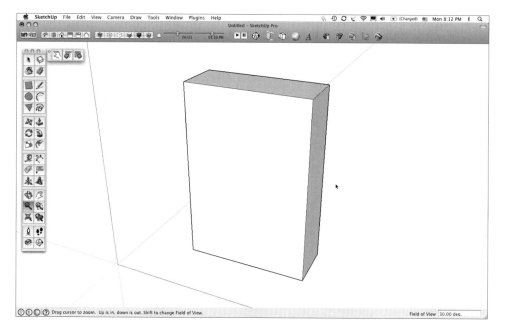

Figure 8.1
Draw a box that measures 36" wide by 14" deep by 52" tall.

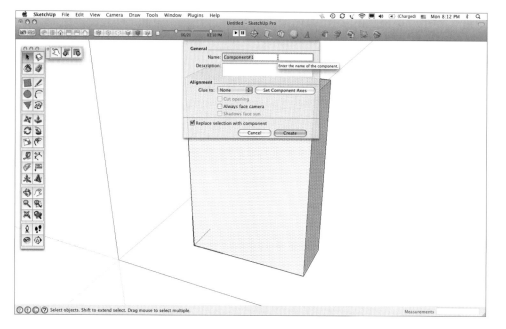

Figure 8.2
The Create Component dialog.

Assigning a Name and Description

The name and description information entered into the Create Component dialog are attributes that will stay with the component. The component name will appear in the Model Info window, Outliner, Component browser window, and the Dynamic Component Attributes dialog.

1. Give your bookcase component the name *Bookcase* and give it a description that includes any relevant information (such as the dimensions 36" wide by 14" deep by 52" high) that you might want to recall later.

2. Click Create.

3. Open the Component browser window, navigate to the In Model library, and click the bookcase component icon. Notice that the name you entered shows up in the Name field of the Component browser window (**Figure 8.3a**).

   In the Entity Info window you'll see the component name listed in the Definition field (**Figure 8.3b**).

   In the Outliner window you'll see the name appear in brackets (e.g., *<Bookcase>*) (**Figure 8.3c**).

   In the Dynamic Component Attributes dialog 🗃, the component name is listed above the attributes list (**Figure 8.3d**).

NOTE If you create leader text in the model by clicking a component using the Text tool 🔤, the default text will autofill with the component name.

Changing the Component Name

If you change the component name in the Entity Info, Outliner, or Component browser windows, the name change will automatically register in the other windows.

However, since a component name is an integral part of dynamic component formulas (as you'll see in later sections of this chapter), once a component has been turned into a dynamic component, the component name in the DC Attributes dialog becomes a separate ball of wax. Name changes in the Model Info, Outliner, and Component browser windows will not be reflected in the DC Attributes dialog, and the same is true vice versa.

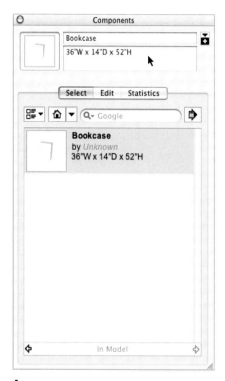

A

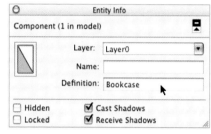

B

Figure 8.3 The component name appears in the Component browser window (a), Entity Info window (b), Outliner (c), and Dynamic Component Attributes dialog (d).

C

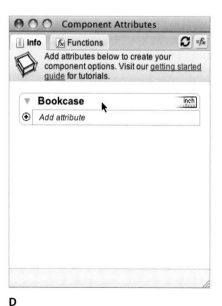

D

Determining the Component Origin

The insertion point of a component relates to the location and orientation of the component axes. Each component has its own axes, which are independent from the model axes. To get a better sense of this feature you can view all of the component axes in a model by going to Window > Model Info > Components > Component Axes > Show Component Axes.

As you may recall from Chapter 4, the origin of the component axes is also the point at which the Move tool has a hold of the component while it's being imported into a project from the Component browser or via the Get Models browser. So the important point to consider when creating a component is, "Can the position of the component axes make it easier for me to place this component into a project?" The answer to that question is typically "Yes!"

For example, if you were modeling a structural column that needed to be placed based on its center point, you would probably be better off locating the component origin at the center of the base of the column to make it easier to position the column when placing copies of it around the model.

Another example might be if you were creating a component of a light fixture that was going to hang from the ceiling; you would probably be better off locating the component origin near the top of the fixture, where it would make it easier to place the component while looking up at the ceiling.

With the bookcase that we're working on, the most intuitive location for the component origin would probably be the back-right or back-left corner.

You can set the component axis location while creating the component initially by choosing Set Component Axis in the Create Component dialog (Figure 8.2). At this point, however, the component axis for our bookcase has already been set, so instead we'll look at the options we have for changing the component axis after it's already been set.

1. Right-click the component and choose Edit Component from the context menu.

2. Zoom out so that you can see the component axis extend beyond the bookcase.

3. Right-click the component axes and choose Change Axes (**Figure 8.4**).

4. Zoom back in, and then place the axes at the back-right corner (**Figure 8.5**).

5. Close the bookcase component.

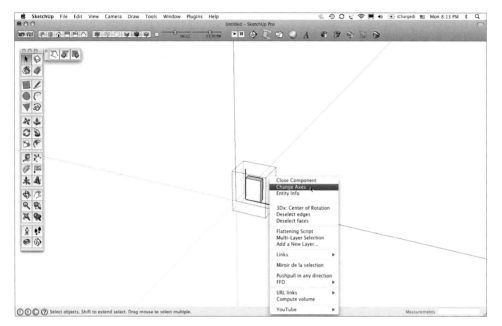

Figure 8.4
You can change the axes location of a component while in Edit Component mode.

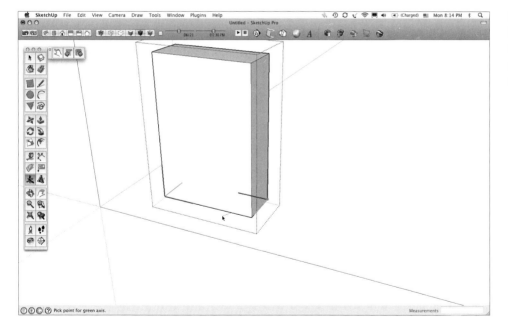

Figure 8.5
Set the component axes for the bookcase at the back-right corner.

Setting a Gluing Plane

When creating a component, choosing one of the following gluing plane options will automatically align the Red/Green plane of the component axes to the type of face that you select.

- **None** will keep the component oriented such that the component axes are always aligned relative to the current position of the project file axes. This option works well for things such as trees, people etc. that are always supposed to stand tall, regardless of the orientation of the face on which they're being inserted.

- **Any** will allow you to place the component onto any kind of face in the existing project. Once placed in the model, the component will glue to the face on which it was placed.

- **Horizontal** will restrict the orientation of a component such that when you go to place it into your project you will only be able to set the model down on an existing, horizontal face—or, onto the ground plane in the model.

- **Vertical** gluing planes restrict the orientation of a component such that when you go to place it into your project you will only be able to set the model down on an existing, vertical face in the model.

- **Sloped** gluing planes restrict the orientation of a component such that when you go to place it into your project you will only be able to set the model down on an existing, sloped face in the model. This option is useful for components such as skylights, solar panels, and other stuff you might expect to put on a rooftop or other sloped face.

Of the available options, our bookcase would probably be best off with a Horizontal gluing plane so that it will always align itself to whichever floor surface it's applied to. Again, you have an option to set the glue-to option when you're creating the component initially (Figure 8.2), but if you've already created your component (as with our bookcase), you can go back and edit the gluing option later on.

1. Open the Component browser, navigate to the In Model library, and then click the bookcase component.

2. Click the Edit tab in the Component browser.

3. Choose the option for Horizontal from the "Glue to" drop-down menu (**Figure 8.6**).

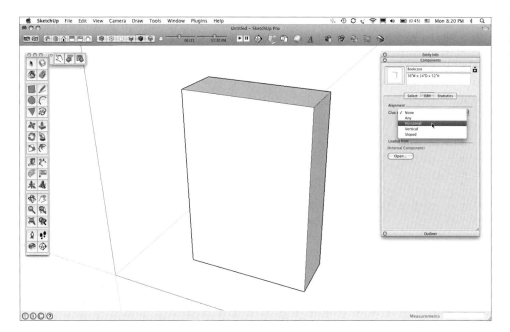

Figure 8.6
Set a Horizontal gluing plane for the bookcase.

Moving a Glued Component

Glued components can only move across the plane of the face that they are glued to. Additionally, if you move the plane that the component is glued to, the component will move along with it. To unglue a component which has been glued to a face, you can right-click the glued component and choose Unglue from the context menu. Keep in mind however that there is not an option for re-glue. To re-glue a component, your best bet would be to reinsert it from the component browser.

Creating Nested Groups and Components

The term *nested* refers to components within other components. When you create nested components in a model, the main component is referred to as the *parent* component, the subparts and pieces are referred to as *nested* components. You can have nested components inside of other nested components and so on, so that you have several layers within a parent component. As a reminder, the general rule of thumb is that any time you're about to create an object and you think you might eventually make several copies of that object in your model, make it a component first. That way, if you ever have to make any changes to the object, you'll only have to change one of the copies, and all the other copies will automatically follow suit. These same rules apply when creating nested components.

For example, our bookcase component would likely be modeled such that the shelves are all the same size. An option in this case would be to create one shelf component and then copy it. That way, if you ever need to change the depth or thickness of the shelves, you would only have to edit one of the shelves.

1. Take the Select tool (V) and double-click the bookcase component to go into Edit Component mode.

2. Take the Offset tool (O) and offset the edges of the front face of the bookcase 2 inches (**Figure 8.7**).

Figure 8.7 Offset the edges of the front face of the bookcase.

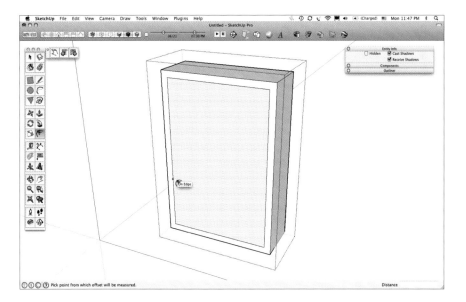

3. Push/Pull (Q) the front face through to the backside of the bookcase to cut a hole through it.

4. Take the Select tool (V) and triple-click the frame of the bookcase to select all the faces and edges.

5. Right-click the frame and choose Make Group from the context menu. (**Figure 8.8**).

6. Draw a rectangle down near the bottom of the frame, and then pull the rectangle up to create a 2-inch thick shelf.

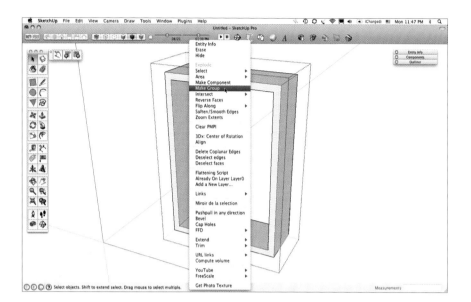

Figure 8.8 Turn the bookcase frame into a nested group.

7. Take the Select tool (V) ▶ and triple-click the shelf. Then right-click the shelf and choose Make Component. Name the component *Shelf,* and then click Create (**Figure 8.9**).

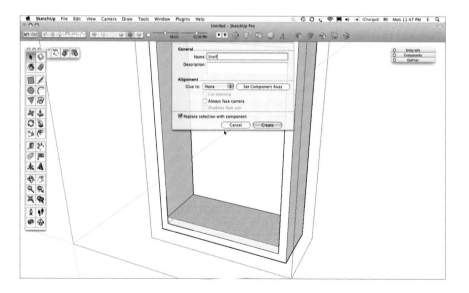

Figure 8.9 Create a nested component for the bookcase shelf.

8. Take the Move tool (M) ✥ and press the Option key (Mac) or Ctrl key (PC) and move a copy of the shelf component up to the top of the frame.

9. Type 4 and press Enter to create five evenly spaced shelves. Then Erase (E) the first and last shelf (**Figure 8.10** on the next page).

10. Take the Select tool (V) ▶ and press Esc to close the component.

Figure 8.10 Copy
the shelves, and then
close the bookcase
component.

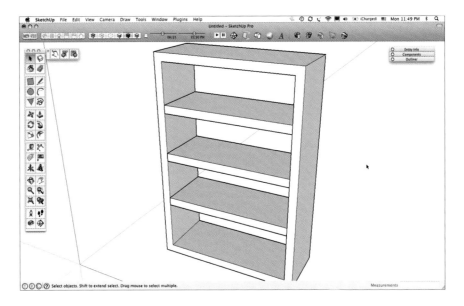

📄 **NOTE** With nested components it's important to get used to making sure you're in Edit Component mode within the correct nested component before trying to make changes to it. Similarly, remember to close the nested components when you're done editing them. The Outliner (Window > Outliner) can be a helpful tool for visualizing and keeping track of nested components.

If you wanted to take this bookshelf to the point where all the parts and pieces were componentized, you could model the left and right sides of the bookshelf as nested components that were flipped along the red axis so that they mirrored each other—again creating a scenario whereby modifying one side of the bookcase would automatically result in the opposite side of the bookcase changing in a symmetrical fashion.

CREATING FACE-ME COMPONENTS

As mentioned in Chapter 4, Face-me components are a great low-poly option for reducing file size and optimizing performance. One of the biggest advantages gained by using Face-me components stems from the fact that they are typically created as flat, 2D components—thereby requiring far fewer edges and faces to represent an object than if it were modeled in full 3D. Despite being modeled as flat objects, Face-me components get their name from the fact that they are set up to automatically rotate so that the component is always facing the camera. Face-me components are especially useful for representing complex organic forms such and plants, animals, and people.

An optional, yet highly effective process for creating 2D Face-me components with accurate outlines and shadows begins in Photoshop. If you use Adobe Creative Suite regularly, you should check out *The SketchUp Show,* Episode 19: "Creating Face-Me Components," included on the companion DVD and online at www.go-2-school. com/Real-World-Google-Google-SketchUp-7. The video illustrates the process of taking an image from Photoshop to Illustrator to CAD to SketchUp—and might shed light on some useful workflows for other stuff you're working on.

For this next example, start by importing the results of the aforementioned process (a cropped PNG image of a palm tree with a transparent background and a DWG outline of the tree). The sample files for this example can be copied from the Chapter 8 Example Files folder on the companion DVD, and the images are also available for download from the Real World Google SketchUp 7 Sample Files Picasa album at http://picasaweb.google.com/tadrosio/RealWorldGoogleSketchUp7SampleFiles.

1. Import the file PALM_TREE_OUTLINE.dwg into SketchUp.

    Warning: This example assumes you're using the Real World SketchUp 7 template (see Chapter 2) or any other template that starts out with an empty drawing (such as the Beginning Training Template Inches). If you're using a template where new files open with a dude standing in the middle of the screen, delete the dude first before executing this next step.

2. Fill in the face by tracing an edge with the Pencil tool (L) ✎ (**Figure 8.11**).

    Note: If you were working on a tree with an outline that had a ton of little leaves or whatever, you could use the Make Faces Ruby script instead (see Chapter 3).

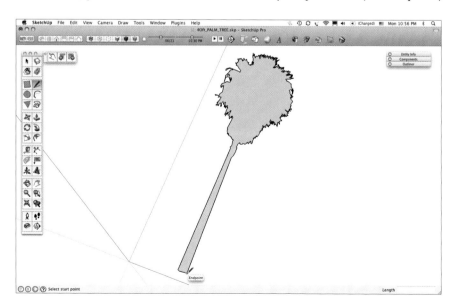

Figure 8.11 Trace an edge of the outline to heal the face.

3. Right-click the face and choose Reverse Faces from the context menu. Remember that it's always better to apply textures to the white side of a face to avoid issues with the textures being misread when exported to other modeling and rendering applications.

4. Scale the tree to a real-world height (such as 40 feet) using the Tape Measure tool (D) .

5. Import the image file PALM_TREE.png. Apply the PNG directly onto the face as an image texture and position it so that it fits within the outline (**Figure 8.12**). If needed, refer to Chapter 6, "Importing Images" for more information about this step.

Figure 8.12 Position the palm tree texture so that it fits within the outline.

6. Rotate the entire tree using the Rotate tool (R) so it's standing upright.

   Tip: Click and drag along the bottom of the tree to set the rotation axis first (**Figure 8.13**) then click a second time to start rotating the tree up, then click a third time to rotate the tree 90 degrees.

7. Double-click the face with the Select tool (V) to select the face and all of the edges. Then press and hold the Shift key while single-clicking the face again to deselect the face.

8. Choose Edit > Hide to hide the edges of the outline around the tree.

9. Double-click the face of the tree again to select the face and all the hidden edges.

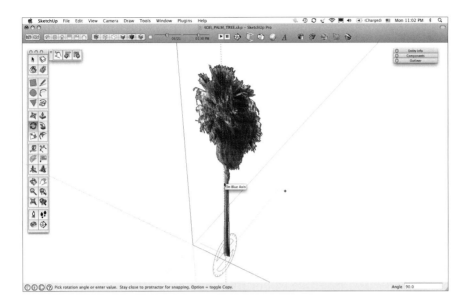

Figure 8.13 Rotate the tree so that it is standing upright.

10. Right-click the face and choose Make Component.

11. Give the component a name (e.g., *40' Palm Tree*) and description (e.g., Coolest 2D Face-me tree ever).

12. Choose Set Component Axes and locate the component axes at the bottom of the tree near the middle of the trunk (**Figure 8.14**).

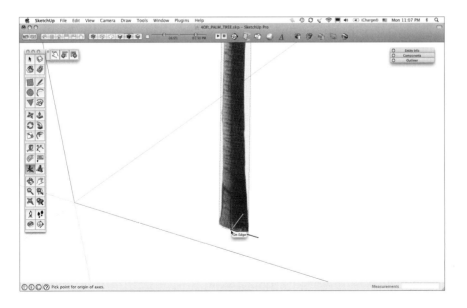

Figure 8.14 Set the tree component axes near the middle of the base to set the point about which the component will swivel as it rotates to face the camera.

13. Choose the gluing option for None, check the boxes for Always Face Camera, Shadows Face Sun, and Replace Selection with Component (**Figure 8.15**). Then click Create.

Figure 8.15
Create the palm tree Face-me component.

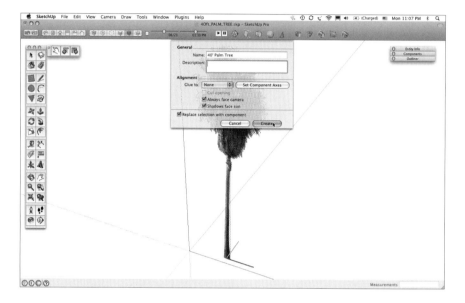

Now the tree is all set up to face the camera from any angle.

Note: If for some reason you didn't want your tree component to face the camera anymore, you could disable the Always Face Camera feature via the Component browser dialog.

Go to the In Model library of the Component browser and select the tree component. Then choose the Edit tab and uncheck the Always Face Camera option.

As a reference, you can download my version of this palm tree component from the Google 3D Warehouse (search for "40 foot palm tree author:blue marble project") and use it to troubleshoot any issues you may have run into while following along with this section.

CREATING DYNAMIC COMPONENTS

SketchUp's dynamic components feature allows you to attach information to any component in the form of data attributes. You could use dynamic components to simply assign basic data attributes, such as an item's real-world SKU number, product name, size, or description. Dynamic component features also allow you to create custom dialog boxes for your components that you can use to easily edit attributes, such as the component size or material, by choosing from options or entering values into the dialog. These features can save a ton of time editing complex components that typically contain many nested groups and components such as doors, windows, and cabinets.

In this section, I'll break down the basics of dynamic components and show you some of the ways you can take advantage of this powerful feature set. First, you'll need to bring up the Dynamic Component toolbar under View > Toolbars > Dynamic Components. **Figure 8.16** highlights each of the tools in the toolbar, two of which (Options and Attributes) can also be accessed via the right-click context menu > Dynamic Components.

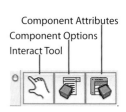

Component Attributes
Component Options
Interact Tool

Figure 8.16
The Dynamic
Component toolbar.

Creating a Dynamic Door Component

In this example, we'll take a look at creating one of my favorite dynamic components: a modern-style door that I created to use in my architectural and interior design projects. I love these kinds of doors and found that I was using some variation of this one in a number of projects—so for me it made sense to turn it into a dynamic component in order to save time when I need to revise the door style for a project. The component we're going to create can be configured in thousands of different ways with just a couple of quick clicks.

NOTE Axis positioning will be very important throughout this example!

1. Draw a 2-foot cube. Start drawing from the origin of the model out toward the solid Red and Green axes directions (**Figure 8.17**).

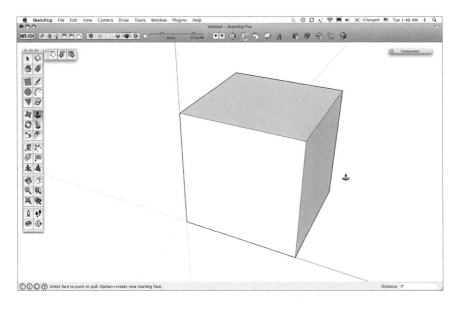

Figure 8.17 Draw a 2" by 2" by 2" cube.

2. Make the cube a component. Call it *Door* and make sure the option "Replace selection with component" is checked before clicking the Create button (**Figure 8.18**).

Figure 8.18 Turn the cube into a component named *Door*.

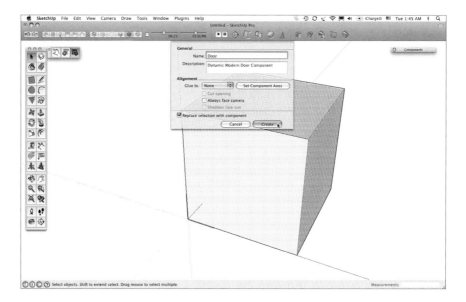

3. Click the Component Attributes icon 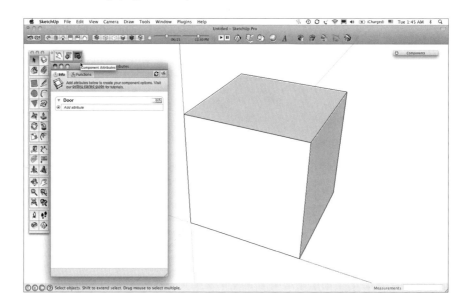 to open the Dynamic Component Attributes dialog (**Figure 8.19**).

Figure 8.19 The Dynamic Component Attributes dialog.

NOTE In the top-right corner you'll see the Toggle Formula View button. You may find it easier to work with that button turned on as we go through rest of the section on creating dynamic components.

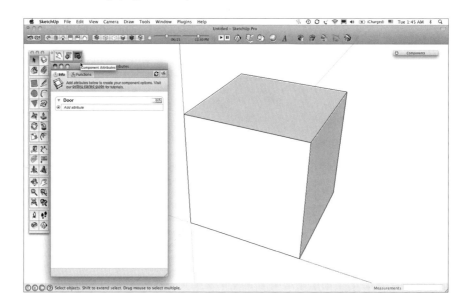

Add Position, Size, and Rotation Attributes

In general, the Dynamic Component Attributes dialog contains two kinds of attributes:

- **Relative Attributes:** The default values are displayed as gray text and can be considered *relative*. These values are simply reporting the current status of the component in the model. Relative values are automatically updated in real time when the component is edited.

- **Absolute Attributes:** You can define an *absolute*, fixed value (one that will not change) for an attribute by putting an equals sign (=) in front of a number or formula. Absolute values are displayed as black text. In addition to simple numeric attributes, absolute values may also include functions and formulas, as you'll see in later sections of this example.

When adding the attributes, consider the following important information regarding the relative position of the component axes and model axes:

- Position values for a nested component are relative to the position of the parent component axes. If a component *is* the parent component, the position values are relative to the model axes.

- Size and Rotation values are always relative to the selected component axes—not the parent or model axes.

1. Add the Position attributes and define absolute values for the door by entering =0 in the PosX, PosY, and PosZ attribute cells (**Figure 8.20**).

    Some procedural notes about entering values:

    - Edit a value cell by double-clicking it.

    - After you enter a value, press Enter to solidify the changes.

    - If you click another value while in Edit mode, the name of the other attribute value will be entered into the active cell. This can be both helpful and annoying at times, so just be aware of when and where you're clicking stuff while editing attributes.

    - To unlock a value, you can delete the cell's contents (including the equals sign) and press Enter—at which point the values go back to being relative.

2. Add the Size attributes and lock in the following Size values to change the dimensions of the box (Figure 8.20):

    LenX (Door Width) =36
    LenY (Door Thickness) =1.5
    LenZ (Door Height) =84

Figure 8.20 Position, Size, and Rotation attributes for the door component.

3. Add the Rotation attributes and enter the values RotX =0, RotY =0, RotZ =0.

   Now try to move, rotate, or scale the box. You'll see that it keeps going back to the 0, 0, 0 model origin—and keeps the same position and size you have set in the Attributes dialog no matter what you do to it.

   For an object such as this door, you would most likely keep the Position and Rotation attributes *unlocked* so that you'd be able to move the door around in the model and place it within any doorway.

4. Go back and delete the contents of the Rotation attribute cells to set those back to their relative (grayed out) values.

Add Interaction Attributes

Interactive onClick attributes allow users to click dynamic components with the Interact tool to initiate a change in state among any values that have been input for the onClick attribute. Examples of basic onClick actions include moving or rotating an object with the Interact tool (as you'll see in this example) or changing the material or size of an object. OnClick attributes could even impact multiple attributes simultaneously.

1. Create a custom attribute named *SLIDE* and enter the value =0.

2. Add the onClick attribute and enter the formula ANIMATE(SLIDE,0,36).

3. Enter the PosX value =0+SLIDE.

4. Click the door with the Interact tool ⛥. The Interact tool will cause the onClick formula to cycle through the SLIDE values 0 and 36, which will animate the change in PosX value of the door.

   You can change the door to function as a swinging door by altering a couple of attributes.

5. Change the PosX attribute back to =0.

6. Add a custom attribute for SWING and enter a value =0.

7. Edit the onClick formula by replacing =ANIMATE(SLIDE,0,36) with =ANIMATE(SWING,0,90). Remember to press Enter to solidify the changes.

8. Delete the SLIDE attribute by clicking the minus symbol that appears next to the attribute name when it's highlighted. When SketchUp asks if you're sure, click Yes.

9. Change the RotZ attribute to =SWING.

10. Click the door with the Interact tool to see it swing open, and then click it again to see it swing shut.

Comma-delimited strings, such as the animate function above, can contain multiple states. For example, you could add a third rotation value to the onClick formula so that it reads, =ANIMATE(SWING,0,90,180). Then click the door with the Interact tool to see it animate through all three stages.

You can right-click the door and choose the context-menu option Flip Along to flip-flop the door along the Red or Green axis to get the door swing to go in whichever direction you prefer.

Add User-Defined Attributes

The Component Options dialog essentially functions as a graphic user interface (GUI) for viewing and modifying dynamic component attributes. In other words, the Options dialog provides a more user-friendly way to edit your components. However, you first have to enable the component attributes (such as size, rotation, etc.) that you want to be able to edit via the Options dialog so SketchUp knows which of those attributes to display.

1. Go back to the LenX size attribute and click the Details tab ◗ .

2. In the Details pane, set the Units option to Default: Inches and select the Display rule "Users can select from a list" (**Figure 8.21**).

Figure 8.21 User-defined LenX attribute details for the door component.

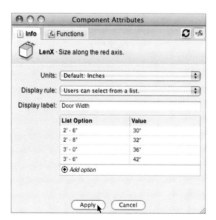

3. Enter a Display Label as you would like it to appear in the Options dialog—for example, Door Width.

4. Add list options for the door width.

    The *List Option* will be the visible name in the list and should be typed out as you want it to appear—for example, 2'-4", or 3'-0". You can add as many of these options as you think are appropriate.

The *List Value* is the number that affects the values and formulas in the Component Attribute fields and should be typed out numerically—for example, a 2'-6" list option would translate into a list value of 30.

5. Click Apply to exit the Attribute Details dialog.

6. Open the Component Options dialog , choose a door width from the available options, and then click Apply to see those changes reflected in the model (**Figure 8.22**).

   Another type of user-defined attribute you can create allows users to enter a value for the attribute via a text box in the Options dialog. This option is especially useful for the kind of components that can be sized to just about any dimension. Rather than having to create some big long list of values for users to choose from, you can just leave it up to the user to decide which value to enter into the text box.

7. For the LenZ size attribute, click the Details tab ⬗.

8. In the Details pane, set the Units option to Default: Inches and select the Display rule "Users can edit as a text box."

9. Enter a Display Label as you would like it to appear in the Options dialog, such as Door Height, choose Inches from the Display In option, and then click Apply (**Figure 8.23**).

Figure 8.22 To change the width of the door, choose a new door width from the Options dialog and click Apply.

Figure 8.23 User-defined LenZ attribute details for the door component.

10. Set up two more custom, user-defined attributes that you'll need for the next part of this example:

- Name: `FrameThickness`; Value: =6. Edit details > Units: Default: Text; Display rule: "User can edit as a text box"; Display label: Frame Thickness; Display In: Inches.

- Name: `KickHeight`; Value: =10. Edit details > Units: Default: Text; Display rule: "User can edit as a text box"; Display label: Door Kick Height; Display In: Inches.

Creating Nested Dynamic Components

Dynamic component attributes can trickle downstream from a parent component to a nested component. For example, the width value of a nested component can reference the width of its parent component, but the same is not true vice versa. For starters, we'll explore some of the nuances of nested dynamic components by giving our current door a bit more flexibility.

If you remember a few steps back, I had you reset the value for the RotZ attribute back to being a relative value, thus making it such that you could rotate the door around in the model to align to any opening. Well, now the RotZ attribute is determined by an onClick attribute, which limits the door to being able to rotate only to a few select degree angles.

Ideally, we'd still be able to rotate the door anywhere, and then click it with the Interact tool to watch it swing open and shut relative to whatever position and angle it's in.

In order for that to work, you need to effectively create a door within a door and set it up such that the parent door can be free to go anywhere in the model while the nested door rotates in relation to the position and angle of its parent component.

1. In the drawing window, double-click the door with the Select tool ▸ to edit the door component.

2. Triple-click the door to select all of the edges and faces.

3. Right-click the door and choose Make Component. In the Make Component dialog, give it the name *DoorSwing* and choose Create.

4. The Component Attributes dialog 🔧 will automatically show the options for the nested component DoorSwing. Once you close the DoorSwing component, you'll be able to see it along with the parent door component in the Attributes dialog. I prefer working in this way so that I can get a better sense for how the nested components relate to the parent.

NOTE The syntax for referencing another attribute is to include the name of the component you are referencing followed by an exclamation mark, followed by the name of the attribute you are referencing. The quickest way to reference an attribute is to click it while the other attribute cell is still active.

5. At this point, go ahead and fill out the attribute values for the DoorSwing component as shown in **Figure 8.24**. You'll notice that many of the attribute values reference those created for the parent component—for example, the LenX value for the DoorSwing component, =Door!LenX.

6. Remove the onClick and SWING attributes from the parent door component (by clicking the Delete button that appears next to the attribute name when the attribute is highlighted), and then add those attributes to the nested DoorSwing component instead (**Figure 8.24**).

Figure 8.24 The attributes for the DoorSwing component are set up to reference the values for the door component attributes.

Now the door can be positioned/rotated anywhere in the model and still swing open and shut using the Interact tool. Before you test all that, however, let's keep going with the rest of this section, which illustrates the process of turning our basic slab door into one that's got a bit more style.

7. Double-click the Door Swing component with the Select tool to go into Edit Component mode. Then triple-click the door again to select all of the edges and faces.

8. Right-click the door and choose Make Component. This time give it the name *Left* and choose Create.

NOTE Keep in mind that now the Position and Size attributes for any nested components will be relative to the parent component axes. In this case, the parent component is DoorSwing.

9. Close the DoorSwing component so that you can see the attributes for both the Left component and the DoorSwing component.

10. Enter the following values for the Position and Size attributes for the Left component (see **Figure 8.25**):

Position Attributes: PosX: =0; PosY: =0; PosZ: =0

Size Attributes: LenX: =DoorSwing!FrameThickness; LenY: =DoorSwing!LenY; LenZ: =DoorSwing!LenZ

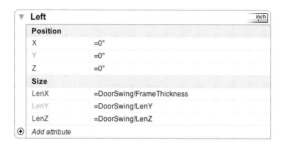

Figure 8.25
Left component
attributes.

11. Edit the DoorSwing component and draw a new box. The box can be any size for now, as we'll set the dimensions using attributes in just a minute.

12. Select the box and make it a component named *Right*.

13. Close the DoorSwing component and enter the following values for the Position and Size attributes of the Right part of the door (**Figure 8.26**):

Position Attributes: PosX: =0; PosY: =DoorSwing!LenX-DoorSwing!FrameThickness; PosZ: =0

Size Attributes: LenX: =DoorSwing!FrameThickness; LenY: =DoorSwing!LenY; LenZ: =DoorSwing!LenZ

Figure 8.26
Attributes of the
component Right.

14. Edit the DoorSwing component and make a new box component called *Top*.

15. Close the DoorSwing component and enter the following values for the Position and Size attributes of the Top part of the door (**Figure 8.27** on the next page).

Position Attributes: PosX: =DoorSwing!FrameThickness; PosY: =0; PosZ: =DoorSwing!LenZ-DoorSwing!FrameThickness

Size Attributes: LenX: =DoorSwing!LenX-(DoorSwing!FrameThickness*2); LenY: =DoorSwing!LenY; LenZ: =DoorSwing!FrameThickness

Figure 8.27 Attributes of the component Top.

Top	inch
Position	
X	=DoorSwing!FrameThickness
Y	=0
Z	=DoorSwing!LenZ-DoorSwing!FrameThickness
Size	
LenX	=DoorSwing!LenX-(DoorSwing!FrameThickness*2)
LenY	=DoorSwing!LenY
LenZ	=DoorSwing!FrameThickness
Add attribute	

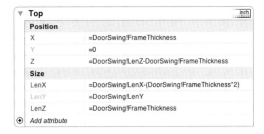

16. Edit the DoorSwing component and make a new box component called *Bottom*.

17. Close the DoorSwing component and enter the following values for the Position and Size attributes of the Bottom part of the door (see **Figure 8.28**):

Position Attributes: PosX: `=DoorSwing!FrameThickness`; PosY: `=0`; PosZ: `=0`

Size Attributes: LenX: `=DoorSwing!LenX-(DoorSwing!FrameThickness*2)`; LenY: `=DoorSwing!LenY`; LenZ: `=DoorSwing!KickHeight`

Figure 8.28 Bottom component attributes.

Bottom	inch
Position	
X	=DoorSwing!FrameThickness
Y	=0"
Z	=0"
Size	
LenX	=DoorSwing!LenX-(DoorSwing!FrameThickness*2)
LenY	=DoorSwing!LenY
LenZ	=DoorSwing!KickHeight
Add attribute	

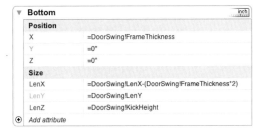

18. Edit the DoorSwing component and make a new box component called *Center*.

19. Close the DoorSwing component and enter the following values for the Position and Size attributes of the Center part of the door (see **Figure 8.29**):

Position Attributes: PosX: `=DoorSwing!FrameThickness`; PosY: `=0.5`; PosZ: `=DoorSwing!KickHeight`

Size Attributes: LenX: `=DoorSwing!LenX-(DoorSwing!FrameThickness*2)`; LenY: `=0.5`; LenZ: `=DoorSwing!LenZ-DoorSwing!FrameThickness-DoorSwing!KickHeight`

Figure 8.29 Center component attributes.

Center	inch
Position	
X	=DoorSwing!FrameThickness
Y	=.5
Z	=DoorSwing!KickHeight
Size	
LenX	=DoorSwing!LenX-(DoorSwing!FrameThickness*2)
LenY	=.5
LenZ	=DoorSwing!LenZ-DoorSwing!FrameThickness-DoorSwing!KickHeight
Add attribute	

20. Edit the DoorSwing component and make a new box component called *Mullion*.

21. Close the DoorSwing component and enter the following values for the Position and Size attributes of the Mullion part of the door (see **Figure 8.30**):

Position Attributes: PosX: =DoorSwing!FrameThickness; PosY: =0; PosZ: =DoorSwing!KickHeight

Size Attributes: LenX: =DoorSwing!LenX-(DoorSwing!FrameThickness*2); LenY: =DoorSwing!LenY; LenZ: =2

Figure 8.30
Mullion component attributes.

Add Hidden Attribute

If for some reason at this point you wanted to hide the entire door component…no problem; you could easily right-click it and choose Hide from the context menu. However, if you wanted to hide one of the nested components, that process is a bit more involved, requiring you to either go into Edit Component mode or use the Outliner to get to the right part and then hide it. The Hidden attribute is useful for nested components such as the door mullions in our current example because it allows you to control the visibility of an object via the Component Options dialog. This feature is especially useful for modeling real-world products with optional accessories that you may or may not want to include within your design.

1. Create a custom attribute for the parent door component named *Mullions*.

2. Edit the Mullions attribute details (**Figure 8.31**) as follows, and then click Apply:

Display rule: "Users can select from a list."

Display Label: Door Mullions (Optional)

List options (as name: value pairs):

• Yes: 0

• No: 1

Figure 8.31 Hidden attribute details for the Mullions component.

3. Add the Hidden attribute to the mullions component. Enter the value
=Door!Mullions.

SketchUp will interpret the Hidden attribute as true or false, determined by numeric
values, with 1 being true and 0 being false. If the user chooses the parent door component option for no mullions, the value would equal 1, which means the Hidden attribute for the Mullions component would also equal 1, which in turn means that
SketchUp will interpret the Hidden attribute as true. Therefore, choosing No
Mullions means the mullions *will* be hidden.

Add Copies Attribute

The Copies attribute can be used to parametrically control the number of copies of a
given parent component and/or nested components. You can use this feature to create
evenly spaced copies of the mullions component based on whatever dimensions you
input for the door height.

1. Add a custom attribute to the door component named *MullionCopies*. Enter the
initial value =3.

2. Edit the MullionCopies attribute details as follows:

Definition: "Users can edit as text box."

Value: Whole Numbers

3. Add a custom attribute to the DoorSwing component and enter the value
=Door!MullionSpacing

4. Add a Copies attribute to the mullion component and enter the value
=DoorSwing!MullionSpacing-1 (**Figure 8.32**).

Figure 8.32
The Copies attribute for
the Mullion component.

The total number of mullions will equal the number of mullion "copies" plus the original mullion. In this formula, we're subtracting one copy from the total so that the total number of mullions matches whatever number is input in the Options dialog.

5. Enter the PosZ value for the mullion component:

=DoorSwing!KickHeight+(((DoorSwing!LenZ-DoorSwing!FrameThickness-DoorSwing!KickHeight)/(Copies+2))*(Copy+1)) (Figure 8.32).

For the formula in Step 4, the term *Copies* refers to the value of the Copies attribute that was added in Step 3. The term *Copy* refers to the specific copy number of the copied mullions. For example, the first copied mullion knows that it is Copy number 1, so, for that particular copy, the value 1 is substituted in the formula above. For Copy number 2, the formula would yield a different result, since the value for Copy would equal 2, and so on.

You can now open the Component Options dialog and determine the number of mullions you want to include for your door (**Figure 8.33**), or you can decide not to have any mullions at all and use the Hidden attribute option to turn off the mullions entirely. Notice too, that if you change the height of the door, the mullions will automatically adjust so that they remain evenly spaced. The same goes for the options to edit the thickness of the door frame and the kick height.

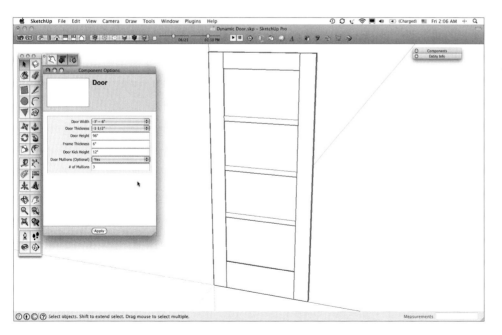

Figure 8.33 Use the Mullion attributes to determine how many you want and to turn them on and off.

Add Material Attributes

When a material is dynamically attributed to a component, the textures are applied to the component wrapper at the parent level.

Materials are applied dynamically in essentially the same way as if you applied the material with the Paint Bucket tool. One of the limitations of this is that it's difficult to predict the direction that the materials will run. When applied dynamically, materials will only show up on the default blue/beige surfaces within the component. If you've preapplied materials to any faced or nested components within the parent component, the Dynamic Material attribute will not affect those materials. This distinction can come in handy if there are surfaces that you don't want to change when the dynamic materials are applied.

To get a feel for what that all means, we'll actually start out by painting all the faces of the door *frame* with a wood texture.

1. Go into Edit Component mode and select all of the faces of the Left side of the door.

2. Take the Paint Bucket tool, choose a material from the Wood texture library (for example, Wood_Bamboo_Dark), and paint the faces of the Left side of the door.

3. Repeat Steps 1 and 2 for all other parts of the door *except* the Center part (**Figure 8.34**).

Figure 8.34 Paint the actual faces within the nested components of the door frame.

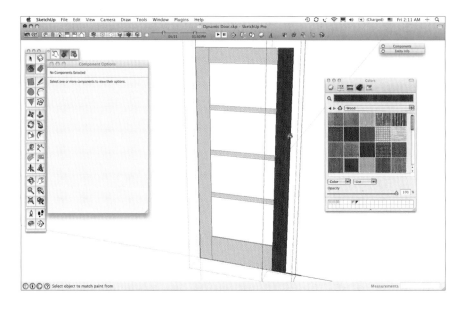

Next we'll set up a dynamic attribute that will allow us to choose a material for the Center part of the door via a drop-down menu option in the DC Configurator. But first we need to create the materials that we'll make available as choices for this door.

1. Select Window > Materials to open the Material browser.

2. Create a new material named *Translucent_Glass_Gray*. Give it a color value of R=221, G=224, B=228, and an Opacity value of 70 (**Figure 8.35**).

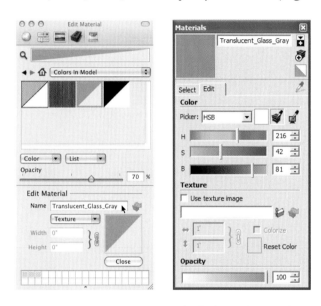

Figure 8.35 Create a new material called *Translucent_Glass_Gray*.

3. Create another new material named *Clear_Glass*. Give it a color value of R=221, G=224, B=228, and an Opacity value of 5.

4. In the Component Attributes dialog , add a Material attribute to the door component.

5. Edit the Material attribute details as follows (**Figure 8.36** on the next page), and then click Apply:

    Display rule: "Users can select from a list."

    Display label: Material

    List Options (as name: value pairs):

    *   Wood: Wood_Bamboo_Dark
    *   Frosted Glass: Translucent_Glass_Gray
    *   Clear Glass: Clear_Glass

Note that the Material attribute refers to the actual material name of the textures in the In Model material library. If you decide to use materials other than those described here, make sure that the exact names for the materials you use are entered in the list options.

Figure 8.36 Details of the attribute Material.

6. Go to the Component Options dialog , choose a new material from the drop-down list, and click Apply to change the material for the center panel of the door.

> **NOTE** The material inherits its scale from the properties in the Material library and will stretch based on the size of the component. In some cases, you may want to consider doing a little pre-planning so that the textures don't get too stretched out in the model. For example, if your component is going to range from 4 feet wide to 8 feet wide, set the texture width for a middle value of 6 feet. That way the texture will only vary a maximum of 2 feet in either scale direction.

A common issue encountered with Dynamic Material attributes is the fact that the materials have to exist in the In Model material library in order for them to be applied dynamically. The danger with that is that if you purge the model of unused materials, you'll end up losing any materials other than the one currently applied to the component. Here is one method you can employ to keep that from happening:

1. Create tiny (1/16" by 1/16") rectangular swatches for each of the materials listed in the Dynamic Material attribute list.

2. Group each of the swatches separately.

3. Place the swatches within the parent component, near the parent component axes.

4. Hide the swatches.

Add Scale Attributes

You can end up with some funky results if you try to scale a component that has its size attributes on lockdown. If you don't want people to mess up your dynamic component by trying to scale it, you can actually disable (turn off) the scale grips.

Add a ScaleTool attribute and then click the Details tab. You'll then be able to choose from a list of available scale handles for scaling along the various axes, planes, and corners and decide which, if any, you'd like to remain turned on. You'll also see a clever diagram that illustrates which scale grips will be available when scaling your component (**Figure 8.37**). In this case, since we've set up our door such that the dimensions are controlled via the Component Options dialog, it's probably best to just go ahead and disable all of the scale handles.

Figure 8.37 The ScaleTool attributes dialog. Scale options can be turned on/off using the check boxes on the right. Disabled options will disappear from the diagram on the left.

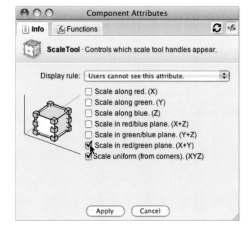

The dynamic Picket Fence component (search the 3D Warehouse for "Fence is:dynamic author:google") showcases a cool use of the Scale tool. The Size attributes for the parent component are left as relative values so that you can control the overall dimensions of the fence using the Scale tool.

If you look at the Position attributes and Copy attributes for the nested picket components, they still reference the relative values of the parent component size attributes. The LenX and LenY size attributes for the nested picket components are fixed, which is why the pickets won't distort their shape when the entire fence is scaled.

The dynamic Framing components (search the 3D Warehouse for "Framing is:dynamic author:google") are also good examples of ways in which the Scale tool can be used. For example, the framing wall component is set up so that when you scale the wall lengthwise, the 2 × 4s will remain the correct size, and copies of the 2 × 4s will be added or removed to compensate for the overall change in the size of the wall.

Add Component Info Attributes

The Component Info attributes are useful for identification, marketing, and reporting purposes, as the information input in these cells will be displayed in the Dynamic Component > Choose Options dialog 📇 (a.k.a. the DC Configurator).

It's also worth noting that the description field recognizes HTML tags for formatting stuff such as paragraph breaks (<br>), bold type (bold type here), italics (<i>italic text here</i>), and URL links (<a href=*URL*>Linked Text</a>) for linking back to a Web site or other online resource that contains more information about the model (**Figure 8.38**).

Figure 8.38 Component Info attributes for the parent door component.

The ItemCode attribute cell is a space you can use to input the product SKU code or order number code.

Take a minute now to type in some information about the dynamic door component we've been working on, and then see how that information is displayed in the DC Configurator.

The Component Info attributes can be especially useful for generating dynamic component reports from SketchUp, as you'll see in the next section.

After it's all said and done, **Figure 8.39** shows what your door might look like, alongside its customized Component Options dialog.

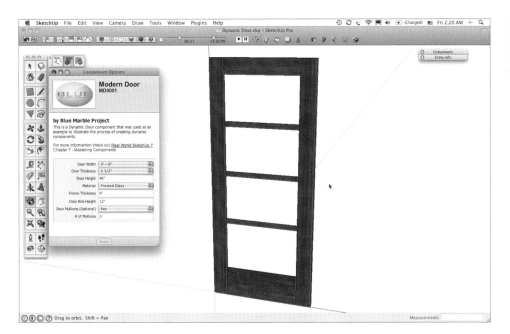

Figure 8.39 The completed dynamic door component and Options dialog.

As a reference, you can download my version of this dynamic door component from the Google 3D Warehouse (search for "Modern Door Dynamic Component author:blue marble project") and use it to troubleshoot any issues you may have run into while following along with this section.

Generating Reports

The Pro version of SketchUp 7 includes an export option located under File > Generate Report. The Reporting tool allows you to export the data attributes for a preselected set of dynamic components, or for all of the dynamic components in the entire project. The reports are exported in either XLS or CSV format, and, once exported, the files can be opened in Microsoft Excel, Mac Numbers, or Google Spreadsheets, and then formatted for whatever purposes the information may be relevant.

While this isn't exactly the most direct way to get project schedules, cut lists, or a bill of materials (BOM) together for a SketchUp project, it's certainly in the ballpark. I suggest playing around a bit with this export feature as it may well influence the way that you end up formatting your dynamic component attributes.

NOTE In order for a dynamic component to retain its attributes, it has to be imported directly into a project. If you download it to your hard drive and then open it, the Dynamic Component features will not work.

Additional Resources

One of the best ways to learn how to create your own dynamic components is to import existing dynamic components from the 3D Warehouse, and then deconstruct them. You can use the information in this chapter to help guide you through the process of learning to read how other components have been created—and then move on to trying to write your own.

At Blue Marble Project (www.bluemarbleproject.com) we've created thousands of dynamic components for building product manufacturers and retailers. You can check out some of the stuff we've done by searching the warehouse for our Blue Marble Project Products collection. Google has also uploaded a wide variety of Dynamic Component models to the 3D Warehouse. A search for "is:dynamic author:google" will retrieve dozens of cool and functional models.

ADVANCED COMPONENT USES

The following are some of the most important and useful context-menu options to try to keep in mind when working with components.

Select Instances

Select Instances is an option that appears when you right-click a component from the In Model component library (assuming that a selectable instance of the component exists and is visible in the model). It's excellent for quickly selecting all of the instances of the component that appear in the model.

Keep in mind, however, that only *visible* components will be selected. Instances of the component that are hidden, or instances on invisible layers, will not be selected.

Make Unique

Generally speaking, any time you edit a component, the changes are reflected in all other instances of that component.

However, the Make Unique option (located in the context menu when you right-click a component in the drawing window) allows you to turn any component instance into a unique component that can be edited separately.

You can also use Make Unique to create a unique subset of components. Say, for example, you had a bunch of instances of the same chair component set up around a table, and all of the chairs had armrests (**Figure 8.40**). You could select all of the chairs from which you wanted to delete the armrests, and then right-click and choose Make Unique (**Figure 8.41**). You could then edit any one of the unique components and delete the armrests (**Figure 8.42** on the next page). The original chair components would retain their armrests (**Figure 8.43** on the next page).

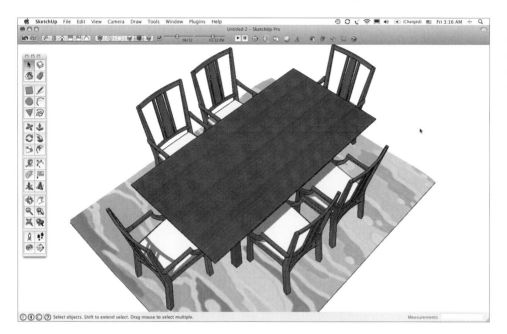

Figure 8.40 A table with instances of a chair component around it.

Thos. Moser, American Bungalow Collection (thosmoser.com)

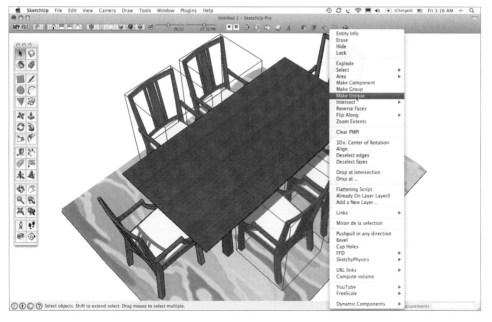

Figure 8.41 Use the Make Unique context-menu option to create a subset of components that relate to each other but are different from the original.

Thos. Moser, American Bungalow Collection (thosmoser.com)

Figure 8.42 Once the subset of chairs has been made unique, you can edit any one of the unique components and the others will follow suit.

Thos. Moser, American Bungalow Collection (thosmoser.com)

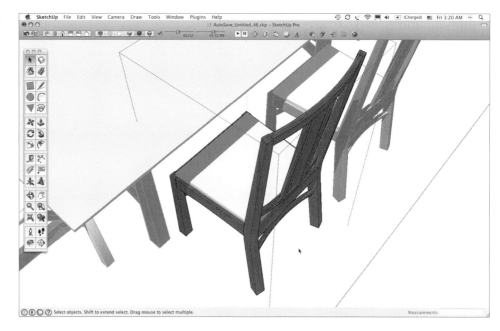

Figure 8.43 The edited dining set now contains two unique sets of chairs—one with, and the other without, armrests.

Thos. Moser, American Bungalow Collection (thosmoser.com)

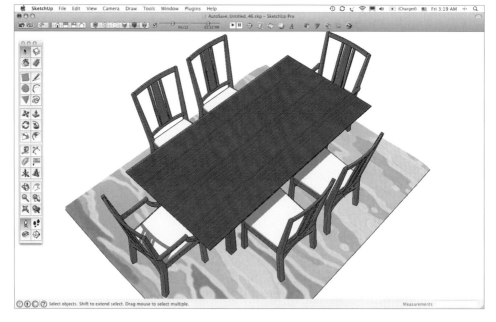

Save As and Reload

Save As and Reload are two separate options (both available from the context menu when you right-click a component in the drawing window or component browser), but I'll discuss them together in this section because I think they're most useful when used in conjunction with each other.

My favorite use of these features is as a method for enabling a team of modelers to work on large projects, similar to the way draftspersons may use X-Refs in AutoCAD to manage large drawing sets.

Save As: Saves a component out from your model as its own file, after which you can open it and work on it separately. For example, if you were working on a massive site model for a master planning project and you needed some help meeting a project deadline, you could turn sections of the model into components and then save those sections out as individual files. Another member of the team could then open that section of the project and work on it simultaneously as colleagues continued work on other sections of the model.

Reload: Related to the preceding Save As option, the Reload option allows you to reload an edited component with the updated version of itself. To ensure a seamless reload process, it's important to preserve the location of the Saved As models relative to their respective model origin/axes, as that is equivalent to the component origin/insertion point back in the main file.

The Reload option also allows you to reload a component with any other SketchUp file from your hard drive. For example, say you had a bunch of oak trees in a project, but you later determined that the climate zone was more suitable for palm trees. You could right-click any single oak tree in order to reload all of the oak trees in your entire project with a SketchUp model of a palm tree.

CAD Workflow Tip

Most 2D CAD programs have a component-like equivalent (like blocks in AutoCAD). Those drawing elements are typically interpreted as components when they're imported into SketchUp. As such, Reload can be an effective option for replacing the 2D components with 3D counterparts.

One tricky part about the process is that the position of the reloaded 3D component will depend on the position and orientation of the original 2D component axes. If you're simply replacing a one-off block for something like a refrigerator or sink, this process is probably more time consuming than simply inserting a 3D component for that object. However, in situations where you've got a bunch of copies of a block in your drawings—such as a bunch of doors, trees, cars, or whatever—the Reload option is a one-shot deal that can save a ton of time, especially if you take the time to get the axis of the 2D component in the right spot before you reload the 2D components with 3D versions.

Upload Component

The Upload Component feature (located in the context menu when you right-click a component in the drawing window) allows you to upload a component object directly to the 3D Warehouse, assuming that you are logged in to the 3D Warehouse with your Google ID. This option works with basic as well as dynamic components.

CHAPTER NINE

Mastering Scenes

Scenes allow you to capture the current state of a model by saving the properties that determine the view of the model and the way it's rendered. This chapter explores the fundamental concepts for creating basic scenes as well as advanced uses of scenes within the context of professional workflows.

Creating a scene can be thought of as simply taking a picture of your SketchUp model that you can keep coming back to again and again. Scenes can also be used as the building blocks for creating different kinds of animated presentations, and they can be used to help manage large files.

The functions for adding, deleting, arranging, and otherwise managing scenes are contained in the Scenes dialog, which can be found under Window > Scenes (**Figure 9.1**).

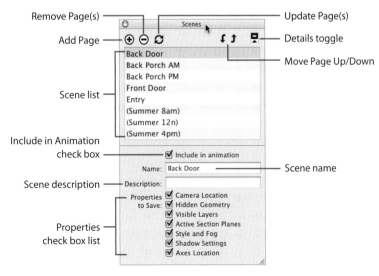

Figure 9.1 The Scenes dialog.

CREATING A SCENE

1. Copy the sample file Mastering_Scenes.skp from the Chapter 9 folder on the companion DVD or download the sample file Chapter 9: Mastering Scenes from the 3D Warehouse. Then open the file in SketchUp.

2. Use the Navigation tools to create a view similar to that shown in **Figure 9.2** and then click the Add button ⊕ in the Scenes dialog to add the first scene.

Figure 9.2 Establish a view of the back porch and then add a new scene.

 **NOTE** Since we're on the subject of scenes, if you download a file from the 3D Warehouse that contains scenes you want to view, save the file to your hard drive and then open it in SketchUp. If you import the file directly into a model, it'll come in as components and you won't be able to see the scenes.

When creating a scene, you have the option to give the scene a name and description. By default, scenes are given the generic name Scene #, where the # is equal to the total number of scenes in the model. In this case, the first scene is called Scene 1. To change the name, you can highlight the text in the Name field and enter a new name.

3. Type in the name Back Porch and press Enter.

You also have the option to save any or all of the following model properties. By default, all of the settings are initially checked on, which is fine for this first scene of the Back Porch. Here's a quick rundown of the general purpose for each of the settings:

• **Camera Location:** Saving a scene in SketchUp preserves the camera position, direction, zoom, and field of view so that you can quickly and easily get back to that one perfect view of your project or have a consistent way to render/print the same view of a project over time as the design changes.

You can use multiple scenes to record different camera positions. If you have at least two scenes with different camera positions, SketchUp will automatically animate the change in view from one camera to the next as you toggle back and forth between the two scenes. This functionality is the foundation for being able to create fly-through animations.

- **Hidden Geometry:** Scenes are capable of remembering which, if any, entities, groups, or components are hidden at the time the scene is saved.

  Once a scene (or scenes) has been established, any new geometry created in the model will automatically appear in all of the existing scenes.

- **Visible Layers:** Scenes will remember which layers you have turned on or off at the time the scene is saved. For example, if you had a simple model of a house, with the roof on a layer, you could turn off the roof layer and create a scene that remembers to hide the roof anytime you want to see through to the interior of the building.

  When you add a new layer to a model with existing scenes, the new layer, by default, will be visible in any of the existing scenes.

NOTE The Ruby script Add Hidden Layer (add_hidden_layer.rb) is available for download from the Ruby Library Depot (www.crai.archi.fr/rubylibrarydepot/ruby/en_sel_page.htm). Once installed, the command is available from the Plugins menu and can be used to create a new layer that will be turned off in all of the existing scenes in your model. Then you just have to go and update the scenes in which you actually want the layer to be visible.

- **Active Section Planes:** Scenes will remember the active section plane and section plane visibility settings. Saving section cut scenes in your model can be an effective method for creating perspective section views of building interiors, communicating building details, and exporting section drawings to CAD.

  You can save multiple scenes with different section settings. If you have at least two scenes with different section settings, SketchUp will animate the difference between the sections. This feature is commonly used to create the illusion of having your model, or a part of your model, build into a scene.

  The section plane settings are located in the Edit > Modeling Settings pane of the Styles palette. If you alter a scene by changing the section plane settings, you will likely also need to update the current style or create a new style in order to effectively save the section settings in your scene. We'll take a look at some of the section plane options later in this chapter.

NOTE I mention hidden geometry here in the list because it's an option. While hiding stuff in your model can sometimes be a nice feature, when it comes to scenes it's probably more efficient and less confusing to control the visibility of objects in the model using layers instead of the Hide function.

- **Style and Fog:** Scenes can remember the current settings chosen in the Styles dialog, such as face styles, edge effects, watermarks, section settings, etc. Remember that styles have to be updated when a change is made in order to save the changes. As you'll see later in this chapter, scenes with particular style settings can help you work more efficiently with large files. Having scenes saved with different style settings can also be a fun way to illustrate a model with different rendering qualities.

  In Chapter 1, I pointed out a preference in the General tab, "Warn of style change when creating scenes." If that preference is turned on, when you create a new scene (or update an existing one), SketchUp will alert you if there are style changes that haven't been updated or saved. A dialog will ask whether you want to:

  - Save the changes as a new style (which is usually the safest option because SketchUp will save the current style settings as a new style without disrupting any of the style settings that may have been saved in other scenes).

  - Update the current style (which may affect other scenes in which the current style was applied).

  - Do nothing to save the changes (in which case SketchUp will revert to the style settings that were current when the original scene was saved).

- **Shadow Settings:** Scenes will record the shadow settings (including time, date, brightness, darkness, etc.).

  You can save multiple scenes with different shadow settings. If you have at least two scenes with different shadow settings, SketchUp will animate the difference between the shadows. You can use this feature to create specific scenes for sun/shade analysis and watch as the sun tracks across the site.

- **Axes Location:** Scenes will remember the position and orientation of the global model axes. Component axes are a different story though; scenes won't remember their positions. You can use the Axes setting to quickly toggle back and forth between different axes orientations. Since SketchUp's drawing tools work more effectively when you're able to work parallel to the model axes, it can be especially useful to create scenes with different axes locations when you find yourself working on projects that have buildings or structures in your model at various angles relative to each other.

SETTING UP A CAMERA FLY-THROUGH

This section covers the most popular use of scenes: creating an animated fly-through of a model.

As mentioned, the basic premise for creating a camera animation in SketchUp is that you have at least two scenes with different camera views. SketchUp will interpolate (automatically animate) the change in view from one camera to the next as you toggle between the two scenes. For example:

1. Change the view in the model by orbiting around and zooming in so that you've got a better shot of the front door (**Figure 9.3**).

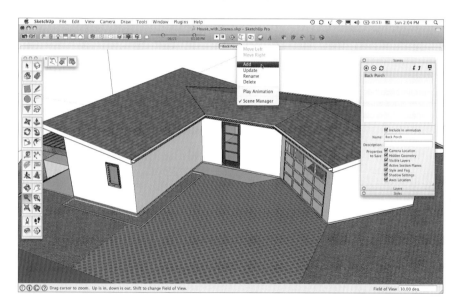

Figure 9.3 Establish an aerial view of the front door and then add another new scene.

2. You've already seen the option for creating a scene using the Add Scene button in the Scene window. You can also add a new scene by right-clicking the Back Porch scene tab at the top of the screen and choosing Add. A new scene tab will be created and is automatically given the name Scene 2 (Figure 9.3).

3. To change the name of the scene, right-click the Scene 2 tab and choose Rename.

4. Then type in the name Front Door and press Enter.

Now you can click either of the scene tabs to toggle the camera view back and forth between the two scenes.

Notice as you toggle between the two scenes that the camera view doesn't just switch immediately from one scene to the next but instead animates smoothly from one scene to the other. The animated camera motion can be exported from SketchUp as a video file.

Positioning a Standard Camera

When you're setting up scenes with different camera views, you can determine your camera position based simply on how you want your model to be framed in camera, or you can set up the camera to represent and communicate a specific vantage point that someone might experience if they were actually there.

1. Select the Position Camera tool ♀ . Before you click to position a camera, the Measurements box displays the *relative* Eye Height at which the camera will be positioned above the face that you click. By default, the Eye Height value is set to 5' 3". Go ahead and type in a value that represents your own eye height (or the eye height of the client you're designing for) and then press Enter.

2. Click the driveway out in front of the front door.

    SketchUp will locate a camera so that it is hovering directly above the point where you clicked, and the camera will be looking out toward the horizon (**Figure 9.4**).

    As soon as you click to locate the camera on the driveway, SketchUp will automatically activate the Look Around tool ♀ and you'll notice that the cursor turns into a freaky set of eyeballs that are looking back at you.

3. Click and drag with the Look Around tool to change the direction of the camera. The Look Around tool is unlike the Orbit tool in that the relative eye height of the camera will stay put, as though the camera were on a tripod and you were just swiveling it around to frame the shot, or as if you were actually standing there, standing in the same place, just "looking around" in the model.

    Since the camera has already been positioned, the Measurements dialog is now displaying the absolute Eye Height of the camera, relative to the model's imaginary ground plane. Since the driveway in this model is coincident with the model's ground plane, the Eye Height value still registers as 5' 3". Had you clicked the roof or something, the absolute eye height would be much taller.

    You can use the Eye Height setting to evaluate multiple view heights for a particular camera location before saving the scene. For example:

4. Set an Eye Height for the camera that represents the average height of someone in a wheelchair: Type in 3'10" and press Enter. Then re-enter the value for the initial view height (i.e., 5'3").

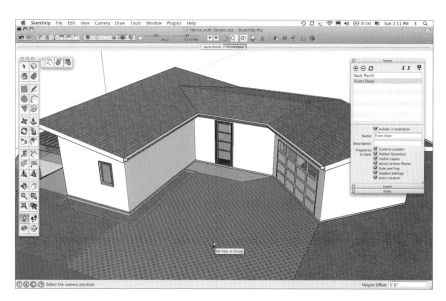

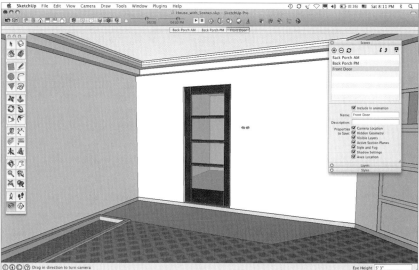

Figure 9.4 Click the driveway with the Position Camera tool to get a view of the front door from eye level.

5. The default field of view for your camera is set to 35 degrees. The larger the field-of-view angle, the more you can see. You have two options for changing the field-of-view angle using the Zoom tool (Z) .

   • Press and hold the Shift key while using the Zoom tool. Zoom In + Shift to decrease the field-of-view angle; Zoom Out + Shift to increase the field-of-view angle. The field-of-view angle will appear in the Measurements box. Try checking out the way your model looks at either extreme. Try out a degree angle of 15 degrees, and then go all the way up to 70 degrees.

- Enter a specific field-of-view angle (such as 45 deg) in the Measurements box and press Enter. You can change your mind about the field-of-view angle as many times as you want.

6. Select the Walk tool (W) 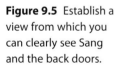 to accurately edit the camera position. Click and drag up to move the camera forward, down to move backward, left to move left, or right to move right.

   Again, the difference between using the Walk tool rather than the Zoom, Pan, or Orbit tools is that the Walk tool will keep the Eye Height value consistent with whichever value you entered. You can even use the Walk tool to walk up and down a ramp, a sloped terrain, or a staircase. And the Walk tool is smart enough to stop before you run into or back into a wall, which can be useful when you're trying to work in tight spaces and might otherwise accidentally zoom out of a room and then have to try and re-establish the view again from scratch.

7. Once you've settled on a view for the entry (see Figure 9.4), add a third scene named *Entry*.

Positioning a Target Camera

In addition to being able to use the Position Camera tool to set up a camera by clicking a face in the model, you can also set up target cameras (cameras that are looking from one specific point to another). For example:

1. Orbit around to the back of the model so that you can see both the figure (Sang) standing on the back patio as well as the back doors (**Figure 9.5**).

Figure 9.5 Establish a view from which you can clearly see Sang and the back doors.

2. Click and drag with the Position Camera tool from Sang's eyes over to the back doors and then let go (**Figure 9.6**).

Figure 9.6 You can click and drag with the Position Camera tool from a point of view to a target in order to visualize that exact line of sight.

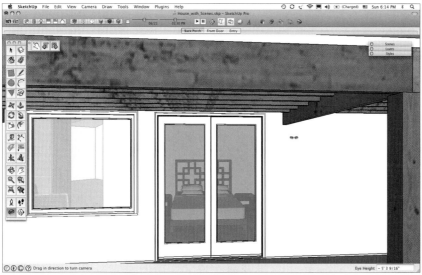

3. Add a fourth scene named *Back Door.*

Playing an Animation

Once you've got a bunch of scenes set up in your model, you can play the animation directly within SketchUp.

On a Mac: You can customize the top toolbar to include Play/Pause animation controls. You also have a "Play animation" option in the context menu that shows up when you right-click a scene tab. When you choose "Play animation," the animation will start; if you choose it again, the animation will pause.

On a PC: The Play/Pause controls will automatically pop up when you choose "Play animation" from the scene context menu. You can then use the controls to pause and restart the animation.

The settings that determine the speed for the animation are located under Model Info > Animation. The Scene Transitions setting determines the amount of time it takes to transition from one scene to the next. The Scene Delay determines the amount of time that SketchUp will pause on a scene before transitioning to the next one. For camera fly-throughs, I typically have the Scene Transitions set to 3 to 4 seconds, and the Scene Delay set to 0 seconds.

Exporting Animations

The animated transitions between the camera position from one scene to another can be exported from SketchUp as a movie file (on Windows you can export AVI files and on a Mac you can export MOV files).

To export an animation from SketchUp, you must have at least two scenes in your model. Once they are set up, you can choose File > Export > Animation.

Prior to saving your movie file, you can choose from a number of export options to customize the output from SketchUp. The export options differ slightly depending on whether you're working on a Mac or Windows, but both platforms include options for specifying the resolution, aspect ratio, frame rate, video encoders, and rendering quality for your movie files.

I've included two videos on this book's companion DVD to help you learn more about the different animation export options for either OS. The videos are excerpted chapters from the *School Series: SketchUp Level 2* DVD, which is available online at www.go-2-school.com/products/view/6.

Reordering Scenes

We currently have four scenes in our model. The most recent scene we created, Back Door, is the last scene. After watching the animation, it looks like it might make more sense to reorder the scenes so that the animation starts out with the Back Door scene. You've got two options for reordering the scenes:

- Select the Back Door scene in the Scene window and then click the Page Up button until it's the first scene in the list.

- Right-click the Back Door scene tab and choose Move left. Repeat as needed until Back Door is the first scene.

CREATING SHADOW ANIMATIONS

One of the coolest ways to take advantage of SketchUp's animation function is to create shadow animations. In this model, the trellis is located on the south end of the house to provide shade in the summer months. Let's take a look at how to use scenes to create an animation of the shadows as they track across the porch from morning to afternoon, and incorporate that into our existing camera sequence.

1. Click the Back Porch scene tab to restore the view that you've already saved.

2. Open the Shadow Settings dialog (Window > Shadows). Check the Display Shadows button to turn on the shadows (**Figure 9.7**).

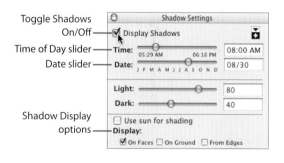

Figure 9.7 The Shadows dialog (with settings described in Steps 2–5).

3. Set the time of day and day/month of year to an early morning time for a day in the summer—for example, 8:00 A.M. on 8/30.

4. Set the lightness and darkness of the shadows to whatever you think looks good (I prefer a lightness value of around 80 and a darkness value of around 40).

5. Uncheck the Shadow Display option for On Ground.

6. Right-click the Back Porch scene tab and choose Update so that the new shadows will be included as part of that scene.

7. Now that the first part of the shadow animation is set, change the time to 4:00 P.M. and then add a new scene called *Back Porch PM*.

    Notice that since the original Back Porch scene was the current scene, the new scene is automatically inserted into the sequence, following its predecessor.

8. If you're as particular as I am about this sort of stuff, you can rename the other Back Porch scene and call it *Back Porch AM* for consistency.

Now (assuming your graphics card can handle it) when you toggle back and forth between the AM and PM scenes, you'll be able to see the shadows track across the back porch. If your graphics card disables the shadows during playback on your computer screen, don't worry; the shadows will still appear rendered when you export the model as a movie file.

Shadow Accuracy

To get an accurate read on how shadows would look on-site for a project, you just need to give SketchUp a couple of pieces of information via the Model Info > Location window (see "Location" in Chapter 2).

Location: You can specify a location either by city, state, country, or by choosing Set custom location to enter exact Latitude/Longitude coordinates.

North Angle: By default, SketchUp thinks that the solid green axis is pointing north, but you can use the North Angle option in the Location dialog to enter a value, or click the Select button to set the north angle in any direction.

Also, keep in mind that SketchUp doesn't take daylight savings time into account. When you're looking at shadows anytime between the second Sunday in March to the first Sunday in November, you'll want to add an hour to whatever time SketchUp shows in the Shadows window.

Updating Shadows

Since the shadows are now saved for just two of our scenes, we need to update the other scenes in the model so they display shadows as well.

In the last section we used the Update option in the scene tab context menu to update the entire Back Porch scene. Updating a scene using the context menu option will automatically update *all* of the properties that you've specified for that scene to remember—including the shadow settings, if applicable. In this section we'll take a closer look at the update function in the Scene window—which, by contrast, allows you to specify which of the properties you'd like to update.

With the Back Porch scene as the active scene, you can still select and update the Back Door (or any other) scene to inherit settings (such as the shadows) from the active scene.

1. Click the Back Porch AM scene to make it the active scene.

2. Highlight the Back Door scene in the Scene window and then click the Update button (**Figure 9.8**).

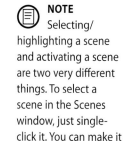

NOTE
Selecting/highlighting a scene and activating a scene are two very different things. To select a scene in the Scenes window, just single-click it. You can make it the active scene by double-clicking it.

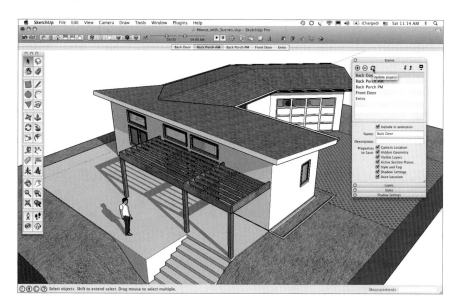

Figure 9.8 With the Back Porch scene as the active scene, select the Back Door scene and click the Update button.

3. Uncheck all of the options *except* for the Shadow Settings and then click Update (**Figure 9.9**).

   Now the Back Door and Back Porch AM scenes share the same shadow settings.

4. Click the Back Porch PM scene to make it the current scene.

5. Highlight both the Front Door and Entry scenes in the Scene window and then click the Update button.

6. Update just the shadow settings for both scenes at the same time.

Now all three scenes (Back Porch PM, Front Door, and Entry) share the same shadow settings.

Figure 9.9 Uncheck all of the properties in the update panel *except* for shadows.

Shadows Only

In addition to playing a role in your animations, scenes with certain shadow settings can come in handy for other uses. For example, you might find it useful to create a set of scenes that display shadows throughout various times of day during the summer and winter solstice for more in-depth shade and day lighting analysis.

1. Click the Entry scene tab to make it the current scene.

2. Add a new scene named *Summer 8AM*.

3. Set the time of day to 8:00 A.M. and set the date to 6/21 (summer solstice).

4. Uncheck the "Include in animation" option in the Scenes window.

5. Uncheck all of the properties in the Scenes window except for Shadow Settings (**Figure 9.10**).

6. Click the Update button and update all of the settings for the Summer 8AM scene (**Figure 9.11**).

7. Change the time of day to 12:00 P.M., and then right-click the Summer 8am scene tab and choose Add. Rename the newest scene Summer 12n and uncheck the "Include in animation" option in the Scenes window.

8. Create another scene with the time of day set to 4:00 P.M., call it Summer 4pm, and uncheck the option "Include in animation."

9. Repeat Steps 2–8 to create three more Winter scenes for 8:00 A.M., 12:00 P.M., and 4:00 P.M. on the winter solstice, 12/21.

Since these scenes are set up to remember only the shadow settings, you can click them anytime to see what the shadows would look like on those dates/times— without having to worry about any of your other settings changing.

Figure 9.11 Update the scene so that it will remember the settings you've altered.

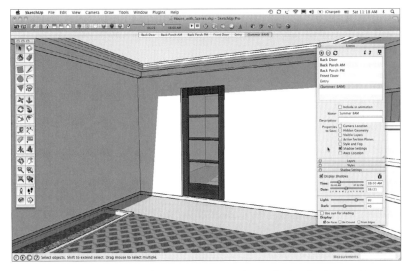

Figure 9.10 Create a scene that is set to remember *only* the shadow settings and uncheck the option "Include in animation."

Using Scenes to Improve Performance with Large Files

Capturing camera positions and animations is probably the most widely used function of scenes, but there are also some pretty cool uses for scenes in which the camera properties are potentially ignored—such as the summer/winter shadow scenes we set up in the previous section, which were set up to remember only the shadow settings.

Layers, styles, and shadows are three of the most critical aspects of your model that you can manage to help increase performance while working on large models.

Having a ton of visible geometry in the model, plus having profile edges and textures turned on, plus having shadows turned on, may all be too much for the ol' GPU to handle. Even though SketchUp version 7.1 drastically improves the performance for higher polygon count models, there are also some useful methods for creating scenes to help manage large files.

Next, we'll set up a scene we can use to turn off all the stuff that might impact SketchUp's performance.

1. Click the Back Porch PM scene tab to make it the current scene.

    NOTE Be careful when creating a new scene if you have utility scenes set up in the model such as the summer/winter scenes in this example. When you add a new scene, it inherits the "Properties to Save" settings from the current/active scene. If one of the shadow scenes were the active scene, this new scene would start out with just the shadow settings checked. This behavior gets a lot of people mixed up in a bad way, so as you're learning to work with scenes, it can be less confusing to start by making the active scene one that has all of the settings checked on, and then go from there.

2. From the Scenes window, click Add and create a new scene named *Working* and uncheck the option "Include in animation."

    Also uncheck the properties for Camera Location, Active Section Planes, and Axes Location.

3. Turn off the shadows for this scene.

4. Open the Layers window and turn off the layers that contain all of the more detailed (and higher polygon count) components in the model (**Figure 9.12** on the next page).

5. Open the Styles window and click the Edit tab.

Figure 9.12
Configure the visible
layers as shown.

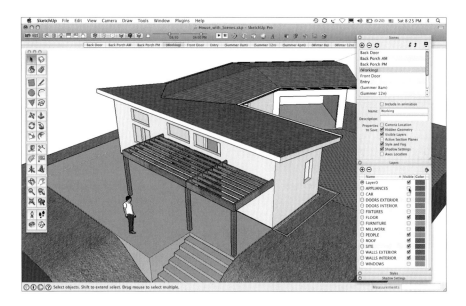

6. In the Edge Styles dialog, uncheck all of the edge rendering options (**Figure 9.13**).

7. In the Face Styles dialog, choose the display option for Hidden Line mode and set the Transparency quality to Faster (**Figure 9.14**).

Figure 9.13 Turn off all of the edge style effects for maximum performance.

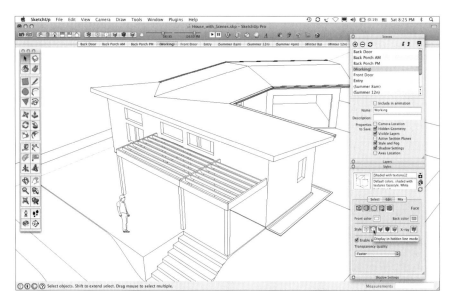

Figure 9.14 Render the faces in Hidden Line mode and set the transparency quality option to Faster for maximum performance.

8. Update all of the properties of the Working scene. When SketchUp asks what you want to do about the unsaved style changes, choose the option, "Save the changes as a new style" and click Update (**Figure 9.15**).

9. Move the Working scene up on the list (or over to the left of the other scene tabs) so that it's the first one in the list.

> 📄 **NOTE** When it comes to arranging the order of utility scenes, I like to keep the ones I use a lot (like the Working scene) at the left of the scene tabs so they're easy to find when I need them. When you have a model with tons of scenes, those that are placed at the bottom of the list end up in a drop-down menu at the far right of the scene tabs and are then kind of a pain to access—which is why I put them at the top of the list (far left) instead.

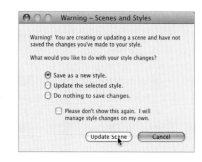

Figure 9.15 Update the Working scene and create a new style when prompted.

The Working scene is now set up so that no matter what you're doing, and no matter what other scene you may be in, you can click it to get back to the settings that are optimized for performance, enabling you to make quick revisions to the model without having to wait for the model view to refresh.

For more information about styles, check out the video *The SketchUp Show,* Episode 37: "SketchUp Got Styles," included on this book's companion DVD and online at www.go-2-school.com/Real-World-Google-SketchUp-7.

SETTING UP ANIMATED SECTION CUTS

As mentioned earlier, creating scenes with section planes can be a useful way to illustrate and present certain aspects of a project, such as a perspective interior view or a construction detail. In this section we'll explore options for creating scenes with section cut information, and we'll also look at ways to create compelling presentations using animated section cuts.

First we'll explore some of the basics for adding section cuts to a model. Sections can cut through an entire model or they can cut through a group or component.

1. Select the Section tool ⊕. Note that when you move the Section tool cursor around in the model, it automatically orients itself to whichever face you're hovering over.

2. Create a cross section of the model by clicking the east end of the house with the Section tool (**Figure 9.16** on the next page).

3. Click the section plane with the Select tool to make sure it's selected.

Figure 9.16 Insert a section plane by clicking the face of the east end of the house.

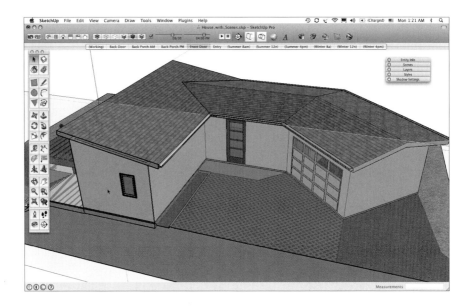

4. Use the Move tool to move the section plane into the middle of the house (**Figure 9.17**).

    One important rule to keep in mind when working with section planes is that you can only have one active section plane within any given context. You can, however, have more than one section plane active at the same time, as long as they're in a different context. By *context*, I'm referring to either the entire model or the context of being within a group or component.

Figure 9.17 Section planes are objects that can be moved and rotated around in the model.

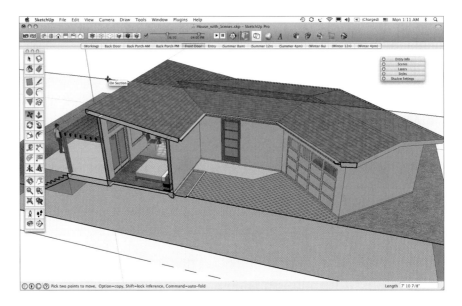

5. Create another cross section by clicking the north face of the garage with the Section tool (**Figure 9.18**). By default, the new section plane automatically becomes the active section.

6. Select the new section plane with the Select tool, and then move it to a spot where it's just shy of cutting through the car (Figure 9.18).

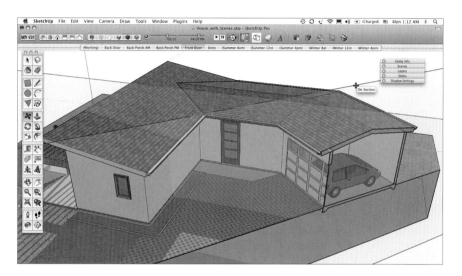

Figure 9.18 Add another section plane that cuts through the garage.

7. Take the Select tool and double-click the first section plane to make it the active section. If you want, go ahead and toggle between the section planes using the same double-click option.

NOTE You can use the Select tool to double-click a section plane to make it the active section.

Updating Section Plane Settings

We're about to look at some options for creating animated section planes using scenes, but first we've got a bit of housekeeping to do. Now that we've added our section planes to the model, you'll notice as you flip through the existing scenes that the section plane objects are visible in all of the other scenes. In some cases, the slightly transparent section plane objects are dulling the view of our other scenes (such as the Entry scene), which is less than ideal.

The process of turning off the section planes is a bit tricky, so we better get through that part now, before things get even trickier by adding more scenes for the section animation.

1. Click the Front Door scene. The active section plane will deactivate, but both of the section plane objects will remain visible in the model.

NOTE When updating groups of scenes, it's best to update scenes with similar "Properties to Save" settings; otherwise you could muck up those settings during the update process. The "utility" scenes we've created for different shadow settings as well as the Working scene should be updated separately.

2. Click the Toggle Section Display tool ⌿ to turn off the section plane objects.

   • On a PC, this option is located in the Section toolbar (View > Toolbars > Section).

   • On a Mac, you can add this tool to the customizable top toolbar.

   • On both platforms, you can also access this Display option in the Styles window under Edit > Modeling Settings > Section Planes.

3. In the Scenes window, select only those scenes that are set up to be included in the animation (**Figure 9.19**).

4. Choose to update only the settings for Active Section Planes and Style and Fog, and click Update (**Figure 9.20**).

Figure 9.19 Select the scenes that are included in the animation.

Figure 9.20 Update the Section and Style settings only.

5. When prompted, choose the option "Save as new style" and click Update.

   NOTE Section settings are saved and updated in the Styles window under the Model Settings tab, so when you save a scene with a new active section cut, SketchUp will ask what you want to do about the style changes. Again, I typically choose the option to "Save as new style" in order to ensure that any existing scenes/styles are not disturbed.

6. Now click the Summer 8am scene tab to make it the current scene. Then repeat Steps 2–5 above. This time, before you update the scene, you can also select all of the other shadow utility scenes and then update the Section and Style settings for those scenes together as a group.

7. The Working scene is the last one that needs to be updated, so click the tab for that scene, and then turn off the section plane visibility. As a shortcut, you can just right-click the scene tab and choose Update from the context menu.

Creating an Animation with One Section Plane

You can create a simple section animation with a single section plane. In order to do this, you need to create a scene in which the section plane is active, and another scene in which the section plane is inactive. When you toggle back and forth between the two scenes, the section cut will start at the extents of the model (or group/component) that it is cutting through and then make its way to where you have positioned it in the model. Keep in mind that the section doesn't actually move; the animation effect is created as SketchUp interpolates the change in state between the plane being active and inactive.

1. Swing back around to the Front Door scene by clicking that scene tab.

2. Toggle on the section plane visibility by clicking the Toggle Section Display tool ⌗ (**Figure 9.21**).

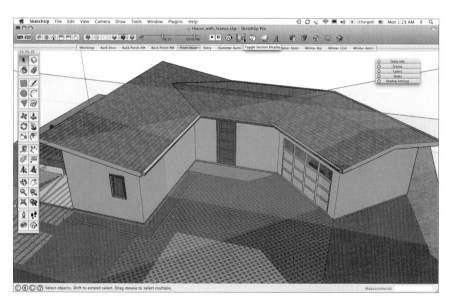

Figure 9.21 Toggle on the section planes so that you can see which one you want to activate.

3. Take the Select tool and double-click the section plane to activate the cross section through the bedroom (**Figure 9.22**).

Figure 9.22 Double-click the bedroom section to activate the section plane.

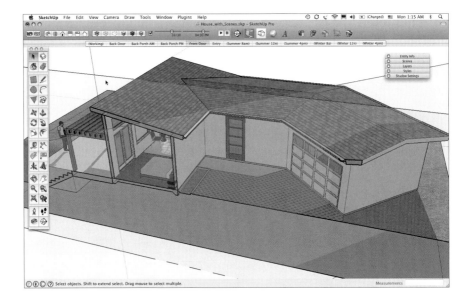

4. Toggle off the section plane visibility.

5. Right-click the Front Door scene tab and choose Add from the context menu.

6. When prompted, choose the option to "Save as new style" and click Update.

7. Right-click the new Scene 13 tab and choose Rename. Give it the name *Bedroom Section* and then hit Enter.

Now you can toggle between the Front Door scene (in which the section planes are set as inactive) and the Bedroom Section scene (in which the section plane is active) and watch the section cut animate into the scene to show a view into the bedroom.

This effect is one that I often use to make it look as though parts of the model are peeling away. To practice with this effect, try creating a scene in which the roof appears to cut away/build up.

Hint: To pull off this effect, you'll have to add the section plane within the roof group, then move the section plane over far enough so that the roof is no longer visible, and then create a scene.

Creating an Animation with Two Section Planes

Similar to the previous section, you can use the second section plane (the one that's cutting through the garage) to create the effect of animating from one active section plane to another.

1. Click the Bedroom Section scene tab to make it the active section.

2. Toggle on the section plane visibility.

3. Take the Select tool and double-click the section plane to activate the cross section through the garage (**Figure 9.23**).

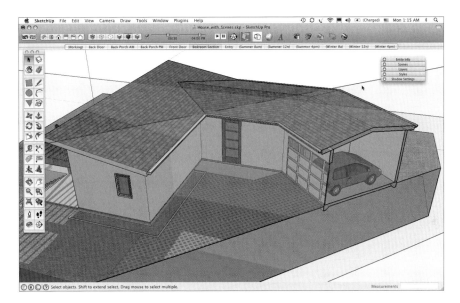

Figure 9.23 Activate the garage section plane.

4. Toggle off the section plane visibility.

5. Right-click the Bedroom Section scene tab and choose Add from the context menu.

6. When prompted, choose the option to "Save as new style" and click Update.

7. Right-click the new Scene 14 tab and choose Rename. Give it the name *Garage Section* and then hit Enter.

Now you can toggle between the Bedroom Section scene and the Garage Section scene to watch as the section cut appears to rotate from one scene to the other.

For an added effect, you could change the view in the model to look into the garage at eye level and then update the Garage Section scene so that the camera moves down to that view as the section cut is animating.

For more information about the Section tool and creating section animations, check out the video *The SketchUp Show,* Episode 31: "The Section Tool," online at www.go-2-school.com/Real-World-Google-SketchUp-7.

CHAPTER TEN

Exporting Graphics from SketchUp

For some projects it may be necessary to print views of your model; at other times you may simply need to send digital images of the model (as JPEGs or PDFs). This chapter focuses on the all-important topic of documenting the work you've done in SketchUp in a presentable or shareable format (i.e., digital or paper-based documents). There are numerous ways to create and export graphics from SketchUp—perhaps more than this entire book could illustrate. With that said, this chapter includes information about the options that almost everyone encounters at some point: preparing your model for presentations, creating scaled graphics, printing from SketchUp, exporting raster graphics, exporting vector graphics, and exporting CAD files.

PREPARING YOUR MODEL FOR PRESENTATIONS

This section explores the options for adding dimensions, onscreen text, and watermark overlays (for logos and title blocks). Adding this kind of information to your model can be a vital aspect of communicating your ideas clearly and giving your presentations that extra layer of professionalism.

Dimensioning Your Model in SketchUp

To add a dimension string to your model, use either of the following methods:

- **From Endpoints:** Click from one endpoint to another endpoint and then pull out a dimension that measures the distance between the two points. This option is especially useful for measuring between points associated with different edges or points that lie in different planes (**Figure 10.1**).

Figure 10.1 Click from one endpoint inference to another endpoint inference to add a dimension.

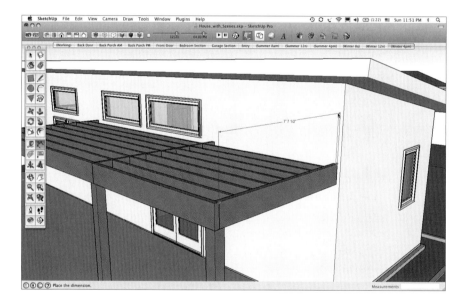

NOTE While pulling out a dimension string, you can pull the dimension out laterally, vertically, or in a direction perpendicular to the vector between the endpoints.

- **From Edge:** Click an edge (look for an On Edge inference) and pull out a dimension string that measures the entire length of the edge you clicked (**Figure 10.2**). Note: If the edge you are trying to add dimensions to is contained within a group or component, you will have to be in Edit Group/Component mode to get the appropriate On Edge inference.

Figure 10.2 Click from an On Edge inference to add a dimension string.

Once positioned, you can adjust the placement of the dimension at any time, using the Move tool. If the default dimension string text is left alone, it will automatically update when the objects that the dimension are attached to are edited. You can edit the default dimension string text by double-clicking the text with the Select tool. Once overwritten, the text will not automatically update if the model is edited.

Chapter 2 briefly discussed the dimension settings and display options available from the Dimensions tab in the Model Info window. The display options are pretty straightforward, so I'll leave those to you.

One of the settings I want to point out, however, is the advanced/expert dimension preference Hide When Foreshortened, which is useful for parsing the dimension strings that are specific to a particular view. For example, if you've created a set of dimensions in the model for a plan view, and another set for an elevation view, the foreshortened option will automatically cause SketchUp to display only the set of dimensions relevant for the particular view.

In situations where the foreshortened options aren't quite getting it done, you can always put dimension sets on specific layers and then hide/show the layers for scenes in which they shouldn't/should appear. For example, you may have an elevation view with overall dimensions and a close-up view of the same elevation with dimensions for a particular detail. In situations such as this, the foreshortened option isn't going to help separate the different dimension sets. You're better off putting the set of dimensions that were created for the overall elevation view on one layer (e.g., S_Elev_Dims) and putting the set of dimensions for the detail view on another layer (e.g., S_Elev_Detail_Dims).

NOTE You may recall the Add Hidden Layer Ruby script mentioned in Chapter 8. Adding layers for dimensions usually happens late in the game, and the layers are typically used in only one or two scenes, which is a perfect situation in which you could save time by using that script.

Once the dimensions are on different layers, you can update the scenes for each view to include the corresponding set of dimensions.

Annotating Your Model

When it comes to annotating your SketchUp model, you can use the Text tool to add notes in the form of leader text or onscreen text.

The type of text object you end up creating depends entirely on how you use the Text tool.

- Create a *leader text* note by clicking the Text tool on any point, edge, or face in the model. Leader text notes will stay attached to the objects to which they were applied. Keep in mind that leader text notes are positioned in 3D space, and the text automatically turns to face the camera.

- Add *onscreen text* notes by clicking in white space, away from the SketchUp model. Onscreen text notes are static text objects that stay put, even when you orbit around and change the view of your SketchUp model.

NOTE When you click a face with the Text tool, the default value for a leader text object is equal to the surface area of the face that you click. If the face that you click is contained within a group or component, the default text will autofill with the name of the group or component.

You can use the Move tool to reposition leader text as well as onscreen text objects.

As mentioned previously with regard to dimension strings, you can create layers to house various text notes that can then be turned on/off for particular scenes.

When deciding on a location for a leader or onscreen text note, consider the various monitor display resolutions that the SketchUp model may be viewed on, and also consider the size of the output of your printouts. If you typically work on a large, high-resolution monitor, you may want to check out what the model looks like at a lower resolution to ensure that the text notes are still legible. Problems are more likely to occur if text is placed while working on a hi-res display and then viewed on a lower-resolution monitor or projector.

Adding Watermarks

SketchUp includes the ability to apply watermarks to your model—either as background images or foreground stamps. The Watermark options are located in the Styles palette under the Edit tab.

Background watermarks are an easy way to create composite renderings of your model that include background imagery such as a landscape, sky, or cityscape. You can use the Background image from Chapter 6 to tinker with the background watermark options.

Overlay watermarks, on the other hand, are commonly used to display a company logo or a title block graphic with information about the SketchUp project. For this next example, you can use the Peachpit logo included on this book's accompanying DVD.

To add an overlay watermark:

1. Click the Add button in the Styles palette (**Figure 10.3**).

2. Choose a file to import and use as your watermark.

3. Give the watermark a name (e.g., Peachpit Logo) in the Choose Watermark dialog, select the Overlay radio button, and click Next.

4. Slide the opacity slider to obtain the desired look for your overlay and then click Next.

5. Choose the radio button "Positioned in the window," pick a location (I typically choose the bottom-right corner), move the slider to determine the scale of the watermark logo, and then click Finish (**Figure 10.4**).

Figure 10.3 Click the Add button to create a new watermark.

NOTE To edit the settings for a watermark you've created, highlight the watermark in the list, and then click the Edit button (which looks like gears).

Figure 10.4 Position the watermark in the bottom-right corner and shrink it down.

The overlay watermark will now sit in the bottom-right corner of the screen, like a sticker. Regardless of whether or not you orbit the model, the logo will always stay put in the bottom-right corner.

Once you've set up your watermark, you'll notice that the preview icon in the Styles window displays a couple of spinning arrows that indicate new, unsaved changes to the current In Model style. You now have a couple of choices for saving the new display settings—depending on how prevalent you want the new watermark to be:

- If you want the new watermark to become part of the default In Model style, simply click the Preview icon to update the current style (**Figure 10.5**). This will effectively include the watermark in any new and existing scenes that include the default style. To view or print the model without the watermark, you must remove it from the watermarks list or choose a new, watermark-free style from the Select tab.

Figure 10.5 Click the Preview icon to update the changes made to the default In Model style.

- To retain the original default, In Model style, click the "Create a new style" icon and give the new style a name (e.g., Peachpit Logo). From the Select tab of the Styles window, you'll then be able to click the In Model library and choose either the original default style or the new one with the watermark (**Figure 10.6**).

Figure 10.6 Click the Create New Watermark button to leave the default style alone and create a new style for the new watermark.

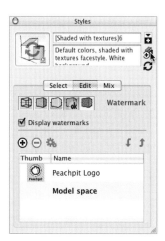

If needed, you can create different styles that contain different watermarks and save them in different scenes.

The most important aspect of watermarks (at least with regard to the subject of this chapter) is that they will show up in printouts, in exported images, and in Google Layout.

EXPORTING TO SCALE

By default, the SketchUp view port is set to display your model in Perspective view mode, which provides a more intuitive experience for working on a model in 3D. With the Perspective display mode turned on, you can print or export any of the graphic formats discussed in this chapter, but the graphics will *not* be scalable.

In order to export scaled graphics you need to do two things: First, view the model in Parallel Projection mode, and, second, choose an orthographic view of the model. For the first part, you can simply choose the Parallel Projection view mode from the Camera menu. (Note: To switch back to Perspective view mode, go to the Camera menu and toggle back over to Perspective.)

For the second part, assuming that your model has been drawn such that it aligns to the SketchUp axes, you can choose from any of the Standard views (Top, Left, Right, etc.) that are accessible via the Camera menu and/or Standard views toolbars in order to find the desired orthographic view of the model.

If your model has been drawn such that it's off-kilter to the SketchUp axes, you can align the camera to any face in the model by right-clicking the face and choosing Align View from the context menu.

> **NOTE** The Align View option will only appear in the context menu if you are right-clicking a face. If you right-click a group or component, you will get options related to groups and components. To align to the face of a group or component, you need to be in Edit Group/Component mode in order to right-click and see the options for the actual face inside the group/component.

PRINTING YOUR SKETCHUP MODEL

Printing views of your model directly from SketchUp is the *de facto* option for those times when you just need to get a view of your 3D model onto a piece of paper. While on one hand the convenience of printing directly from SketchUp is a plus, the downside is that the options in SketchUp for creating dimensioned, annotated working drawings, complete with title blocks, etc. are limited and cumbersome.

In the free version of Google SketchUp, you are limited to the print options found in SketchUp. With Google SketchUp Pro, you have the added option to export your model to, and print from, Google Layout.

This section explores options for setting up scenes in SketchUp for print, and also covers the print settings in SketchUp.

Print Settings

On the Windows version of SketchUp you'll find that the print options are broken up into two separate dialogs: The Print Setup dialog (File > Print Setup) and the Print dialog (File > Print).

On the Mac OS the print options are broken up into three separate dialogs: the Page Setup dialog (File > Page Setup), the Document Setup dialog (File > Document Setup), and the Print dialog (File > Print).

These menus are fairly straightforward and reminiscent of the print options you have in most programs. That being said, there are a few SketchUp print settings worth particular attention:

- The Page Orientation option (located in the Print Setup dialog in Windows or in the Page Setup dialog on a Mac) is where you choose portrait or landscape orientation for the page size you've selected. I typically work on low-rise projects and find myself using the landscape orientation so that I can fit more of the model on a sheet of paper. Landscape orientation also more closely resembles the aspect ratio of your monitor, so it's easier to approximate what the final output will look like before printing.

- In the Windows version, there is an option in the Print dialog that allows you to print multiple scenes from the model in one shot.

- The print size of the model is determined in the Print dialog in Windows and in the Document Setup dialog on a Mac. If "Fit to page" is unchecked, and if the SketchUp model view is set up with an orthographic view and Parallel Projection mode is turned on, you'll have the option to determine a print scale. Enter the print scale dimensions as they would appear in an architectural scale notation. For example, a 1/2" = 1'–0" scale drawing would translate into a half inch in the drawing equaling 1 foot in the model.

- The print quality is determined in the Print dialog on both platforms. The larger the paper size and the higher the print quality, the longer it will take to print. At a minimum, I recommend choosing high-quality printing. Draft quality is a decent option for those times when you just need a quick print of a large, detailed model, but the edges in your model will look chunky and jagged—not an ideal output for presentation graphics.

EXPORTING 2D GRAPHICS

Being able to get views of your model on paper is great, but for those times when you're able to save a tree and transmit your files digitally, SketchUp's got you covered with plenty of options for exporting 2D graphics in a variety of file formats.

This section covers the settings and options for exporting raster images, vector graphics, and CAD files.

Exporting Raster Images

SketchUp exports 2D images in a number of formats, including JPEG, TIFF, and PNG. In Chapter 4, which discussed options for importing image files into SketchUp, you read about some of the pros and cons of different file formats such as file size, lossy versus lossless compression formats, transparent backgrounds, etc.—and the same issues should be taken into consideration when deciding which format to export. This section looks at the options available for exporting raster images of your model from SketchUp.

1. From the File menu, choose Export > 2D Graphic.

2. From the File Type drop-down menu, choose a file format (e.g., *.tif).

    TIFF format is ideal for images that will be post-produced in Photoshop or eventually end up being printed. PNG files are ideal for Web and onscreen uses.

3. Click the Options button.

    The options are primarily intended as a way for you to determine the size and resolution for the exported image. When calculating the image size, you'll want to consider two things: How will the image be used (e.g., will it be printed, or will it be sent in an email or posted to a Web site), and how big does the image need to be (in real-world inch dimensions)? The answer to these questions will ultimately determine both the image size and the image resolution.

4. On Mac: Unlock the aspect ratio ⬚ and set an aspect ratio for the image by typing a number in the top field and the bottom field (e.g., 16:9).

    On Windows: You can choose between 4:3 and 16:9 aspect ratios from the drop-down list to the right.

By default, the aspect ratio is set to 4:3, but you can change it to something wider. I typically use an image-export aspect ratio of 16:9 because nowadays people are used to looking at images on widescreen-format monitors and TVs, and a 16:9 aspect ratio works well for both print and Web use.

5. Relock the aspect ratio (relink the chain) and then set an image size for the exported image.

By default, the image size is measured in total number of pixels. You can use the Units drop-down menus to switch between pixels, inches, centimeters, and millimeters.

With the image units set to pixels, you might need to do a little backward math to figure out an appropriate dimension. For example, if you know that the image will end up being printed at a resolution of 300 pixels per inch (see Step 6) and the overall image size needs to print 11 inches wide, the final image size would need to be 3300 pixels wide (300 pixels per inch × 11 inches = 3300 pixels).

6. When deciding on an appropriate resolution, the end usage for your file is perhaps the best determiner. For Web (or other onscreen use such as PowerPoint presentations), set a 72-pixel-per-inch resolution. For print use, set a 300-pixel-per-inch resolution (**Figure 10.7**).

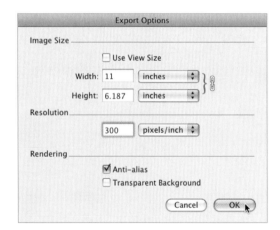

Figure 10.7a Print settings optimized for printing an 11-inch-wide TIFF at 16:9 aspect ratio.

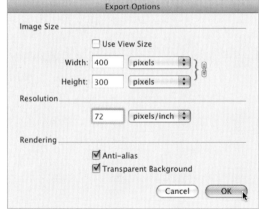

Figure 10.7b Print settings optimized for exporting a 400-pixel-wide PNG for Web use at 4:3 aspect ratio.

7. Check the option for Anti-alias. Anti-aliasing will improve the rendering quality of the edges and textures in your model (**Figure 10.8**).

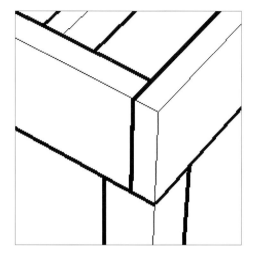

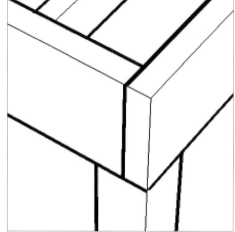

Figure 10.8a Close-up of image with Aliased edges.

Figure 10.8b Close-up of image with Anti-aliased images.

NOTE If you're going to export an image of your model to Photoshop for the purpose of compositing the rendering onto a background image, you can import the background image into SketchUp first (using the "Use as new matched photo" image-import option). You can then use the Match Photo option to align the model to the background before exporting the TIFF images to Photoshop.

8. Mac only: When exporting a TIFF file on the Mac, you can check the option for Transparent background. This option is useful for compositing a rendering of the model onto a background image in Photoshop.

Post-Production Tricks

The following workflow methods can help make the time spent post-producing your SketchUp renderings in Photoshop (or equivalent) more efficient.

Separate Layers

The Transparent background option (mentioned in the previous section) is also useful for SketchUp renderings that require post-production in Photoshop. An effective post-production workflow involves exporting parts of the SketchUp model as separate images, then recompositing the images as layers in Photoshop.

For example, a SketchUp rendering of a building with trees in the foreground would be time-consuming to edit in Photoshop, especially if you wanted to edit parts of the building while working around the trees. By isolating the foreground objects (e.g., people, trees) and then exporting that as an image, followed by the midrange objects (e.g., walls, windows), then background objects (e.g., other buildings, trees), you can then rebuild the composite image as a series of separate layers. Once the images have been recompiled in Photoshop, you will have a much easier time selecting and editing sections of the individual layers.

Hidden Line

Post-producing renderings of models that have been textured with a bunch of photo-real textures in Photoshop can be a time-consuming endeavor without the ability to make quick and easy selection sets. You can typically save a ton of time by simply exporting two additional images of your model rendered in Hidden Line display mode: one with the shadows on, and another with the shadows off—so that you can easily select regions of the image using Photoshop's selection tools (such as the magic wand).

Photo-Realistic Renderings

SketchUp's default lighting options are limited to a single-point light source—the sun. If you're looking to enhance the realism of your SketchUp renderings, there are a number of third-party plug-ins that, once installed, give SketchUp the ability to render more real-istic lighting effects and enhance the way that materials are rendered.

IDX Renditioner (idx-design.com): The IDX plug-in allows you to add multiple light sources and includes material-rendering options for reflectivity and bump maps. A free version is available for rendering low-resolution images. The full version costs $199 and allows higher-quality, higher-resolution rendering options. The IDX plug-in is available for both Mac and Windows operating systems.

SU Podium (suplugins.com): The SU Podium plug-in allows you to add multiple light sources and includes material-rendering options for reflectivity and bump maps. A free version is available for rendering low-resolution images. The full version costs $179 and allows higher-quality, higher-resolution rendering options. The SU Podium plug-in is available for both Mac and Windows operating systems.

LightUp (light-up.co.uk): LightUp allows you to add multiple light sources and includes material-rendering options for reflectivity and bump maps. Unlike IDX and Podium (which render static 2D images), LightUp renders the SketchUp model in 3D. Once the model is rendered, you can walk around in the rendered environment. A fully functioning 30-day free trial version is available. The licensed version costs $179. LightUp is available for both Mac and Windows operating systems.

For more information about third-party rendering plug-ins, check out the recording of the *Photorealistic Rendering Options* webinar series available online at www.go-2-school.com/Real-World-Google-SketchUp-7.

Exporting Vector Artwork

In the previous section you learned some options for exporting raster image files. Raster graphics are flattened, 2D files that are essentially made up of a specific number of little colored squares (pixels). Vector graphics, like raster images, are flattened graphics. Unlike raster images, vector graphics are not a pixilated image file format. Vector files retain endpoints, edges, and polygons—all of which are editable in programs such as Adobe Illustrator. The workflow of going from SketchUp to Illustrator is especially useful for professional graphic designers. Architectural designers who render elevations in Illustrator may also find this section useful.

From the 2D graphic export options, SketchUp offers up export options as vector artwork formats in PDF or EPS file formats.

What to Expect

Here are a few things you should expect when exporting to a 2D vector graphics format:

- The 3D model will be flattened into a 2D graphic based on the current view of the model at the time that the graphic is exported.

- All of the visible edges and faces in the model appear as lines and shapes in the exported graphic.

- Image textures are not exported, and neither are shadows. Instead, the faces are rendered based on the texture's default color and shading.

- Edge colors, edge extensions, and profile edge settings are rendered, but any sketchy edge styles, watermarks, background images, or edge settings for jitter and endpoints are not exported.

- Dimensions strings are rendered and the dimension text is exported as outlined text.

- The leader lines from the Leader text notes are exported, but the actual text from the notes is not.

Once the image files are opened in a vector graphics editor such as Adobe Illustrator, you can manipulate the lines and shapes. All of the elements in the artwork are separated from each other as individual parts and pieces, which can potentially make the selecting and editing of graphics rather time-consuming.

Everything is also lumped into a single layer in Illustrator. In some cases, if you need to edit the graphic, it may be faster to lock the layer that contains the SketchUp artwork and then simply retrace over whichever parts need editing.

Preparing Your SketchUp Model for EPS Export

This section covers some options for setting up your SKP model to make it a bit easier to edit the line weights and fills of the vector graphics once you're in Illustrator.

If the edges in SketchUp are being displayed with different edge colors, the edge colors will render in the exported vector graphics. Certain selection options (such as Select > Same > Stroke Color) in Illustrator are really helpful for editing a SketchUp rendering to quickly assign appropriate line weights (a.k.a. stroke thickness). The following simple example is intended to illustrate the concept.

1. Draw a box.

2. Open the Styles palette (Window > Styles) and click the Edit tab. Select the Edge properties icon, and choose By Material from the edge color drop-down menu (**Figure 10.9**).

Figure 10.9 Choose the option in the Styles palette to view the edge colors by Material.

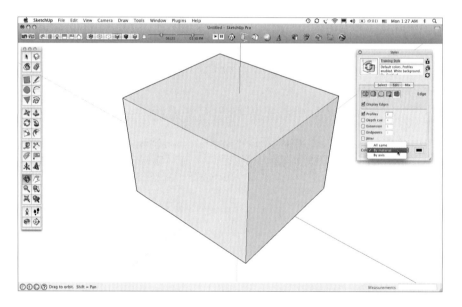

3. Choose Wireframe display mode from the Face Style options in the View menu.

4. Open the Entity Info window and then select the bordering edges with the Select tool (**Figure 10.10**).

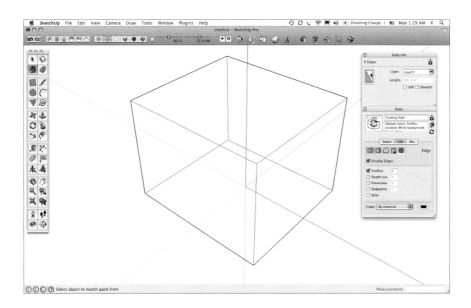

Figure 10.10 Select the edges along the outer rim of the box.

NOTE It is also possible to paint edges using the Paint Bucket tool, but I've found it's often easier to assign colors to edges via the Entity Info dialog.

5. Double-click the color preview indicator and choose a color (e.g., Green) from the color palette. Once chosen, the color will be applied automatically to the selected edge(s).

6. Choose the inside edges and assign a different color (e.g., Blue; **Figure 10.11**).

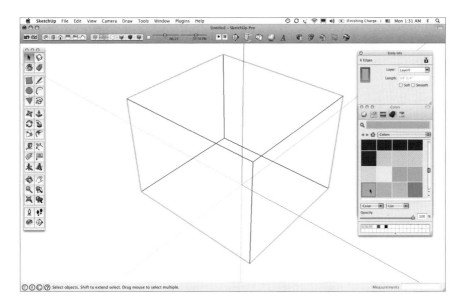

Figure 10.11 Choose the other edges and assign a different color to them.

To preview what your model will look like as a vector graphic, choose the Face Styles option for Shaded View mode. If you don't like the colors for the faces in your model, you can edit the colors of your model in SketchUp (I recommend doing a Save As of your model first), or you can edit the colors in Illustrator once you've opened up the exported vector graphic. Once open in Illustrator, you can use the Selection option for Same > Fill Color to quickly select and edit similarly colored shapes.

Export Options

Once you're ready to export views of your model, choose 2D graphic from the File > Export menu, then choose either PDF or EPS format and click the Options button (**Figure 10.12**).

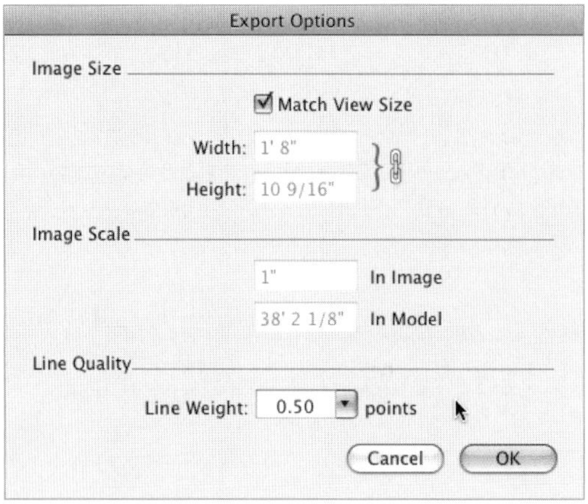

Figure 10.12 The Mac Options dialog for exporting 2D graphics as EPS or PDF files.

The following options can be customized for obtaining the desired output of EPS (and PDF) vector graphic files:

- **Image Size.** As with the previous section regarding raster image export options, this setting determines the overall image size of the exported graphic. Keep in mind that SketchUp will export the entire model, regardless of the closeness/zoom/cropping of the SketchUp camera, and the image size refers to the size that the entire model will be rendered out as.

- **Graphic Scale.** You'll recall that the option to export scaled vector graphics is only available for orthographic views while in Parallel Projection camera mode (see previous section, "Exporting to Scale").

- **Line Thickness.** SketchUp gives you the option to set a line width (in points) for the regular edges in the model. Any profile edges will be rendered thicker, depending on the thickness defined in the profile edge settings in the edge-settings pane of the Styles window. For example, if the profile edge thickness is set to 5 in the Styles palette, the profile edges will be 5 points thick in Illustrator.

Creating PDF Files

There's no denying that PDF files are the most common and popular document-sharing format. When it comes to turning your model into a PDF file, you can print to PDF or export to PDF.

Printing to PDF rasterizes the model so that all of the styles, notes, and dimensions are displayed as they would be if the model view were otherwise printed (on paper) or exported as a raster graphic (such as a JPEG).

Exporting the model to PDF will create a vector graphic—the options and benefits of which were explored in this section.

A third PDF option is to export your SketchUp model as a U3D PDF file. The U3D file format was developed by Adobe to allow interactive 3D models to be added to PDF files. You can export SketchUp files to U3D format using the Render Plus 3D PDF plug-in (downloadable from renderplus.com/wk/RPS_3D_PDF_w.htm) or convert your SketchUp models to U3D format using a file converter like Right Hemisphere's Deep Exploration (righthemisphere.com).

Once created, 3D PDF files can be opened and viewed by anyone using Adobe Acrobat version 8 or higher (get.adobe.com/reader). When exporting to U3D file format, SketchUp will export textures but will not export styles, dimensions, or text objects.

Exporting to CAD

And so here we are, having come full circle since having looked at the options in Chapter 5 for importing CAD files, to this section, which illustrates the options for exporting the work you've done in SketchUp to CAD.

To export a file to CAD, you can choose from among a number of CAD formats (from ACAD R12 to ACAD 2007) in the file format drop-down menu in the File > Export > 2D Graphic dialog.

What to Expect

NOTE The options you'll explore in this section are similar to those explored in the previous section on exporting vector artwork. The CAD file formats (DXF and DWG) are technically considered vector formats that can be opened in your preferred CAD application or in a vector graphics application such as Adobe Illustrator.

Here are a few things you can expect when exporting your 3D SketchUp model as a 2D DWG or DXF graphic format:

- The 3D model will be flattened into a 2D graphic based on the current view of the model at the time that the graphic is exported.

- All of the visible edges in the model appear as lines in the exported file, and the lines retain whichever colors are visible in the SketchUp model at the time the model is exported (useful for setting up the edge colors in SKP to mesh well with your CAD line weights).

  Before exporting, you can choose the Styles option to display edge color By Material (Window > Styles > Edit > Edge Settings > Color > By Material).

  Otherwise, you can simply determine line weights, colors, layers, etc. after the model has been exported from SketchUp and opened in CAD.

- Edge extensions and profile edge settings (also found under Styles > Edit > Edge Settings) *can* be exported, but any sketchy edge styles, watermarks, background images, or other edge settings such as jitter and endpoints are *not* exported.

- Faces are *not* exported, and thus, image textures and shadows are absent from the exported CAD file.

- Dimensions strings and leader text objects are exported along with text.

Once the exported files are opened in CAD, you can manipulate the lines and shapes. All of the elements in the artwork are separated from each other as individual parts and pieces, which can potentially make the selecting and editing of graphics rather time-consuming.

Depending on the chosen export options (see the following section), it is likely that everything in your SketchUp model will appear in CAD on one or two layers. In some cases, if you need to edit the graphic in CAD, it may be faster to simply lock the layer that contains the SketchUp artwork and then redraw whichever parts need editing.

Export Options

To determine and select your preferred CAD export settings, click the Options button (**Figure 10.13**) before saving your CAD file. The following export options are applicable to any of the CAD file formats that SketchUp can export.

Figure 10.13 The Mac Options dialog for exporting 2D graphics as DWG or DXF files.

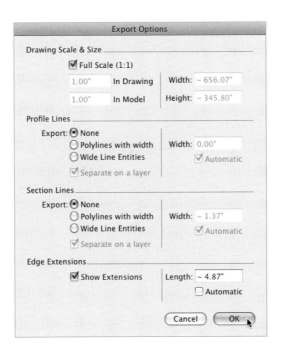

- **Drawing Scale and Size.** If the SketchUp model view is set up with an orthographic view and Parallel Projection mode is turned on, you'll have the option to determine a scale for the CAD file. By default, the scale is set to 1:1. If the check box for 1:1 scale is unchecked, you can enter a drawing scale as it would appear in an architectural scale notation. For example, a 1/2" = 1' – 0" scale drawing would translate into a half inch in the drawing equals 1 foot in the model.

- **Profile Lines and Section Lines** can be exported as Polylines With Width or as Wide Line Entities. Personally, I prefer to leave both of these options set to None, which effectively puts all the lines in the drawing onto a single layer (Layer 0).

  Polylines are effectively the equivalent of a shape with perimeter edges and a fill. The width of the polygons will be equal to the width entered in the Export dialog.

  Wide line entities are a single line with a thickness value equal to the width entered in the dialog.

  If you choose the option to assign a line width automatically, SketchUp will try to choose a line thickness value that proportionally matches the thickness of the lines in the model.

  By default, if you choose to export Profile Lines or Section Lines, the option to export the geometry to a separate layer will be enabled. This can be a useful option regardless of whether you want the lines to have a different width. For example, you could set the width to 0.00" and still choose the option to export to a separate layer. Having Profile and/or Section edges on separate layers can make it a bit easier to assign line weights or other properties to those lines in CAD.

NOTE For sectional views of the model, you can use the option for exporting a 2D CAD graphic, which will effectively create a Section/Elevation drawing. Another option for exporting Section Lines is to export them all by their lonesome by utilizing the export option for File > Export > Section Slice. The export options for Section Slice are similar to those described in this section, but the resulting drawing will contain just the Section Cut lines.

Google Layout

Google Layout is another great option for creating printable presentation graphics of your SketchUp model. Google Layout is an application that comes bundled with SketchUp Pro. As its name suggests, Layout is a multipage graphics application that allows you to import your SketchUp model into a 2D page-like environment for the purpose of creating working drawings.

Layout's features include the ability to add title blocks, notes, dimensions, drawing labels, and graphic entourage, to embed other images, as well as options for creating 2D vector artwork. Best of all, Layout allows you to arrange multiple views of the same SketchUp model on a single sheet. For each view you can choose between Perspective and Parallel Projection, choose a drawing scale, and choose a graphic display style.

Layout is a remarkable program that is certainly worth test-driving (if you haven't already). For more information about Google Layout, check out the *Layout For Everyone* training DVD online at www.go-2-school.com/Real-World-Google-SketchUp-7.

INDEX